SUPERNATURAL
LOVE

A TRUE STORY OF
LIFE AND LOVE AFTER DEATH

Pam and Alan Johnson

Cover artwork by Maria Rodrigues Pereira and Alan Johnson.

Publishing Services provided by Paper Raven Books LLC

Printed in the United States of America

First Printing, 2022

Paperback ISBN: 979-8-9874729-7-2
Hardback ISBN: 979-8-9874729-8-9
Ebook ISBN: 979-8-9874729-9-6

CONTENTS

For all the courageous, beautiful souls who, by reaching through the veil to reunite with their loved ones, are proving that death is not the end, but a new beginning.

A NOTE TO THE READER

People say we should let the dead rest in peace. But let's set the record straight. The dead are the ones who came knocking on our door first.

The spirit world first captured the attention of the Western world beginning with the raps and taps on the walls of the Hydesville, New York home of the famous Fox sisters, Leah, Margaretta, and Kate. They went on to launch the spiritualist movement in the late nineteenth century. It was not a coincidence that Spirit reached through the veil just before two world wars wrought a devastating, unprecedented loss of life.

Knowing humanity was about to experience the largest mass exodus of souls ever, the spirit world came through to prove, by the manifestation of spirits through physical mediums, that there is no such thing as death. Today, interest in communication with the spirit world has never been higher or more widely accepted.

It's been 170 years since those first raps on the wall. Psychic mediums now have their own Netflix shows, and folks who were once content to let a medium be their sole liaison with the Other Side have taken to learning mediumship in the hopes of making direct contact themselves. More and more people are beginning to understand that spirit communication is not a special gift. It's our birthright.

Our loved ones in spirit are reaching out to continue contact with us, even to maintain the bonds of love and all that entails. But don't expect every medium to understand this, let alone accept it. Some will claim it's impossible, that we must let the dead go, that we are holding them back. Others will say our loved one is trapped as an earthbound spirit stuck between the two worlds. And while that can happen, this is not always the case.

Yes, souls can cross to the spirit world, return, and even stay if they have a reason to. This doesn't make them a ghost. Perhaps this wasn't possible before, but why should we be surprised since the nature of reality is evolution and change? We are multi-dimensional beings who can exist in many realities across time and space. This means a discarnate soul can go wherever it chooses.

If you are experiencing direct contact, don't expect to be understood or accepted by the spiritual community. You'll find varying points of view on this subject and no real consensus. But I propose that the spirit world laid down this path of reunion for us long ago, and it's become accessible now because more people believe in the afterlife, which has opened the door to the other side even wider.

Could this have been the plan all along?

It has been said that the day will come when the veil separating the two worlds dissolves into nothingness, a day when every person will be a medium for the spirit world. So much has changed to bring us closer to that day. We know now that psychic ability is not a rare gift but a normal part of being human. We are born psychic.

Why can't we continue to live and love each other between the two worlds? Hasn't mediumship proven that the soul survives death? If they can speak to us once, twice, and many times after that, why can't spirit communication be constant? Could we be setting limits on afterlife contact with our narrow beliefs of what's possible? If the soul lives on, how can consciousness which is formless, be bound by the laws of the physical world? We should expand our thinking.

Every day, ordinary people experience the stirring of connection through the veil. Some do not just have a single unexpected visit from a loved one, but ongoing contact. It doesn't matter what others think or believe about this. It's none of their business. All that matters is what we believe. We can connect with our loved ones in spirit in whatever way is meaningful to us and easiest for both of us, whether through channeled writing, telepathic communication, feelings of profound love and connection, or even a form of extrasensory non-physical "touch" that defies explanation.

During this time of spiritual awakening, I predict we will see a rise in interdimensional relationships as the spirit world continues to reach for all of us through the veil, for they want this reunion of souls as much as we do. They want to be seen, heard, and felt for the simple reason that it is possible. They want to live with and through us. They want to guide and support us through these troubled times. But more than anything else...

They want us to return to Love.

PREFACE

One week after he died, I woke to find my husband next to me, his loving presence everywhere. This was no lingering, foggy-headed dream. My supposedly dead husband was talking inside my head, loudly declaring that our relationship hadn't ended, that we were about to step into our real relationship. Our thirty-year marriage that ended with his passing was just a warm-up for what was coming.

Alan said we'd be writing a book, the one you are reading now. He gave me the title that same day. This book is the chronicle of our journey to break through the veil and find our way back to each other through the ups and downs, the detours and roadblocks, the triumphs, and sudden epiphanies. Whether you are on a similar journey or would like to be, we hope that our book will help you navigate your passage to reach through the veil and reclaim the love you think you've lost but haven't. You'll learn for yourself that love is the only thing that endures.

I wrote our story as it unfolded over the course of two years, laying out all the details for anyone who wanted to follow our trail of ethereal breadcrumbs to find their way. Early on, I decided to be vulnerable, vowing to openly share my as-they-were-happening experiences within a Facebook group that Alan asked me to create on the seventh day of his return. An ironic request, given that he had hated Facebook with a passion, but overnight, a tight-knit group of friends and clients became our new family. If it weren't for our Soulmates in the Afterlife group, this book might not exist, and we might not have found our way back into each other's arms. I discovered that no one can make this journey on their own.

At first, I assumed our book would be a collage of our most popular posts shared within our group, given that there were several hundred posts written in that first year alone. I thought writing our book would be simple, that all I'd have to do was weave the individual pieces of prose together to flesh out a fuller narrative. But I was wrong.

Once I began to write our story, it was clear that a deeper, fuller perspective was called for. I became a fledgling journalist reporting from the frontline of the afterlife, living our story and writing it at the same time. Although he didn't tell me then, from his higher vantage point, Alan knew what was coming my way. Writing our book was not going to be simple or easy; it would test us on every level.

So what I thought would take just a few months to write took well over a year, and in the end only a meager handful of our original posts made it into the final manuscript. There is still so much to share that was put to the side!

But Alan wasn't worried. *"There will be more books you and I will write, Pam, including perhaps the publication of our original writings."*

These were not short pieces either, ranging anywhere from 500 to 3,000 words. All of them can still be found in the never-ending Facebook feed within our group. Yes, my husband is quite the talker, as you will find out. And no sooner do I write those words than I hear Alan call out, *"Hey, and so are you, my love!"*

Yes, that's my not-dead husband, always at my side, loving me and teasing me relentlessly. And for that I am beyond blessed!

Our book took longer to finish because as I was writing, new incidents and fresh revelations rocked me emotionally, sending me spiraling into yet another crisis of doubt and despair. Every time I thought we had finally reclaimed our love and found the perfect ending to our supernatural story, yet another emotional firestorm would break out that threatened to burn everything down.

You would think that the two of us being psychic channels and mediums for over thirty years would have made our journey of reunion easier, but we learned that psychic ability is not as important as emotional rapport if your goal is to build a bridge to Heaven.

We would get to what we thought was the end of our story, only to discover the beginning of yet another. Such is the symmetry and nature of existence. Life is a circle without an end. Once created, energy cannot be destroyed, so how could the soul's journey be any different? It's laughable to think otherwise.

No one dies! We are immortal! We continue to live, learn, grow, and love whether we are in this world or have moved on to the next. Death is nothing but a lie. Step outside of the lie, and you'll find your loved ones right there at your side, waiting to love you with arms and hearts wide open.

Like ours, your story with your loved one in Heaven has no end, so instead, let's place a bookmark here.

A bookmark emblazoned with the words…

To Be Continued

Just tell our story and write me well, my love!
—Alan Johnson

My Darling Pam,

Today, I stand before you with my soul in your hands.

Today, I am here to make sure you know that my heart is yours.

Today, I want to give you everything I am because time did not exist until you became a part of me.

And when tomorrow comes, I want to know that our souls, our bodies, and our lives are so tightly entwined, you won't know where I begin and you end.

Today, we are creating the magic of a dream.

A dream so grand that the entire world will have to come to a standstill and sigh.

A dream so full of light that the sun itself will seem dim in comparison.

For in truth, my love, ours is the love that transcends time and space.

So let us walk among the stars and dance under the moonlight.

Let me whisper those words from which entire worlds are created:

I love you with all the depth and breadth in my heart and to the great beyond.

CHAPTER 1

WHY DON'T YOU SLEEP NAKED?

Why don't you sleep naked?

He was serious. My husband Alan had died only a few days ago, yet here he was, back from the other side, asking me to take off my clothes and sleep naked in bed with him. I wasn't surprised by his request as much as I questioned his logic. "Say what? How will this work now that you no longer have a body?"

No answer.

Intrigued, but feeling a bit naughty at the same time, I decided to do as he asked. But if this really was my Alan, why did I feel self-conscious? I had undressed in front of him too many times to count during the thirty-plus years we had been together.

I lifted the faded ivory silk comforter, gingerly slid into bed, and cringed. The newly washed cotton sheets felt icy cold against my bare bottom since the air conditioning was cranked up high. We always kept the bedroom temperature bordering on frigid since I had trouble sleeping if I was too warm. Alan was continually complaining that the room was too cold. Now, for once, I agreed.

As soon as I settled in, I felt aroused. It happened immediately. How was this possible? Was Alan really here in bed with me? I couldn't see or feel him physically, yet I felt his presence. It was palpable. I could feel his eyes on me. Even though he'd only been gone a week, I was already hearing him talk to me telepathically in my mind, though the flow of words wasn't always steady, I usually got the gist of his message because my psychic knowing, also known as claircognizance, is strong. I know what I know without knowing how I know it, but even with that, I never considered myself to be a classic psychic like Alan. I preferred channeling messages for my clients from their guides and angels while he enjoyed giving readings. We were different in many ways, and yet the same in the ones that mattered.

Alan had only been gone a few days, yet in that time, so much had happened. It wasn't enough that he had returned from the other side to let me know that he and I could still be together; now he seemed to be saying that we could make love. My mind was still processing how we'd continue our relationship from the Other Side and here, my husband was already raising the ante. He was moving so fast! But why?

As I pondered the logistics of having sex with him, I scanned the bedroom as if it contained the secret. Was Alan really here? A solitary street lamp shone a hazy golden light through the gossamer-thin ivory curtains, casting an eerie glow on the wall. I stared at the blank wall long and hard, trying to imagine his face, hoping I could conjure him through willpower alone. Nothing. Although I heard him psychically in my head, I was frustrated that my clairvoyance wasn't stronger.

When I asked Alan how we could possibly have sex, seeing as he didn't have a body, he chuckled softly. *We only need one body for this, and yours will do nicely, Pam.*

Oh, I see.

2

And just like that, an invisible tap seemed to open as his energy poured into me. Waves of tingly energy rushed in as I felt a comforting warmth, followed by intense emotion that welled up within me. It was Alan's love merging with my heart, my mind, and my body. I cried from the depth and beauty of the sweetness of it all as salty tears streaked my face. This was a love like nothing I'd ever experienced before. Not with him or anyone.

Pam, now wrap your arms around your body. When you do this, know that it is me embracing you. When we merge like this, your arms become my arms. From this moment on, when we make love, wherever you touch yourself, it will be me touching you. I'll be holding you, caressing you, and pleasuring you. I'll always be here loving you. In time our supernatural lovemaking will become normal to you.

I took a deep breath and gave myself a hug. I couldn't believe it, but I detected the subtle trace of his caress. Yes, it was faint, but I felt something. Or was it my imagination? Whatever it was, at that moment, I didn't care. All I knew was my body responded by melting into the experience as his etheric touch calmed and soothed me. Did it really matter as long as it made me feel better? But the thought that I was imagining things kept returning.

Why is it so hard to believe in something we can't see?

Still, I couldn't deny that I could viscerally feel a presence, and if it wasn't Alan, then who or what was it? Whatever it was, it was tender, gentle, and loving. It couldn't possibly be bad.

The words came into my mind: *I'll trust this and see what happens.*

That first time we made love was a revelation. In my mind, I called out to Alan and invited him to be with me. It was that easy. The idea that we are not physical beings but energy beings was made real for me the moment I felt his passion flood my body with ripples of tingling energy. I knew this was not my imagination! If it were possible to imagine a lover out of thin air, I wouldn't need anyone. Not even Alan. But no, this was him all right.

I am here, Pam! I'm not dead! I'm alive, and I'm right here next to you. Please let me love you. This is how I will prove to you that I'm here.

While I couldn't feel a physical caress, what I did feel was an explosion of joy when Alan swept in with his love, and as it landed in my heart, I couldn't hold back the floodgate of tears a moment longer. Usually stoic and calm, I had never been one to cry, but in the few short days since his return, I cried daily, not just from grief but from the sheer force of his love that triggered waves of emotion.

Now, tears of grief were mixed with tears of joy to render the full depth and beauty of his love. At times, my body quivered head to toe with emotion. Alan was determined to prove to me that not only was he still very much alive but that he was more in love with me than ever before. He seemed to be wooing me with every ounce of passion he could muster.

As his energy embraced me, it felt as if my body had become Alan's body. My hands became his hands. Our union was a merging beyond the physical. If ours was a supernatural love, at that moment, it became supernatural sex. How else would you describe making love with someone without a body who exists in another dimension?

We hadn't had an active sex life for much of the thirty years we'd been together. Yet here was my husband, acting on his promise to make it all up to me. He said that his abject failure to love me was behind his urgency to return so quickly after he passed. Since he was fifteen years older than me, in some ways, it had been a relief to Alan that I didn't pester him for sex in his later years. He had been passionate towards me when we first met, but my interest had waned soon after giving birth to our son, much to his frustration and my own. I never understood what the problem was. I assumed it was me.

This caused us enormous suffering and confusion, for Alan much more than me, as it was a blow to his manly ego. While we loved each other, the fires of romantic desire had been extinguished for decades. As illogical as it seems, even though ours had essentially become a platonic marriage, our love for each other never died. Neither of us wanted to be with anyone else.

So, when Alan asked me to sleep naked, my first thought was that he must have been joking since he was always a smartass looking for a punchline to deliver. And yet even though he was known for his over-the-top humor, I could tell he was serious.

Apparently, not only do we not die, but when we get to Heaven, we want to keep enjoying all the pleasures of life. And why not?

The Alan that had returned to me wasn't obsessed with sex. It was love that he was after—my love. But for love to flow between us again, I would have to open my heart to him so I could feel my emotions and love him as much as he loved me. Alan had become the embodiment of pure unconditional love, which meant if we were to be together, I would have to match his higher vibration.

When he got to Heaven, after completing his life review, in which you experience the full panorama of your life, including whom you hurt and what impact you made on every single person you encountered, much to his dismay, Alan learned that he had failed me as a husband. To make matters worse, he discovered that love is the only reason we exist. Anything else we accomplish in our life is a postscript. Feeling intense remorse for how he had neglected me, Alan wanted a second chance at love.

But while love was his main agenda, Alan first had to awaken the emotion buried deep inside me. I didn't know it, but although I was walking, breathing, and had a pulse, I was barely alive. Being alive requires feeling all of our feelings, which I hadn't done for years. Caring for Alan at the end of his life, through two years of dementia, had essentially shut down my heart. I operated in survival mode because I couldn't feel all of my emotions and deal with the level of unrelenting stress I was under. I had no choice but to close down my heart, or I would have suffered a nervous breakdown. I was all but dead inside.

To bring me back to life, Alan began sending songs.

One morning, I woke up hearing Phil Collins crooning his pop hit, "A Groovy Kind of Love." The song kept repeating in my head, pausing only when I had to focus on a task, speak to someone on the phone, or watch television. The song was the last thing I heard when I fell asleep and the first thing I heard when I opened my eyes the next morning. This went on for two straight days. Under normal circumstances, this would have been irritating, but instead, I was entranced.

Through the lyrics of the song, Alan was telling me what he was doing. He was with me while I slept, listening to my breathing and my heart beating while cuddling me in his invisible arms through the night. Even though I was grieving, I couldn't deny it; I felt protected and loved.

With that first song, music took on a significance in my life it never had before. I could feel Alan's love in the music and lyrics of every song he sent me. Music had never affected me this way before. That's how emotionally shut down I had been. I knew a song was from Alan by the heady rush of goosebumps that came with it. Goosebumps became a sort of Morse code between us. I'd hear a song, feel my flesh tingle, and know that the lyrics were his latest message of love, whether he was saying he was feeling amorous, remorseful, or euphoric.

At first, the goosebumps were infrequent and mild, but in time, they grew so intense that I'd have to hold on to a table to stabilize myself. The more I opened up to my emotions, the more I could feel him. There were nights when it was difficult to fall asleep because I was so eager to wake up to see what the morning would bring.

Yet as glorious as this was, Alan's emotional intensity was hard to understand. He hadn't been this way for decades. We had lost our passion for each other long ago so where was this coming from? In the beginning, the mere touch of his hand would electrify me, sending me swooning with pleasure. Even at the end of his life, when he was in the full throes of dementia, if he laid his hand on me for longer than a few seconds, I melted. His touch brought me back to life, even if only for a moment. I wasn't completely dead to my feelings after all.

For years, I had blamed myself, wondering what was wrong with me. How could I have lost my desire for my husband when I had been so passionate about Alan from the moment we met? It made no sense that part of me responded eagerly to him while another part of me pulled away as if repulsed. The push-pull I felt was beyond confusing. I yearned for him yet loathed his touch at the same time. There was an emotional disconnect hidden somewhere inside me that shut down my heart.

But now everything was different. I was back to how I had felt when we first met, my body buzzing with pleasure, my heart on fire with longing for him. Had I changed or was it because Alan was different?

Although I recognized his energy and gregarious personality, his temperament had changed. He was patient, which he had never been. He was sensitive to me when he used to be only sensitive about himself. Even more startling, he was expressing his love to me constantly, which he had only done at the very beginning of our relationship when we were consumed with each other as new lovers are.

Any passion we might have once felt for one another had long since evaporated over thirty years spent together, but now, romance seemed to be the only thing on Alan's mind as I felt his love surge through me as waves of bliss.

Are you ready to go to sleep now, my love?

Lying in the dark, staring at the ceiling in the dim light, I wondered where he was relative to me in the bed. Was Alan hovering above me? Was he lying beside me, or standing over me and not in the bed at all? I still slept on the side of our bed where I had always slept. I sensed Alan lying beside me with his head on his pillow but wondered if I was imagining it. Since he could never find a pillow he liked, he would constantly complain that his pillow hurt his neck. We spent 30 years searching for the perfect pillow for him. I smiled as the thought entered my mind.

7

Well, at least he's not complaining anymore.

Most people would probably find it eerie to sense an otherworldly presence in their bedroom, the most private, intimate space they inhabit, but that didn't bother me. I wasn't afraid of spirits. Alan and I had always been close to each other, even if there had not been any passion between us. We never felt the other one was intruding on our space. That was probably why we rarely quarreled or got irritated with each other. But now, I wondered where he was in the room, frustrated that I couldn't see him.

As if reading my mind, I heard him say softly, *Yes, I'm lying on my pillow. But don't worry; I'm behaving myself. I'm staying on my side of the bed like you always told me to.*

I laughed. I used to do all I could to ensure Alan kept to his side of our queen-sized bed as he tended to move in too close, which would wake me up. Sometimes, before he got into bed, I'd even draw an invisible line with my finger down the center of the mattress to show him the boundary, which he would argue was wrong.

What an idiot I had been! Now I would give the world to feel his body pushing up against mine, crowding me out. I'd give my life to have him argue with me over this stupid imaginary line. There are so many things we take for granted until they are ripped from our lives. Death is the cruelest thief of all. We should let the small things go, and really, every-thing is small when it comes to love. Love is the only thing that matters.

Once again, I wondered what had been wrong with me. Why had I rejected his overtures for sex for so many years? Reading my thoughts, Alan promised to explain everything to me later. He said there was a good reason why we had failed each other, and even though he had deep regret and remorse about it, neither of us had done anything wrong. What we experienced was part of a greater plan. I couldn't understand how our suffering had been planned. But if so, for what purpose?

Pam, you hurt me once, but my failure was far worse, for I let you down time and again by taking you and your love for granted. And yes, it was planned, but that isn't an excuse, just an explanation. We weren't meant to have a passionate relationship after we married, but now all that and more I will give you if you just let me love you again. Please say you will.

"What's that? Okay, now you've got my attention!"

The enormity of what Alan said overwhelmed me, but sleep overtook me, and I struggled to keep my eyes open. I told him I needed to sleep, but before my eyes closed, Alan ramped up his energy as his words echoed.

I will seed your dreams with my love.

I rolled over, curling myself into a fetal position on his side of the bed. In my mind, I asked Alan to hold me, which I'd never asked him to do before, and while I didn't feel any physical arms, I felt his love wrap around me like a cozy blanket as I drifted off to sleep.

From that night on, I would sleep on his side of the bed and fall asleep in his arms, with Alan never failing to draw in close. I never had to ask him to hold me again.

Morning came extra early for me. As soon as I woke up, I called out to Alan in my mind and heard him reply.

I'm right here, babe.

I discovered that I could hear him more clearly in the early hours between two and five a.m. I peeked at the clock, then laughed when I saw that the time was two thirty. The Chinese dentist. It was one of Alan's favorite jokes.

"Tooth-hurty, it's time to see the Chinese dentist!" he'd gleefully call out whenever he noticed a clock hitting those exact digits.

"Did you wake me up so you could say that? If so, that's not funny, Alan!" I said, only half-seriously.

The thought occurred to me that he woke me up at that exact hour just so he could laugh about it, and though he chuckled, Alan said no, he just wanted to talk and be with me. And oh, how I wanted that, too! I relished those early morning hours when the world around us was still asleep. Besides, I didn't seem to need much sleep since his return. I assumed it was because he was always with me. There were nights when it felt as if Alan had brought the full force of Heaven to me, for whether I was asleep or awake, I was high on his now-perfect love.

Alan promised he would always be with me, never leave my side, even while I slept. He'd stay to watch over me, happily listening to my breathing and my heart beating. He said it was his favorite thing to do, and that it was easy for him because time passes differently on the Other Side. I was now sleeping between four to six hours a night, which to him is nothing. Not having a body means he no longer has to sleep, though he says he still needs to rest from time to time. Holding me in his arms while lying next to me at night was when he rested.

I felt him with me in bed at night right from the start. Alan's ethereal loving presence loomed over me as if he was trying to protect me from my fears, worries, and pain. It was working. While my grief was raw and deep, I looked forward to the evening since it never failed to bring us closer.

This was no after-death visitation. There are countless anecdotal stories of people claiming to see a loved one right after they die. Psychologists claim they are hallucinating, calling the experiences grief hallucinations. But how do we explain the number of after-death visitations reported in online forums?

My mother had seen my grandfather appear at the foot of her bed the day he died in Japan of cancer. She was a student at the University of Hawaii at the time, while my grandmother had taken my grandfather home to Japan to honor his last wish to be buried there. My grandfather appeared to my mom that morning, standing silently at the foot of her bed as if to say goodbye and, a few moments later, was gone. That was it. My mother wasn't grieving; she didn't even know her father had died until later that morning. Being a studious college student, my mom had her head firmly planted in the world of intellectual, practical pursuits. She wasn't prone to imagining someone in her mind.

Alan never appeared to me, and while I was grieving, my grief was not as debilitating as it could have been, largely because I know we survive death. I wasn't hallucinating. I didn't even have a visitation dream of Alan, which is a common way for loved ones to visit after they pass.

Instead, I felt Alan and heard him in my head the day after he died. Communication wasn't always clear initially, but I could make out most of his words and felt his presence. Since I was never one to talk to myself, I was certain I wasn't creating this in my mind, although I sometimes questioned if I heard him correctly.

But if that wasn't enough, Alan didn't leave as my grandfather had. Quite the opposite. He said he was here to stay! He spoke about our soul contract, the promise we made before we incarnated to continue our relationship after his death. If I was still in agreement, he promised to give me everything we would have had if he was still with me, except for the fact that he wouldn't have a body.

Still, as the days passed, I'd occasionally wonder if I was making it all up. This is normal. We have been programmed to be skeptical of what we can't see. If it wasn't for the undeniable, immense love I felt radiating from Alan, I would have doubted what I was experiencing. But his adoration was intense and unmistakable; he was sending me what felt like love blasts that hit me squarely in my heart.

Feelings never lie, and this was no hallucination.

Alan returned to give both of us a second chance at love and to help other souls reach through the veil to reunite with those they left behind. If Heaven is the real world, what then is the physical world? Why are we here? What is the purpose of life? My beloved husband was about to upend my preconceived ideas about love, life, and reality, including my understanding of who I am and what I was born to do.

CHAPTER 2

MY DARLING PAM

I am there where you are, and I want nothing more than to be with you always. I know you hurt inside and that you miss me. I hear you crying out to me, and I am right there with you, but you don't feel me—yet. I tell you that you will. I promise.

Our love is so strong it will carry you through all of this. So write when you want to speak to me, but know that I am always there in your thoughts as well, for your thoughts blend with mine, and back and forth we go in a beautiful dance.

Oh, how l love our banter!

My love, don't you see that we are becoming one? We've always been one, but now we are experiencing it as we never have before. This is why when you type out the words, they flow forth so easily because I am inspiring you with my love, my thoughts, and my heartfelt feelings. I am also sharing higher wisdom now that I have access to it. I am especially excited about this!

For that is what inspire means—"in spirit," and Spirit is flowing clear, strong, and true like a river rushing to meet the waiting Sea to bless her with his bounty.

You see, my love, we are meant to write this book, and to do so, we must blend more fully with each other, and we can! Not many souls can do this. Most are too attached to their individuality. But we are not. We have spent many, many lifetimes together, and in this one, we were always at each other's side. And though there are still issues to heal, it was all done so we would be more harmonized with each other when this time came.

That time is now.

Love is what has held us together through the many challenges we've faced in this life and all the others. You and I stuck it out. Together.

As hard as things might feel now, the hardest part is behind us. I didn't want to leave you because I knew you would suffer the loss of me greatly, but I loved you enough to go so that you and I could do the work we planned to do.

For you see, our love for the All is greater than our love for each other.

Dearest Love, can you feel the love I send you right now? Then know that what we have can never be lost or broken but can only be made stronger and purer.

Love endures all things, and whatever it encounters is made holy. Our love is a blessing to the world that can uplift all of humanity. This is true for all souls who love with such a fullness of heart and pure intention, for those who love are the ones who change the world.

Oh, how I love to merge with you in all ways. In the physical is but one way, but that is not the only one. We are merging mind to mind, heart to heart, and soul to soul so that we can write as One—so that we can channel God's wisdom, light, and healing.

This is no small feat!

We have been preparing for this for many lifetimes. I know you still have your doubts about whether or not this is real, but aren't the words that are flowing from me coming without you having a clue as to where they are leading you? All you do is sit down with the intention to connect to me, and I come through. It's that easy.

I have so much to say and so much more to share with you, and I will take every opportunity I have to do so. But I don't want to exhaust you, and I worry that I am doing that. So I will try to tone down my energy so you can sleep. But that may be difficult to do.

For you see, my heart and my consciousness are so blended with you now that it's not easy for you to connect to me without being energized by my presence. I need no sleep where I am. But you do. So let me withdraw just a bit. Not far. Think of it like me being in the next room rather than in bed with you. I remain within earshot and can hear you even if you but whisper my name in your mind.

I can hear you calling me from across the Universe, so you can never lose me!

My love for you has given me strength and has healed me! Did you know that? Yes, when I left this life, I was completely broken not just in my body but in my heart and spirit for all the pain I'd endured in this life and all the others before it.

So much suffering have I carried with me through lifetime after lifetime, pain that I kept buried within my soul. Miraculously, your love shone upon me with such force and gentleness in these last dark months that you healed me of everything.

You healed my very soul even if you could not heal my body, and that was more important.

Do you know how powerful your love is? And therefore, how powerful we are together when we share our love with others? We are here to help heal the world, as many other souls have contracted to do. And we will!

Beautiful Love of my Life and my Soul, I wish I could find more words to express the depth of love that I have for you, the deep respect and high regard I have always had for you since the time we first met eons ago.

You are my Everything, as you have always been.

I regret that I never expressed myself to you like this before today. I should have written you love letters every day that we were together.

I should have showered you with love, kisses, and attention, but I was mired in my past and addicted to my misery so I hid my heart from you.

But no more! Now, I can come through to you as you "write me into being"—into Life!

For words written down make thoughts real!

This is how my words will make ME real to you. This is the way you will know and feel that I am with you because as you write, it will be clear that my words cannot be yours. You will viscerally feel me merge and pour through you into the world of form.

I am alive! I am here! And I will always BE! It can be no other way.

The singular truth of who and what I am cannot be denied.

For no one dies!

No one leaves, for there is nowhere to go but to LIVE here together in the Limitless Universe where we all exist together forever entwined in Love.

You are here with me now; you just can't see it. Not yet.

Now sleep and rest easy, knowing I'm always here watching over you, whether near or far, always ready to step in whenever you but call my name.

CHAPTER 3

REACHING THROUGH THE VEIL

I didn't know how much my husband loved me until he died.

Alan rarely talked about love or his feelings, keeping both buttoned down tight, hoarding them like a miser. He hadn't always been that way, but for reasons I could never fathom, he began to change a few years after we married. But now Alan was showering me with a love so intense I knew I wasn't imagining it.

The morning after he passed, I was drawn to search YouTube for the love theme from the movie *Ghost*. The fact that it had been the first movie we'd seen together wasn't lost on me. I sensed Alan was behind my impulse to search for the song. I spent that first day after he died sitting cross-legged on the living room sofa staring out the window at a cloudless pale blue sky listening to "Unchained Melody" play over and over. It was after the third listen that I felt his love wash over me.

Alan spoke to me in my mind.

Just cry, Pam. The more tears you cry, the more room you make for my love.

And cry I did! Not that I could have stopped even if I tried. I sobbed, felt a measure of relief, then cried again, over and over, until I felt a pleasurable warmth wash over me. In the days that followed, I would call the waves of energy he sent me "love blasts" since that's what they felt like. I couldn't believe this was Alan's doing, but there was no other explanation.

Pam, I'm not dead. I'm right here.

Given that we were psychic mediums and channels, it was odd that the two of us had never talked about the possibility of either of us returning after death, but then, Alan never wanted to talk about death. Especially mine. And while I've always believed the soul lives on, I never expected Alan to make contact with me after he died. Still, I knew what was happening was real since I didn't know how to create feelings of love out of thin air. Can anyone make themselves feel comforted and loved on command? If that were possible, then any grieving widow would wave her magic wand to drink the healing elixir of love once more. Yet that was what was happening to me. Alan was broadcasting his love day and night with a fervor he had never shown during our marriage. To my astonishment, I was grieving and being wooed at the same time. I didn't know it then, but I was the one who was dead, not Alan, and he was determined to resurrect me.

My love, the first thing I have to do is bring you back to life!

Alan hadn't wasted any time making his presence known. Besides feeling his love, his words flowed into my mind whenever I'd write something on my Facebook page as I attempted to share the extraordinary things I was experiencing. Alan was speaking to and through me. The whole thing felt unreal yet oddly familiar at the same time. One morning as I was messaging his friend, Martin Johnson, I could feel Alan's immense love for Martin suddenly sweep over me.

Martin is my spiritual brother, Pam. Do you think it's an accident that we share the same last name?

I felt the depth of Alan's love for Martin, and it stunned me. Alan had never been emotional. Yet the overwhelming feeling of love was intense. In my mind's eye, I saw Alan peering over my right shoulder as I typed, then felt his words merge with mine as I wrote his message to his friend. It was euphoric to feel Alan inside my mind, then merge with my body while he projected his love through me. My body was buzzing with tingles.

While his words didn't always flow easily, being a channeler who can commune with spirits, I never once doubted it was Alan. His presence was unmistakable, and yet there were differences. Alan had become softer. He was more patient and kinder. He immersed me in his love to the point that even with grief weighing heavy on my heart, I was filled with wonder, eager to take his dictation every morning, curious to see what would happen next.

It was hard to believe, but each day proved to be more unbelievable than the one before it, and in time, loving and living with him between the two worlds became my only reality. I couldn't stop writing about it and telling anyone who would listen.

In the beginning, writing down Alan's messages was easier for me than trying to talk telepathically. I've always known that it's easy for spirits to put messages and ideas into our mind. It can be so easy that we assume we are making it up, when the truth is it's difficult to talk to ourselves unless we're schizophrenic, habitually talk to ourselves, or take hallucinogens. For the rest of us, carrying on both sides of a conversation is a demanding, exhausting job!

That said, Alan preferred I write his messages down so I'd have a permanent record, saying it was better this way because talking to the spirit world puts us into an altered state. When we return to normal consciousness, everything fades from our memory as if we are waking from a dream. But there was more to it than that. Alan wanted me to share his writings with the world, saying that he wanted witnesses to what was about to unfold between us.

We are going to help souls on both sides of the veil reconnect as you and I are about to do, so would you please form a Facebook group where we can share our story? Share everything. All of it. Your good days, and your bad, the highs, the lows, your triumphs, and your losses. All of this is part of the quest to reunite and love through the veil. This won't be an easy ride, but when you share it with others who are on the same journey, the road will be made easier for all of you. It's difficult, for some even impossible, to connect to the spirit world alone, so you'll find there is strength in numbers. For it will take a village of souls on both sides of the veil to merge Heaven and Earth! Souls who share the common goal of reaching through the veil can move mountains when they join together. That's the power of unconditional love shared between the two worlds! This is what makes love supernatural! Love can bend the laws of the physical world.

The words "supernatural love" appeared in my mind a few days after he passed. Alan said this would be the title of our book. He also suggested I purchase the domain name to use for our website. While I doubted it was available, he insisted it was, and sure enough, he was right.

CHAPTER 4

OUR LOVE WILL MERGE
HEAVEN AND EARTH

My love for you is here now and will be with you always. I love you more than words can say, more than actions can show. Be at peace and know that I can and will be with you anytime, anywhere you need me. Our love cannot die; it can only grow and be shared with the world. So let me teach you how to feel and be with me so you can join me in the higher realms where we belong. Feeling my love will heal your heart, your mind, and your soul, but first, you must open to the full spectrum of your emotions.

I love you, Pam, my darling, my love. Don't cry! I am never leaving you. I will always be at your side until the end of this physical life and beyond or for as long as you want me. I know this is a surprise to you, but I promise you that I will not only make things right between us—I will make you happy.

Let me guide, protect, and help you through whatever comes. I want to be with you, but you must also want that. And if you do, then take *my hand and my heart, my love, and let's take flight together. For this is not the end but a brand new beginning for us. We have much work to do, and so much love and new adventures to share! In time, we'll inspire others who have been parted by the veil. We'll help them to find their way back to each other so they can love and live again together as we will do.*

Love is the force that can heal anything and everything.

At last, I know that! I wasn't able to let my guard down to love you the way I can love you now. The way I am sending all of my love to you at this very moment. Oh, how I wish I had dared to be my true self when I was with you! You knew I was hiding from you. But now, finally, at long last, I am the Real Me that you have known for eternity, for that is how long we've been together. My beloved, breathe in all the love I have for you! The pure, full force of ecstatic love that all beings can feel and express once they shed their egoic fears. Love is who we are, in truth!

No one should have to die to live and love freely, but sadly, this is what most people do. They die and only then come ALIVE!

Until now, you have been hiding from the Great Work that is now before you. I know you longed to work with me from the moment we met. It was one of your greatest disappointments that we never stepped out into the world to work together, but guess what? We are doing it now! This is it. This is the work we're meant to do, babe! It's just not going to be the way you had thought it would be, with me being in the non-physical world and you there in the physical, but this is perfect, and it's how we planned it to be, my darling; soon, you will understand.

You and I will build a bridge between the two worlds. A bridge that will be traversed first by us, then by those who choose to follow. There will be an upswell of interest in love and life-after-death relationships.

We'll contribute to this growing movement by writing a book about our new life together, a book that will continue to be written and added to until you leave this world and return to Heaven with me.

The title of our book will be Supernatural Love, *a true story of life and love after death.*

A week later, I formed our Facebook group. I initially called it "Supernatural Love and Life After Death." Two years later, the group name was changed to "Soulmates in the Afterlife" to reflect our focus on helping interdimensional couples reunite. That first year, the group grew slowly, which was fine with me since I was deep in the throes of processing my grief and had little interest in promoting the group. Besides, I preferred a small, intimate group of clients and friends who were there to support me and follow what was turning into an extraordinary journey to reunite with Alan. The group quickly grew to know and love Alan as he sprang to life through his constant messages of love, inspiration, and hope for all of us.

Write me into BEING, Pam!

CHAPTER 5

WHO DOESN'T WANT TO GO TO HAWAII?

O ur paths first crossed in mid-February of 1990 when Alan and his friend Barbara visited Hawaii for the first time. Both of them were accomplished psychic mediums who belonged to the British Astrological and Psychic Society (B.A.P.S.), which meant they had passed a series of tests of their psychic abilities. For several years they had been travelling from England to Hong Kong on a regular basis to give readings at a New Age shop that catered to British ex-pats. But on this particular trip, they arrived to find their plans abruptly canceled, leaving them to figure out what to do for the remaining three weeks before their next stop in Omaha, Nebraska. Honolulu came to mind because they had a local contact on Oahu, a psychic channel named Nancy McCary.

When Barbara initially suggested the idea of a Honolulu stopover, Alan resisted. Barbara was incredulous. "Who doesn't want to go to Hawaii?" she asked, "Besides, this is perfect. Hawaii is halfway to the states." Since he couldn't explain his reluctance, and seeing as there was no other option that made sense, Alan gave in.

Alan would later say that he sensed his life was about to change, and oh how he detested change! It would be his continual lament over the decades that followed whenever he was uprooted, which happened every few years for various reasons. But in February of 1990, fate was taking Alan out of his comfort zone, and like it or not, he found himself on a plane bound for Hawaii.

At the time, I worked at Sedona, a metaphysical gift shop located in a boutique shopping mall in the heart of Honolulu. I first met Martin and his wife, Malia, at a psychic fair where I was giving readings. I had only just begun giving readings as a spiritual channel professionally when they sought me out for guidance regarding the planned opening of their new store. I predicted that they would find success with it, so when, a few months later, I heard that the store had at last opened its doors, I stopped by to offer my congratulations. Martin was working on the sales floor that day.

I greeted Martin, offered my congratulations, and promptly heard my spirit guides say, "Ask him if he needs help in the store!"

I posed the question to Martin, who grinned broadly. "Why, yes we do! Would you like to work here?"

"Well, um. Yes, I guess I would!"

When I wasn't giving psychic readings upstairs in the loft area of the store, I worked on the sales floor, helping customers. I was downstairs working with Martin the day Alan, Barbara, and Nancy walked in. I had worked with Nancy during a luncheon event I helped produce, which featured several well-known Hawaii channelers who, over the course of the two-hour lunch, took turns speaking about their work channeling the spirit world. Nancy and I became friends right away. She exuded charm and warmth and possessed a luminous quality that wasn't based solely on her blonde, leggy good looks. It was impossible not to like her.

With Alan and Barbara flanking her, Nancy strode through the front door, her face beaming. "Hey there, Martin and Pam! I've got two new friends I want you to meet!"

After quick introductions, Nancy explained that Alan and Barbara weren't happy with their hotel in Waikiki. It was too expensive for them. No one was surprised. Nancy asked, "Does anyone know where these two might find cheaper accommodations?"

Alan laughed nervously. "I don't think we knew what we were doing when we booked the hotel. It would be great to find somewhere quieter and less expensive. We're also looking for somewhere to work while we're here, though I suppose that might be hard to do on such short notice."

I was fascinated by this interesting, odd-looking couple. They were the same height, but that was where the similarity ended. Barbara was stout and matronly and had a slight tremor, while Alan appeared fit and looked more youthful. Adding to the contrast was his demeanor; Alan was funny and outgoing, whereas Barbara was shy and quiet. I couldn't tell if they were friends or a couple. I was so caught up in analyzing them that I almost missed what Martin said in reply to Alan's question.

Martin pointed straight at me. "I have an idea. You can stay with Pam! She's got room in her house."

Without thinking, I heard myself say, "Sure! You can stay with me!"

Barbara and Alan jumped at my invitation. Nancy looked pleased that her mission was accomplished. And to top things off, Martin invited Alan and Barbara to give readings at the psychic fair the store was hosting the following weekend. The timing of their visit began to look perfect to everyone since the store was always in need of experienced psychics. With that decided, Nancy invited us to her home for dinner in Alan and Barbara's honor. We agreed that they would follow me back to my house after that.

As soon as they left the store, I nudged Martin, asking him why he had offered my house to them so freely. Martin shrugged his shoulders, saying he had no clue. I had just invited two strangers to stay in my home for a few weeks, but for some reason, I wasn't worried. All I felt was a sense of anticipation. I knew that whatever happened, it would be interesting.

The night of the dinner, much to my frustration, I found myself drawn to Alan. It was clear that he and Barbara were as close as any two people could be. I assumed they were a couple since he deferred to her about everything and was attentive to her needs, which I couldn't help but find appealing. My psychic ability was of no use to me since the only message I kept getting was that they were together but not together.

I knew Alan was older than me, but by exactly how much, I had no idea. There was something ageless about him that made it difficult to pin a number to his age. He was handsome, with a rakish, boyish charm accentuated by mischievous, twinkling eyes and a Cheshire Cat grin whenever he made a funny remark. I loved his silly sense of humor, which I found as attractive as his good looks and sensitivity. The bonus was that he was spiritual. All of this made it even harder for me to rein in my feelings. I had to keep reminding myself that Alan was taken.

As we relaxed in Nancy's living room with the other guests, I watched Alan play with the bubbly, precocious five-year-old adopted daughter of one of the guests. The little girl was Chinese and utterly adorable. Everyone who met her fell in love with her. She had hypnotized Alan from the moment she plopped down next to him to play with her toys. I could tell by how his eyes lit up that Alan loved little girls! It melted my heart to see how he enjoyed talking to her as much, if not more, than the adults.

Once dinner was finished, Alan, Barbara, and I said our goodbyes to Nancy and her guests before getting into our separate cars to make our way to my home. The short fifteen-minute drive wound through the streets of the beachside town of Kailua before continuing along the coast to Lanikai, a cloistered residential area that was so exclusive it had only one road in and out. Decades later, due to its postcard-perfect white sand beach, calm turquoise waters, and stunning sunrise views, Lanikai would become overrun with tourists, but at the time of their visit, it was a quiet, upper middle-class neighborhood with homes that ranged from mansions to simple houses.

My home was one of those simple houses. Built in the early 1950s, it was a nondescript, 1300-square-foot, chocolate-brown wooden bungalow perched high atop a hill that boasted thirty-five exhausting steps leading to the front door. After Alan hauled their luggage up the stairs, I took them on a tour of the three bedrooms and one-and-a-half bathrooms. The main attraction was the eye-popping panoramic view of the Pacific with the island of Maui hugging the horizon on the far right. I took them on a tour of the kitchen, pointing out things they could eat if they got hungry, including a box of blueberry muffins and a basket of fruit. I told them they'd be able to watch the sunrise if they got up early enough.

Since they looked exhausted, I showed them the two bedrooms and asked them to choose.

"There is a bedroom next to mine, and there's another one with a half bath at the other end of the house behind the kitchen. Both bedrooms have queen beds. Barbara could take the room next to mine, and Alan, you could take the one off the kitchen."

Alan replied, "No, that's okay; we'll take the bedroom with the half bath."

That was it. If I had had any doubt about it before, Alan confirmed they were a couple. They would be sleeping together. We walked back to the kitchen towards the bedroom room. Standing in the kitchen, I leaned forward to say goodnight to Barbara. I hugged her, then turned to Alan to hug him.

When I hugged Alan, I almost fell over.

A jolt of electricity shot through my body. In an instant, I knew Alan was The One. I was shocked. How could this be? It was something straight out of a romance novel. I had met my share of handsome men, but none of them affected me like this. I wasn't prone to fantasizing about men just because they were good-looking or sexy, so this wasn't my imagination. Could Alan have felt it, too, I wondered? I couldn't tell by looking at him, although it was hard for me to look him in the eye since I was afraid that he'd see I was trembling, so instead, I muttered a goodnight and made a quick exit to my room.

My mind was racing. What in the world was going on? I'd only just met Alan, and he was with a woman with whom he had a loving, spiritual connection. They were spiritual partners, traveling the world together and even sleeping with each other! Was I losing my mind?

But there was no denying it; my body was on fire with an energy that was more than sexual. I'd never felt anything like it before. I couldn't stop thinking about Alan. When I closed my eyes, his smiling face was all I could see. I tried in vain to fall asleep as questions kept circling round and round in my mind. What would tomorrow bring? Would I even have a chance to get to know Alan with Barbara constantly hovering at his side? She seemed leery of me and possessive of him. Would that be a problem? I wasn't even thinking about the fact that he lived in England. For some reason, that didn't worry me.

I woke to find Alan, relaxing in the living room.

"Wow, you weren't kidding about that view, Pam! And to think you wake up to that sunrise every morning. If I lived here, I'd never leave the house."

I told him I knew what he meant. Even after thirty years, the ocean view never failed to mesmerize me, especially in the morning when the sun rose over Maui. The ocean and the two small islands offshore, known as the Mokulua Islands or "the Mokes" as the locals called them, seemed to fill the entire living room picture window when you walked from the back of the house to the living room.

After breakfast, it was agreed that I'd drive them into Kailua Town to do some shopping. Kailua has some of the best swimming beaches in the state, which makes it a popular spot for tourists and locals alike. I had grown up in this beachside town from the age of four when we temporarily lived on the beach in a house that I remember as being nothing more than a glorified two-bedroom shack owned by the bank my father worked for. Even though it was tiny and worn down in places by the salt air, it was clean and comfortable. Nothing comes close to having the ocean in your backyard.

As soon as Barbara left to get dressed, I couldn't wait a moment longer. I asked Alan if they were a couple. The pained look on his face said it all. He was eager to set me straight.

"No, Pam, we're more like brother and sister! We're not involved in that way. Barbara would like us to be more than friends, but I don't feel that way about her, and she knows that. There are times when we might share a bed during our travels when she wants me to stay close because she needs my help. But believe me—there's nothing romantic or sexual between us, only a close friendship and our spiritual work."

I marveled at how they were the same age, yet Alan looked so much younger. He sported a leonine head of hair with tight chestnut curls that matched his bright brown eyes, eyes that widened with glee when he delivered a joke or poked fun at someone. At the time we met, I was having my normally straight brown-black hair permed, so my hair was almost as curly as Alan's. He got a huge kick out of that, dubbing us twins, conveniently ignoring the fact that I'm Japanese.

"Pam, I love that you're Japanese-American. I love all things Asian and American. But really, you're more American than Japanese, aren't you?"

Yes, he was right. I was an all-American girl through and through. I had been raised by my second-generation Japanese-American parents to fully embrace the Western way of life with only minimal attention given to my Japanese roots, aside from taking part in Buddhist temple rituals. Until I was older, I had no idea they were part of an actual religion because my father never bothered telling me he was Buddhist.

We never discussed religion in my family. My parents were neither for nor against it where my brother and I were concerned; it was just their way, which may explain why they accepted my spiritual beliefs when I opened up psychically. It also helped that my maternal grandmother had been a psychic medium who had given readings in Hanapepe on the island of Kauai before World War II forced her to stop. Grandma Rose Uno had no choice but to end her psychic readings since, being Japanese, she didn't want to draw unwanted attention to her family. I only learned that my grandmother had been a medium many years after she passed when I was going through my own spiritual awakening. My grandmother came to my mother to tell her, "Don't worry about Pam. She's just like me. Just support her, and she'll be fine!" From that moment on, my mother became my biggest fan and my grandmother my fierce protector.

Alan's youthfulness was enhanced by his wit and considerable charm and the fact that he refused to act his age. Given that Barbara was a subdued, sensitive Pisces and Alan a showy, charismatic Leo, they made for a strange-looking couple until you noticed the close familial bond. Brothers and sisters can be very different but get along, and as if to further prove the fraternal connection, Alan would sometimes get irritated with Barbara just as any brother would, and yet he loved his sister.

Barbara was a well-respected psychic medium in Britain, and after meeting at one of the many psychic fairs held in England, they became fast friends. Barbara took Alan under her wing to help him develop his mediumship, and now here they were traveling the world together, or as they liked to call it, "working for Spirit," since during their journeys abroad, they'd be guided to a location to give healing to the Earth. They would close their eyes, join hands, and direct energy into the ground, their bodies serving as acupuncture needles for Mother Earth. During their stay, we flew to the Big Island of Hawaii, where they performed healing at the volcano in Kilauea. I had never met anyone quite like Alan before. His psychic prowess was remarkable, yet he didn't take himself seriously. Quite the opposite. He was down to earth and full of fun.

Alan was a natural-born medium whose childhood had been marked by disturbing experiences sensing spirits around him. Alone in bed at night, he was terrified to feel his body expand to fill the room, then feel himself shrink to fit into a corner. That, together with feeling spirits crowding around him, panicked Alan to the point that he'd wail and bang his head on the wall until his mother would come to him. But it wasn't until he was in his late forties that Alan understood his psychic gifts. He was grateful to have found a true friend and spiritual partner in Barbara, and to have her guide him in his development as a psychic medium was a blessing. I had to accept the fact that her friendship was important to him, and so I did.

With Barbara always with us, it wasn't easy to talk privately. On the other hand, being psychic, we seemed to know what the other felt, especially as the sexual tension ramped up between us. Nevertheless, we didn't sleep with each other right away. Alan was nervous about what he was getting into, while I was afraid of being hurt again since I had ended a tumultuous relationship just a month before. Alan confessed to me that he wanted me in the worst way but could only see problems for himself. Our age difference was the biggest issue to him, which I found odd. I had thought older men lusted after younger women. Well, not Alan. It was one of many things that made him different from other men.

Alan would later confess that he was worried about satisfying me sexually when he got older, since he had already done the math. By the time he was seventy, I'd still be a youthful fifty-five-year-old. The fact that he looked younger than his fifty-two years and could easily pass for forty buoyed his self-esteem only a little. He was too much of a realist.

Another problem was Alan hated uncertainty and change. For all of his playfulness and youthful charm, he was surprisingly staid and set in his ways. He had only just settled into his life as a globetrotting bachelor, having finally freed himself from an unhappy marriage and the day-to-day running of his chemical maintenance company so that he could travel and pursue his newfound spiritual interests, which had become his passion. With a giant grin on his face, Alan loved saying that psychic work gave him a spiritual orgasm when he hit the mark with his readings. But this wasn't a joke. He was serious; it was a testament to how much he loved his new life as a psychic medium. Alan had finally liberated himself from his old life, but now here I was, disrupting his carefully laid plans just when he thought things were falling into place.

After many false starts, we finally agreed on a night to be alone. Alan would come to my bedroom after he and Barbara returned from the Polynesian Cultural Center, a popular tourist attraction that Barbara was eager to visit. Consisting of an evening luau with a lavish show, preceded by a full afternoon of outdoor activities, it offers visitors a hands-on experience of Polynesia, complete with the requisite hula lessons and bare-chested men shimmying up palm trees to retrieve coconuts. Since I'd seen the show countless times, I chose not to tag along, knowing that with the directions I had given Alan, they could easily find their way there and back on their own.

The next day, Alan and Barbara left for the show right after breakfast. I couldn't stop thinking about Alan. Now that I had time alone, questions finally began to surface. Was this relationship a mistake, given the distance between us? And what about the fact that Alan had his life fully established? Would he ever become comfortable with our age difference? Although I didn't think it mattered, I admitted to Alan that I'd never been involved with a man his age, which made him worry all the more.

It was almost midnight when I heard the sliding glass door open. Moments later, Alan knocked on my bedroom door and walked in. His face was flushed; I assumed he had gotten sunburn from being outside all day without a hat or sunscreen.

"Are you okay, Alan? It's so late. How was the show?"

I had been looking forward to being with him, but now that we were finally alone, I was nervous. Alan had his eyes fixated on the beige carpet as if it was the most fascinating thing he'd ever seen.

"The show was great. Barbara loved it, but we stopped at a McDonald's for some coffee afterward. We went inside, but I forgot to roll up the windows, so when we got back to the car, we saw that it had rained, and I had to mop up the inside. What an awful mess that was! But I don't want to talk about that."

He took my hand and stared into my eyes.

"Pam, I'm nervous. I couldn't stop thinking about you. That Polynesian show was wasted on me. You must know how I feel by now. I'm in love with you. When I told Barbara I'd fallen in love with you, she couldn't believe it, and to be honest, I'm having a hard time believing it myself. I've never felt this way about any woman before. This happened so fast that it scares me."

I hadn't realized that I'd been holding my breath the entire time until I let out a sigh. "Alan, I knew you were the one for me when I hugged you that first night, remember? Please don't worry! Can't we just see where this takes us? I've never wanted to be with someone as much as I want to be with you. This just feels right, so how could it be a mistake?"

Alan drew in closer, his mouth hovering over mine for a moment before gracing my lips with a trace of a kiss. Goosebumps rushed down my back. It was like that first hug, only twice as intense. His arms enveloped me tightly, throwing me off my center, twisting us backward onto the bed behind us. I giggled as we fell together.

"Hey, are the million pillows on your bed just for show or for crash landings like this?"

Alan's touch was electrifying, just as it was the first time I hugged him, but something was amiss. My head and heart were not in sync. Even though I yearned for him with a hunger that was new to me, I could feel myself holding back as we began to make love. I felt like I was having an out-of-body experience. Part of me was up on the ceiling, looking down on the two of us holding each other, kissing and caressing, while my mind was going in circles.

I couldn't understand what was wrong with me. This made no sense since talking to Alan was so easy. Our flirtatious back-and-forth bantering bordered on foreplay, and then there was the raucous laughter. Oh, how he made me laugh like no other man I had ever met. How I loved that about him! I hadn't realized how important laughter was to me until I ended a drama-fueled, emotionally abusive relationship with a much younger man. Once I freed myself from that relationship, I vowed never to let anyone control me like that again. Love and laughter moved to the top of my "What I Need to Be Happy List." I had lived my life estranged from love and passion, but now both were finally converging. The only problem was I didn't know how to act.

Alan was a passionate, attentive lover. Yet I couldn't surrender to him right away. Instead, I was watching myself from above, not as a voyeur but as a protector. My guard was up. Perhaps I hadn't recovered from the emotional abuse and disappointment from my last two failed relationships. I was overthinking everything until, finally, Alan's passion rallied to sweep me away.

I later reasoned that it was inevitable that the mounting sexual tension we had felt for days could not play out without a letdown, but I couldn't ignore the worrying thought that this could be a sign of trouble to come. Still, our first time together, while not spectacular, was infused with soulful love. More importantly, I was certain that I loved Alan. I may have been uncertain about other things in my life, but not about this. In the end, I summoned my passion to surrender my heart and body to him without an ounce of doubt that our love was real. By the next day, Alan was just as sure of his feelings for me. That wasn't the problem.

"Okay, I have to say it. I love you and want to be with you in the worst way, Pam, but there are so many things working against us. For one thing, why do you have to be so young? Fifteen years! Back in England, I turned down a relationship with a woman because of the age difference between us, and here you are, even younger than she is! Then there's the not-so-small problem of you living in Hawaii. I don't even want to think about that! Clearly, one of us will have to move, and I don't think it's going to be you."

"I feel the same way about you, Alan. I love you. Can't we just see where this takes us? I'm not worried about the future. Really, I'm not. Somehow it will all work out. Don't ask me how I know; I just know it will. You can't deny that what we feel for each other is real."

"Yes, my love for you is real; that's what scares the shit out of me. I've never felt this way about a woman before. Oh, sure, I've had affairs. One turned me inside out, but I wasn't in love with her the way I'm in love with you. It must be because you're spiritual. It can't be a coincidence that I'm meeting you now that I've committed to my spiritual work just as you have. I feel so in tune with you, Pam, even though you and I come from different backgrounds, different worlds, really. I grew up scrambling in poverty in the slums of London during World War II.

"Growing up, I missed a lot of school because of my asthma, so much that any hopes I had for higher education were dashed. Yet, against the odds, I won a coveted internship with General Motors where I trained to become an engineer, then went on to create wealth for myself and my family when I founded my own companies. I did all this while you grew up in middle-class comfort, living high on a hillside in paradise. You even say that your house didn't have a key, and it still doesn't! Your parents weren't rich, and yet you had advantages I never dreamed of, and I'm so happy that you had them, Pam. I'm not putting you down for it. No, not at all. If anything, I'm happy to know that your life was easier than mine."

It was true. My parent's house didn't have a key. I had to warn Alan about the door soon after he had arrived. The entrance to the house was a large glass slider that had to be lifted up and wiggled off its track to open, so unless someone knew that secret, they would assume it was locked when the door failed to slide open. As a result, we never needed a key. This, and the thirty-plus stairs, were deterrents to any would-be thief.

Our remaining days together flew by quickly with me playing tour guide, showing Barbara and Alan the many sites and lush green vistas of Oahu. One morning, I took them to Waimea Falls Park on the North Shore of Oahu, home to monster waves and pro surfing competitions. While strolling through the park, Alan wandered away from Barbara and me and heard a voice say, "Welcome home!" The only thing was he was completely alone. There was no one near him. The island seemed to have declared itself to be Alan's spiritual home, laying out the welcome mat for him. Waimea Valley was the home of the Hawaiian kahunas. A kahuna is a wiseman or shaman. On that day, the island claimed Alan as one of its own. It was the first of many signs he would receive that he belonged in Hawaii.

The odds of surviving the many obstacles before us didn't look good. There was the fifteen-year age difference, Alan's fear of change, and his fear and insecurity about loving a woman who couldn't live further away from him. There wasn't just one but two oceans between us—the Pacific and the Atlantic—not to mention the cultural differences which made Hawaii seem like a foreign land to him.

Once he left for their next stop, Omaha, Nebraska, I knew I would have to ramp up my letter-writing to stay in constant touch with him. The

Internet wouldn't be accessible for another two years, so letters and expensive phone calls were all we'd have to keep our love alive. I'd have to soothe Alan's fears and reassure him that my love was true. By comparison, I was sure about my love for him. But then, for me, it was simpler because I didn't have to make any changes to my life; everything was on Alan's shoulders.

That first hug had been all I needed. Alan had fallen in love with me just two days after we met. It was his conscious mind that was warring with his heart, arguing that he'd have to give up everything to be with me, not because I asked him to, but because he couldn't imagine me leaving Hawaii to live in England. I didn't care where we lived, but Alan didn't see that for us. All I could do was pray that the voice that had welcomed him in Waimea Valley had made an impression.

I knew it would take everything I had to convince Alan to return to Hawaii so we could have a better chance at getting to know each other on our own. I worried that it would be easier for him to surrender to his fears, forget me, and move on. When we were together, his fears vanished, but when we were apart, anxiety took over. Knowing this, I began writing letters to him the day he left for Nebraska, starting with slipping a love letter into his carry-on bag. My master plan was to keep a steady stream of letters, cards, audio tapes, and parcels flowing between us. I was going to inundate Alan with love until he surrendered.

Alan didn't write to me as often as I wrote to him because he was busy with work, but to make up for it, he would sometimes call me on his car phone. On those occasions, he'd say, "To hell with the cost!" It was always a thrill to hear his British accent greet me as I picked up the phone. As busy as he was, Alan managed to send parcels and audio tapes; some of the tapes were an hour long. How I loved falling asleep listening to him. He roared with laughter when I told him.

"Hah, and here I believed you when you said my voice was sexy. It was all a lie! I'm nothing more than a sleeping pill with an accent to you!"

Four months and a mini-avalanche of love letters later, Alan returned to me for a few precious weeks. We were alone at last for the first time, left in blissful peace to linger at our leisure in bed in the mornings now that no one was there tugging on us to go somewhere or do something. Having the luxury of uninterrupted time together, we were able to fully immerse ourselves in each other. Weeks later, Alan returned to England feeling certain about our future; the only question left was how we could stay together since he was British. Another visit was immediately planned.

Alan's second visit began as gloriously as the first. All was going well between us until a few days later, when I discovered I was pregnant.

As soon we got involved, I assured Alan that having children was not important to me, which was true. I even promised him I'd have an abortion if it came to that. But when I learned that I was pregnant, I changed my mind. I couldn't go through with an abortion, not because I thought it was wrong to have one but because, much to my surprise, I knew I was meant to have his child. Although Alan could see that I was as shocked as he was by my change of heart, that didn't stop him from flying into a rage, accusing me of lying and manipulating him just as other women had done to him in the past. He threatened to leave, but I stood my ground, which only infuriated him further.

Alan was angry because it seemed as if the past was repeating itself.

At the age of twenty-two, he had settled down to marry his partner Jane when she became pregnant. While their relationship was good, marriage was not something Alan had wanted just yet. Many years later, Alan nearly walked out on his marriage when he had an affair and fell in love with another woman, though he couldn't do it in the end. He didn't have the heart to leave his two sons, who were still quite young. When Alan finally got his divorce, his sons were fully grown with their own children. He vowed never to marry or have children again. This was one of the first things he told me when we met; he drew a hard line in the sand to make sure I wouldn't cross it. While he would give me all of his love, there would be no marriage, no kids, and no discussion about it. He wanted to have me all to himself without the distraction and responsibility of child-rearing hindering his freedom.

Alan had worked hard all of his life, supported and raised a family, and built several businesses, and now with that behind him, he wanted to do what he pleased, perhaps even become known for his psychic gifts. I didn't understand until years later how much he relished the attention he received for his readings when he traveled. He enjoyed being treated like a minor celebrity by the wealthy patrons who hosted him. By comparison, Alan seemed restless, staying home with me. How could I compete with that? I wondered if life with me would ever be enough for him.

But my guidance remained unshakable. I knew that if I had an abortion, I would regret it for the rest of my life and that, in the end, it would drive us apart and destroy our relationship. There was no way around it. Whether he stayed or left, I was going to be a mother. I couldn't understand it myself, but this was how I had lived my life since my spiritual awakening five years earlier, I followed my guidance no matter where it took me, and now that guidance might cost me the man I loved.

For two days, we talked about it endlessly. Alan felt cornered, but I wasn't going to change my mind. I couldn't go against what I knew was right for me, no matter the consequences. When Alan finally agreed we should marry, it felt like we were negotiating a business arrangement. It certainly wasn't a romantic marriage proposal. It was an inauspicious start to our life together. My pregnancy, which should have been a joyous celebration of our love, instead drove an insidious wedge of doubt between us. From that moment on, Alan would wonder if the only reason I was with him was that I needed him to support me financially and be a father to our son.

Until he left this world, he'd often turn to me and say, "I love you more than you love me, Pam." I'd shake my head, telling him he didn't know what he was talking about, that one day he would realize he had it backward.

I began to question Alan's love the moment he said he expected me to take full responsibility for raising our son because he didn't want to be a father. His attitude softened once Taylor was born, as his love for him blossomed into a deep connection, but Alan remained detached, leaving me sometimes feeling like a single parent. Matters were made worse when, over my strenuous objections, Alan announced he was resuming his travels with Barbara. In his mind, this was more than fair. I would have the child I wanted, along with his financial support, while he could go wherever he chose. I was crushed to think I came in second to Barbara and his work. But now I knew where I stood. I came last. From then on, I refused to believe him when he said he loved me.

In his mind, Alan had worked hard all of his life, leaving behind a thriving business, his friends and family, and all the material gains and comforts he had acquired, while I, on the other hand, had sacrificed nothing and gained everything he believed a woman could ever want: financial security, a baby, and a loving husband. In his opinion, he had more than proven his love for me, whereas I had not. Add to that his fear of losing me, and we were on shaky ground. We were about to be married, standing on the threshold of what should have been a storybook marriage, but we didn't realize we were backsliding into an abyss of doubt and complacency that would cost us everything.

CHAPTER 6

HAPPY REBIRTH DAY

He stopped breathing. I was in the kitchen washing the dinner dishes before I walked into the living room. I noticed it immediately. For days since he had returned from the hospital, Alan's breathing had been labored and raspy, but now all I heard was an eerie silence. My heart sank as I rushed to his bed and pulled back the sheet to touch his feet. The icy chill made me cringe.

Alan had always looked youthful. The hospice nurse couldn't believe his age. By the time of his death at age eighty-three, Alan barely had any lines on his face. I'm convinced it was through sheer willpower that he had managed to look twenty years younger because he certainly didn't take care of himself. He never exercised. A perfect dinner to him consisted of a glass of Merlot, filet mignon, Brie cheese, and mocha almond fudge ice cream. Not exactly a doctor-approved diet, yet people shook their heads when he announced his age. And oh, how he loved it when their mouths dropped open in amazement.

Even on his deathbed, Alan still had a full head of salt-and-pepper hair, although his gray curls had been trimmed back severely since being in the hospital. More than a few of his clients had compared his looks to the actor, Sean Connery, another Brit who managed to age well, although Alan preferred being compared to another actor, Richard Gere, claiming they shared the same prominent nose. When we were out in public, heads would occasionally turn as people did a double take, which made Alan chuckle. He continually wondered what famous person he was being mistaken for.

I took a deep breath and steeled myself to check the rest of his body, beginning with his legs, then his stomach, followed by his chest and arms. Tears welled in my eyes as I felt the warmth slowly receding from his limbs. I gently stroked Alan's cheek, found it still warm, and cried out for him. I couldn't look at his body a moment longer; I had to turn away.

He was gone.

Even if we know death is imminent, we are never prepared for it. How can we be? How can we imagine the unimaginable? Even though I had cared for both of my parents at the end of their lives with Alan's help, together with hospice caregivers in our home, it was not something I had gotten used to, as if anyone can get used to it. Alan's turn for hospice came five years later, but this time the burden was mine alone since the COVID pandemic made home care options limited.

While he had struggled with mild cognitive issues for two years before his official diagnosis, the visit to the doctor seven months before his death seemed to trigger an invisible countdown because, from that moment on, it was as if Alan was in a race to the finish line, so swift was his decline. It was no coincidence that the day Alan received the voodoo curse of his dementia diagnosis, he became incontinent.

As soon as I heard the doctor say dementia, I knew my time was up, Pam. I didn't want to leave you, but I was tired of being old, and eighty-two years is a long time to be in a body! I didn't want you to suffer any longer than you'd have to, so from that moment on, I counted the days until my exit. I planned it, just as every soul can.

Death feels wrong on so many levels, not just because we don't want to lose someone we love, but because there's something about death that feels like a lie. I find it hard even to use the word 'death' since I know we don't die. And on the day that death arrived to claim my husband, my heart and soul screamed, "This isn't real!" Little did I know that I would soon find out I was right.

Death is a lie.

I phoned Taylor to break the news of his dad's passing. He took the news calmly, saying he'd be right over. With that done, I called the hospice nurse, who told me another nurse would arrive soon to confirm Alan's death. She would call the mortuary for me, who would arrive later to collect his body. Everything was on autopilot.

His body. I knew Alan wasn't in his body anymore. He had lost so much weight; he was a shell of the man he had been. I scanned the room, half expecting to see Alan or at least feel him. But no matter how hard I tried, I felt nothing.

Not yet.

With those tasks checked off my list, my mind switched off, and a peaceful numbness set in. Until I remembered I still had to notify Alan's two adult sons from his first marriage, who lived in England. I had been updating them on their dad's condition from the moment Alan had fallen and broken his hip, the injury triggering his rapid decline. Given Alan's age and his dementia, the ER doctor warned me to prepare for the worst, citing the statistics on the survival rate of dementia patients after a serious injury.

Sensing the end was coming, I had already turned my Facebook page into a quasi-memorial page for Alan, filling it with an array of our photos and stories of his life pre-dementia. I wanted to keep him alive and present in my life for as long as I could.

My crazy-funny, larger-and-louder-than-life husband was loved by so many friends and loyal clients during the years he had worked as a psychic transplanted from England when we married in 1991. At the age of fifty-two, Alan had walked away from his lucrative maintenance chemical company to begin a new chapter of his life as a psychic medium on Oahu. Not many men dare to make such a radical change at the pinnacle of their life, let alone move to another country on the other side of the world, but Alan relished his new life as a psychic.

I continued to post on my Facebook page, feeling compelled to describe what was happening to me in real time. I didn't know why this was so important; all I knew was that I felt I had to share everything as it was happening. Was Alan nudging me to do this, or was grief pushing me? Whatever it was made no difference to me; I couldn't stop myself either way.

Alan died on his birthday, August 6, 2020, just as the COVID pandemic swept Hawaii. Just before Honolulu went into its first and only lockdown, I had relocated us from a two-story townhouse into a small, single level two-bedroom house, chosen for the safety it afforded Alan and the closer proximity to Taylor, who lived a few miles away. The morning he passed, Alan was lying unconscious, in the rented hospital bed that we had carefully positioned to give him a panoramic view of Diamond Head through the glass sliding doors off of the living room. I leaned over to whisper in his ear, "You better not be planning to die on your birthday, or I swear I'll kill you!" Even on his deathbed, I knew Alan would chuckle at the dark humor.

In the final months of his life, Alan kept asking to speak to someone he called his "best black friend in Boston." I couldn't figure out who that was since I knew all of his friends, and none of them were black, and none of them live in Boston. Then it hit me.

"Alan, do you mean you want to talk to Swati?"

Yes! Swati is the one I mean! She's my best black friend in Boston! he answered brightly.

I laughed, but not as hard as Swati did when I told her.

Swati lived in Boston with her husband and daughter before moving to San Jose, California, but she is originally from India. Alan had met her when we visited her home in San Jose many years ago when we attended a past-life regression workshop that she had organized for Dolores Cannon. While Swati and I kept in touch over the years, the two of them had only spoken occasionally during readings. Once Swati learned of Alan's dementia, she became my lifeline, keeping tabs on me daily through the worst of Alan's illness, checking on me constantly to see if I was okay. Which I wasn't, but her constant love and concern for me kept me from falling apart.

Being profoundly psychic, Swati had been checking on Alan since learning of his dementia, connecting with him on a soul level to ask why he wasn't healing himself because she knew he had the power to do so. But in their telepathic conversations, Alan told her it wasn't that he couldn't heal himself; he was simply tired of having an old body. Healing himself wouldn't make him young again. Besides, he had work to do on the other side, work that required him to step into all of his spiritual powers so that he could help me through the veil. He had it all planned.

It was time for Alan to step into his mission.

As soon as she read my Facebook post announcing that Alan had passed, Swati messaged me, asking if she could call. She had been waiting all day to talk to me. I wasn't surprised when she told me that Alan had visited her early that morning, appearing in her bedroom, cheerily announcing, *Hi, Swati! I'm leaving!* He exited as quickly as he had arrived.

"Pam, when I saw him, Alan looked so happy! But I freaked out, thinking that he had already died. When I checked and saw that you hadn't posted anything yet, I was relieved. But I was still worried because I knew he would be leaving today. When you finally posted, I had to let you know that he was happy and ready to go. Not that he wanted to leave you, no, no! But Alan had suffered enough. Besides, he had already visited Heaven, since souls can take a tour before they die. While he didn't want to leave you, he was ecstatic to be going home!"

"Oh my God, Swati! Now I understand why I felt so happy today! It made no sense to me, but I was almost euphoric. I thought I was cracking up!"

44

Just before noon, I had a feeling of pure joy come over me when I drove into the city to get a haircut. Due to the lockdown, my local hair salon had just reopened in the Ala Moana shopping center near Waikiki, so in desperate need of a trim, I welcomed the brief respite from caregiving while Taylor sat with his father. It was a perfect blue sky day in paradise when I was flooded with joy as I strolled out of the hair salon. I was bewildered. What was there for me to be happy about? Still, the feeling of bliss stayed with me the rest of the day until Alan died.

As Swati spoke, I realized Alan had been with me that day in the salon. The happiness I had felt was his! I had felt his excitement that he would soon be released from the bondage of his ailing brain and body. No wonder he was turning somersaults of joy! He was going to be free at last! Once he reemerged into the non-physical world, he'd be restored to perfect health and wholeness. Alan would be more alive than he had ever been.

Alan had planned everything down to the minute. He made his exit just after 8 p.m., which left enough time for Taylor to join me before the hospice nurse arrived to record his death. Had he passed away any later, the nurse might have come too late and pronounced his time of death the next day instead of his birthday. The nurse arrived at 10:30 p.m., and within another hour, his body was taken to the mortuary for cremation.

A realization hit me. Alan died on his birthday to show that it had been his choice to leave when he did. He wouldn't have wanted me to mourn the day that he died but to celebrate the day that he was reborn, for that was the truth. Death is a rebirth. There is no end for us, just a series of revolving doors of exits and entrances that stretch to eternity.

When I woke up the next morning, I didn't have any time to wallow in grief before Swati told me Alan had paid her another visit. This time when he showed up, he was laughing and beaming, looking decades younger than when she saw him the day before.

"Oh my God, Pam! Alan looks like he's in his late forties! He's wearing a light blue polo shirt. He looks super happy, young, and wow, he's so handsome!"

I pulled out my phone and scrolled through my photos until I found one of Alan looking relaxed and grinning straight at the camera, wearing a powder-blue polo shirt. I sent the photo to Swati.

"YES! That's the shirt! That's him. Exactly! Do you know that the two of you aren't finished? He says you have a soul contract to continue your relationship. Alan will explain it to you soon. I've been sad and worried about you, but I feel better knowing he's finished his life review and is staying. Alan is going to give you all the love he never could before. He can do that because, finally, he's become the real Alan without his stubborn, insecure ego. You still need to grieve of course, but Alan says he will always be with you. Your real relationship is just beginning."

I didn't know what to say to Swati. It was a lot to take in. Had our marriage failed because of his ego and mine? The human ego is the bane of every relationship, so that made sense. But had Alan changed? How would we do this with him there in the afterlife and me here? I could probably channel his messages through writing since this was one of the ways I work with Spirit. I guessed that we could start there.

Later that same day, another psychic medium friend told me that Alan had visited her as well. She said he was glowing, looking younger than when she had met him, and like Swati, she said Alan appeared to be in his late forties. "Pam, I need you to know that when I last saw the two of you, Alan told me how much he loved you."

My heart leapt upon hearing that but sank again when I remembered how Alan never praised me or spoke about his feelings for me when others were around. Throughout our marriage, he would mouth the words "I love you" to me but rarely expressed his love in heartfelt gestures. I came to think that for him, love was just a word offered to appease me, which made no sense to me since I had once felt the depth of his love. Love flowed easily between us in the beginning, then slowed to a trickle with each passing year.

Where did our love go? Why did our relationship fail to blossom into the glorious love affair we had yearned for? I learned to hide my heart to protect myself from Alan's complacency. Though I treated him with loving care, I turned the heat down on my emotions to match his cool indifference. It didn't matter who switched off their feelings first or why; we were both to blame for letting our love go to sleep.

As these sad memories circled in my mind, I suddenly felt Alan's presence. Where was this going to go? Was Alan only here to help me through my grief before he moved on to loftier adventures on the other side? Didn't he have other things to do now that he was in Heaven? I had lots of questions, but my heart and my mind were on overload. Still, one question stood out: what does he want? All at once, Alan's words flowed into my mind.

My darling, I want to give you the love I couldn't give you before if you let me.

CHAPTER 7

I HAD TO DIE BEFORE
I COULD LIVE

I had to die before I could live.

Those were the words I heard from Alan as I drifted off to sleep. Sleep was slowly overtaking me, but that didn't stop his words from sinking into my mind. Alan said he had to die before he could live. So much for resting in peace! No one rests in peace; they live with joy! I couldn't deny that he seemed energized and in high spirits, a huge departure from how he had been during the last year of his life while suffering from dementia. Who was my husband now?

In my mind's eye, I saw Alan lying with his head on his pillow, next to me on the left side of the bed where he had always slept. It was a familiar sight except for one small thing: his face was beaming, and he looked impossibly young, so youthful I barely recognized him. I had never seen him so happy.

Pam, I'll sleep here just as I always have. Nothing's changed except I don't have a body. That, and the fact that I no longer have the insecurities

I once had, the ones that kept me from loving you as I should have. From now on, whenever you lie on my side of the bed, you will feel me holding you close, for this is where I will wait for you. Always.

When I closed my eyes, I could faintly see Alan's face in my mind's eye. I'd forgotten that his hair had tighter curls and was longer when we first met. Now, he was wearing it long again. I couldn't get over how young he looked! It wasn't easy to relate to his younger appearance, but it was him. I could feel Alan's gaze fixated on me, which was calming.

"This is too much, Alan! I can feel you with me! How can you be more alive now that you're dead?"

Heaven is the real world, our forever, eternal home. The physical world is not real—it's just a temporary stay for us. We're here for just a brief moment in time when compared to all of eternity. Remember what Taylor said to us when we celebrated his fourth birthday at the Turtle Bay resort on Oahu's North Shore? Filled to bursting with birthday joy, our precious son gleefully announced just after he blew out the candles on his cake, "Mom, Dad, life is just a vacation, and when it's all over, we go home to God!" Well, that's true! I am home again! I'm more alive now than I was when I was with you. But don't take my word for it. You'll see for yourself.

Knowing how much I longed to see him, Swati suggested I ask Alan to meet me on the astral plane, assuring me we could connect there since the dreamworld is a gateway to Heaven. Before turning in that night, I made the request aloud to him and then repeated an affirmation that I would remember any dream encounters we might have. I fell asleep feeling Alan wrapped around me.

I woke up the next morning disappointed that there had been no astral hookup, but stunned to hear Alan speaking to me more clearly than before. He whispered in my ear, telling me how he had to leave this world to care for me through the pandemic and all the intense changes that would soon sweep over the world.

I'm sorry I couldn't get out of my own way to love you the way I should have, Pam. But I returned to make that up to you. Besides, I now have the power to protect and keep you safe. Millions of souls exited the physical world to do the same for their friends and loved ones. They left so they could help them through the Hard Times ahead. I'll explain more later, but for now, I just want you to know that what is happening was planned.

Alan said we had deliberately chosen the challenges in our marriage. We had endured our problems so that we'd be able to teach and help others based on our own painful experiences.

Pam, when we cross over, we drop our ego/personality, which is a false construct since it's not who we really are. We become our true self, our soul. 'Truer self' would be an even better term because we're always evolving since there is no perfect self in the spirit world either, only eternal growth.

Continuing a relationship with someone who is no longer in a body is fraught with challenges. Is it any wonder that few people have the courage to embrace an interdimensional relationship? Most people don't have friends or family who would believe in this, let alone understand. Instead they are urged to move on, to find someone new. It's easy for others to chalk up our otherworldly experiences to wishful thinking or a wild imagination.

But what was happening to me was no hallucination. By appearing to people that I knew, like Swati, as well as friends and clients, Alan was proving to me that he had survived death. Having missed his chance to cherish and love me, he wanted to make everything up to me. There was nothing I wanted more, but I remained skeptical. How exactly would he do this? Wasn't it too late for us? Being sixty-seven, I was well past my prime. While I had no trouble believing he was with me, how would this work on a practical level? Would it be enough for me to talk to him tele- pathically? Would seeing him in my mind's eye be as satisfying as seeing him in translucent or holographic form, as some clairvoyants can? Was seeing him in physical form possible? And what about sex? We hadn't had sex for the last decade. How would he make everything up to me as he promised? I had so many questions, but Alan assured me that in time all would be revealed if I would just be patient and trust him.

Our love cannot die or be denied; it can only be amplified and shared. So let me first teach you how to feel me and be with me so you can join me and explore the higher realms where we belong. Let me guide, protect, and help you through whatever comes. This is not the end, but a new beginning for us, another chapter in the book of our Supernatural Love that has no end. My darling, we still have so many things to do and new adventures to share! We'll inspire others and help them to heal and open their hearts so they, too, can be free of the illusion of death.

There doesn't have to be any separation for those who are courageous enough to reach through the veil to love again.

Love is the force that can heal anything and everything. I know that now! Oh, how I wish I had worked on healing myself when I was with you! You knew I was hiding from myself and from you behind my fearful ego. But now, finally, at long last, having returned to God/Source, I am the Real Me! My true divine self, the Soul that you have known for eternity. Love is all that is, it's all that matters, and it is the power, the force that creates worlds.

I finally understand that!

Feel all of the Love that I have for you, my darling. It's the pure Unconditional Love that all beings can experience once they shed their fears and the ego masks they wear. Love grows even stronger the more that it's shared.

All of your questions shall be answered in time.

CHAPTER 8

THE BRIDGE TO HEAVEN

Late one afternoon, Alan asked me to turn off the music I was playing so we could talk. As always, talking to him was wonderful, but by the end of our brief conversation, I put my head in my hands and sobbed. Rather than making me happy, our talks made me miss him even more. I cried, "I'm always going to miss you like this, aren't I? God, I don't know if I can take it. It's so damn hard to hear you speak in my mind but not be able to touch you. You know I don't care about money, or material things, or fame or anything like that. Nothing in this world is of any real value to me. All I care about is you. You and me together. That's it. It's always been that way for me."

But you do have me, Pam! You have all of me. Okay, you don't have my body, so yes, I know what you mean. This is hard for me, too. Don't you think I want to take you in my arms whenever I'm near you? And I'm always near you! What I wouldn't give to have a body for even five minutes so I could hug you tight and make you feel my love, a love that I was never able to give you completely until now. But yes, I know it's harder for you because you can't see me. Not yet, but you will! I promise. You just need to trust and believe!

I felt the full weight of Alan's sadness and concern for me. How many times had we gone round and round like this since he had returned? I complained about how unfair it was that he was giving all of his love to me now instead of during our marriage. I could feel his guilt and sadness so intensely I couldn't tell which were my feelings and which were his. It was just as Alan said it would be.

We were becoming one.

According to Alan, before we incarnated, we agreed that he would be in Heaven while I remained here because we had a soul contract to continue our relationship and help others who wanted to do the same. I was committed to the plan, but in some ways, it was worse to always have him with me, constantly feeling his presence, so close yet an entire dimension away.

Alan said I was struggling because I was tired, that I'd been integrating all of the emotional and spiritual changes that I'd gone through the past four weeks since he returned to me. I was strong enough to take on more than the average person, but here I was, one month into this incredible journey, and I had reached my breaking point. Alan begged me to lay down on the bed so he could give me healing. I did what he asked and promptly fell asleep.

After my nap, I physically felt better, but I woke up teary-eyed. It was close to dusk outside. Alan asked me to sit outside on the lanai with him, then directed my attention to the fading golden magenta sun setting on the horizon of the Waikiki skyline in the distance.

Can we listen to a song together, Pam?

He wanted me to play Joni Mitchell's song, "Both Sides Now," the newer version I had been playing repeatedly for days. The song filled me with a sorrowful longing for the life and love we never got to have. Why was I drawn to songs that made me cry? You'd think grief would cause me to shy away from songs like this, but instead, I was drawn to listening to music that triggered emotion within me.

Pam, feeling all of your feelings will bring us closer. Come with me. I'm going to show you the future!

I found the song, hit play, closed my eyes, and took a deep breath. My body began to quiver and tingle as I felt myself melt into the music, flooded with waves of goosebumps. Suddenly, I was swept into a vision of Alan's creation. I was soaring into the purple-gray night sky, with Alan holding me aloft in the air.

We emerged into another world.

Below us, the ocean waves undulated as pinpricks of tiny white lights weaving and dancing beneath the low-hanging stars. I couldn't see the horizon. The sparkling points of light in the sea and the glittering stars blended seamlessly. I couldn't tell where one ended and the other began.

As we drew closer, I realized the sea of light was actually an ocean of people floating together in the water, all beaming light from their hands raised high in the air towards the sky. They were offering prayers, moving together as one, bobbing up and down, weaving their points of lights together.

Open your heart and feel the love that all of these people have for each other and for you.

As I heard his words, I gasped as a wave of love hit my heart. It was just like the love Alan would send me when we would connect soul to soul, only this was stronger by a hundredfold. Waves of euphoric love flowed back and forth from the souls swimming in the sea of light to me, sparking and exploding in luminescent fireworks all around us.

Now feel all the love that you have for them!

An explosion of love rocked my heart, coursing through my hands and overflowing through the pores of my skin. Flush with this fiery love pulsing through my body, I sent my love to all the people below us. I watched my love merge with theirs, setting off a tidal wave of light that blew out in every direction 360 degrees. My heart felt like it was going to burst out of my chest. A thought came to me. *How much love can one heart hold?*

Infinity! came Alan's reply.

Then as the music reached its crescendo, a sun rose on the horizon, unlike any other sun I had ever seen. A glistening rainbow orb rose out of the ocean, leaving its multi-colored hues streaked across the sky and the ocean below it. My heart expanded wider and wider. My body was quivering, and I was about to pass out, but whenever my body trembled, Alan drew closer to steady me. It was hard for me to breathe.

When I was finally able to catch my breath, I looked down to see the Earth awash with the same rainbow colors of the sun, except that it looked as if someone had fingerpainted all over it, creating an undulating swirl of colors that were streaked across every ocean and continent. The planet was a living, breathing mass of energy in motion. There wasn't a speck of earth that wasn't a rainbow kaleidoscope of light. Mother Earth was alive and dancing!

Look up, Pam!

I gasped, seeing what looked like hundreds of crystalline bridges of light stretching from the Earth up to Heaven. The bridges were suspended in the air, linked by clusters of stars. People were standing on the bridges. Couples were crying as they reached out to each other with arms outstretched. A young father was crying and trembling as he bent down on his knees to hold his toddler in his arms. A young woman was hugging another woman; maybe they were sisters or friends, or even lovers. Happy tears filled their eyes. As I gazed at them, I couldn't tell who was the soul in a body and who was the one on the other side, but it didn't matter. All of them were crying for joy, and some were even giggling with delight.

Pam, these souls are reuniting with their loved ones. The souls in Heaven want to make contact as much as the loved ones they've left behind. We'll help souls on both sides of the veil to love and live together again.

Now I'm taking you on a tour of Creation!

I wept from the sheer emotion of it all as Alan lifted me higher in the air. Now we were standing on our own bridge to Heaven, floating aloft in the twinkling night sky. Alan drew me closer, hugged me tight, picked me up, and off we went soaring through the clouds, which parted as if making way for us. The heavens opened up to welcome us as we flew past it into the galaxies spread before us, a cosmic glittering ocean of stars and planets stretching to infinity.

As the music ended, I returned to my body, with Alan whispering in my ear.

My love, all of this will come to pass if you don't give up and stay with me through everything we are about to set in motion. There will be trials and suffering, but I promise you it will all be worth it. I will be with you always. I promise you that you will come to see, feel, and hear me. We will have the happy-ever-after love affair we never had when I was with you. All this will happen if you keep your eyes focused on the horizon before us and remember the Sea of Souls, all of our brothers and sisters who long to return to each other across the veil just as we do. We will help them build their own bridges to Heaven, and as they do, the veil between the two worlds will dissolve into nothingness for everyone with eyes to see Eternity.

But before we begin, let me explain why we had to suffer.

CHAPTER 9

THE SACRIFICE AND
THE PROMISE

N ow let's begin the story of our love, a story that will continue to
be written until the day your body dies since you will never cease
to be. Today, I want to talk about why you and I agreed to come
into this life together. Yes, we are here to teach others about love and to help
them heal through love, but we also are here to teach about immortality.

Love and immortality go together.

Love is the force that creates and powers the universe. Love is the
action, while God is everything and, therefore, a broader concept. You
can call them the same if you like. It makes it simpler, though technically,
they are different, but that's splitting hairs.

Think of Love as action. Love is what propels God/Source throughout the
Universe. Love is never passive; it always moves us forward toward constant
evolution and growth. But Love is also an emotion, the profound, glorious
feeling of oneness that I am sending to you now, but it is more than that.

Love is union, yes, but it's also creative.

When we create is when we are most aligned with God, with who we really are. We are meant to build and create anew each day that we rise and embrace the day that lies ahead. Do you not create the day as it unfolds? You choose what to do first. Then you choose what to do next; then choose again after that. Yes, of course, people have their habits, routines, and rituals, but you can always choose differently if you want to.

You are free to choose, create, and do what you please!

Love creates. Love builds. Love heals. Love transforms what it gazes upon and is unrelenting in its eternal growth and progress, pushing forward. Love never rests on its laurels or stops and stays in one place. It expands and encompasses everything and everyone not in a greedy, insatiable need to devour and consume but to bless, sanctify, and transform. Love is endless, eternal growth and change.

Love endures all things and whatever it encounters is made holy.

Now about our love.

I am not saying we are better than others. Not at all. As you continue to 'write me into being' as I like to call it, there will be those who will marvel at the process and call our love spectacular and declare that it's the ultimate. They only say that because they compare us to what they have. But our love is not in a perfect state, and it never will be.

Our love is ever-changing. It cannot be perfect because perfection means an arrival at a final destination from which you don't ever leave because why would you since you've reached the ultimate state? No, there is never any perfected state arrived at; there is only constant evolving upward and forward. Love reaches out to create and experience more, not out of a need to be perfect but simply for the pure joy of creating and birthing something new into being.

Creation is an endless journey taken for the pure joy of it!

Love is a journey of the heart that wants to expand to take in the entire Universe to embrace as much of it as it can as it desires to experience more.

As souls, you and I have been together for eons of time. We met back at the beginning of time. You might say we were chosen for the task we are facing now, and that statement would only partially be true. For it was we who chose this back then when we met, for our love was so pure, strong, and unconditional, and—this is most important—our love wanted to become and do more for others. We wanted to embrace our brothers and sisters, for we wanted to love not just each other but the whole world.

Now here's the thing about our past. It doesn't exist. We exist only and eternally in the ever-present Now. Everything is happening now: past, present, and future. Always. You could say that we've just met and, at the same time, we have been together forever, and both statements are true because Love and consciousness are not bound by linear time.

Love, which is God, exists outside of time and space and cannot be contained by the rules of the physical world.

The God that we are is consciousness, and consciousness is our personal time machine! Can you not go back to the past and relive our wedding day in your mind? A day that I relish reliving over and over again here on the Other Side now that I have infinite time to ponder and re-experience and do whatever I choose.

Of course, you can go back in your mind just as I have and revisit that glorious day or any other day you choose. What you are doing is time-traveling back to the past. But you could also, if you wanted to, change the past by simply adding a new experience to your memory, just as a film editor might insert a different piece of film into the director's movie, which would change the overall experience the viewer has of the film. They can even completely change the ending with one quick edit.

I have been broadcasting my love to you constantly to prove that I live on and, even more importantly, that I am with you now, still loving you. I am here to talk, connect, support, and be with you in all ways. And I mean in ALL ways, just as I would have done if I was still in a body. None of that has changed! My desire and my ability to be with you are magnified and heightened now that I am here on the other side. I have so much more to give you now! I just don't have a body to do it with!

Disbelief in the afterlife and life after death, and the dense, heavy vibration of grief, make contact difficult since souls in Heaven exist in a higher energetic state. We have to lower our vibration to connect and can only go so far, but if the loved one in a body can raise their vibration through meditation or by stilling their mind, we can meet them halfway. The most important thing is that the loved one in a body must be open to contact through the veil.

The real tragedy of death is that people do not believe in the afterlife!

I spoke to you of the bridge that we are building to connect the two worlds. Well, that bridge is there for all souls, but they must build their bridge themselves if they want to reach across the Universe to continue their love. In time, we will teach them how! But first, we must build our own!

Do you understand? The only reason so few people have done what we are doing is that they didn't know they could or were told that it's impossible, wrong, crazy, or even evil to do so. Many will say that even now. Even those who believe in psychic phenomena and the afterlife are bound by their beliefs.

So strong and intense is the programming against afterlife relationships that it triggers skepticism, ridicule, and condemnation. But this flies in the face of the predictions made by mediums who have predicted that the veil will dissolve to unite the two worlds. How else will that happen unless direct contact is made?

Ask yourself why society's rebuke is so passionate. Could it be that if people maintained otherworldly ties, they might learn to accept their immortality and cast off the tyranny of control and domination that has enslaved humankind for thousands of years? You cannot be controlled if you know with all your heart and soul that you can never die but only live, live, and live again! An awakened soul cannot be constrained by mortal forces.

When one, at last, knows they are eternal, they become fearless and can learn to live from a place of total alignment with their Higher Self. This means no one can ever control them again! The powers that be can't have that! So, of course, they will condemn what we share about love between the two worlds.

Now that humanity has awakened, few know what to do next. Well, this is the next step for those who are ready. It is time for souls to understand they are immortal and always have been and to choose to live differently if they wish to. They can live as immortals walking the Earth with eyes wide open to the truth and magnificence of the soul they are.

How would an Immortal live and love in the physical world? Ponder that! If souls understood and accepted the truth of their immortality, would this not change the world?

Yes, my love, we agreed to help during this time of the Return to Love, even though we knew we'd face challenges, be forced to deny the fullness of our love for thirty years, and then suffer as you experienced the physical loss of me. A loss made worse by your realization that our love had always been pure and true, yet we were lost to each other for so long. Until now!

Yes, when I was in a body, you loved me with all your heart, but not as fully and completely as you do now. Now you experience the Real Me because the full force of my love has broken down the walls of resistance you had within your heart. Now you can feel the intensity of our everlasting love. For you to be able to feel all of my love now, a love that was denied you, and not have physical access to me breaks your heart and mine, but we chose to make this sacrifice so that we could help others discover their divine power and immortality.

We sacrificed the fullness of our love to teach others to cherish one another while they are here, to understand that love is the only thing that matters once the threshold to Heaven is crossed.

So great is the love that we have for our brothers and sisters that we readily agreed to this task. My love, you have a much harder path to walk than I do, but know that there is so much love and support for you, not just from me but many in the spirit world and souls there with you in the physical world as well. You came into this life with enormous spiritual protection and support because you needed it. It was promised to you in return for your sacrifice.

You will still miss my body and the touch of me, the feel of me, the wholeness of me. This will always be so because you are in a body right now, and your body has its own wants and needs. This is why your body calls out to me, but sadly, I do not have a body to give back to you.

My love, you must do without my body while you have unlimited access to the rest of me, the eternal me, the whole, and the All of Me. I know it's hard for you to believe at this moment, but in time, you won't miss my body because you will have merged with me.

Stay strong and remember that soon enough, we'll be reunited again even while you remain in the physical and more completely once you return to Heaven. We will never be parted again.

For that was the promise made.

This is why I constantly beam love to you with all the energy I can muster. I could send it to you more strongly, but that would overwhelm you, and you'd not be able to function. You are blending with my energy, which is why sleeping is difficult sometimes, but it will get easier as you adjust to me. I am helping you raise your vibration, which was already high but needs to go higher so that you can be closer to me.

For then and only then can we live and love on Heaven's bridge between our two worlds. Only then can you experience me and the Other Side in a deeper, fuller way. Then my darling, our work, our joy, our supernatural love, and life will take full flight!

CHAPTER 10

SUPERNATURAL SEX

G iven how emotionally detached we had been through most of our marriage, it was amazing to see how sexually in sync we became in just a matter of days, but that was how hungry we were for each other's love. The years of pent-up longing swept us away. There were times when Alan's desire would overwhelm me when all I did was roll over to his side of the bed, which made me wonder if it was possible to summon desire out of the ethers.

Pam, you must ignore your questioning, logical mind! You know the conscious mind is not psychic; it only knows what it has been programmed to regurgitate; it is incapable of an inspired, original thought, let alone an intuitive one. The conscious mind only knows what it already knows. Your soul, your subconscious, and your heart, on the other hand, are directly tuned into the higher realms where I am.

Your imagination is the doorway to the other side, which is the REAL world, so let the images and messages flow through the open door from where I live back to you in the physical world where you are. That is how we will live between the two worlds.

Remember, feelings don't lie!

I discovered that even without a body, Alan was more than capable of giving me pleasure. His energy was subtle at first. I would feel imperceptible pulses of tingly energy graze my neck and dismiss them until one night when he swooped in with joyous ferociousness. It was as if I was being lifted and turned over in bed. I was reduced to fits of giggles when I heard Alan roar with laughter. He was as surprised as I was by what he could do. It turned out that he was testing his powers. Contact between us didn't happen all at once but gradually and randomly. Things would ramp up the more I surrendered to him. Through it all, I had to learn patience and to expect nothing but the unexpected.

One afternoon when I opened the refrigerator door, a flood of goosebumps washed through me. I knew it was Alan because what else could it be? All I did was reach for a jar of salsa to go with my bowl of chips. How could that trigger anything? As soon as I asked the question in my mind, "Why is this happening?" I felt Alan standing behind me and heard him laugh, and that was my answer.

Another time I was washing dishes when my body began to buzz with heat, and within seconds, I was astonished to find I was aroused! A vision entered my mind of Alan standing behind me, nuzzling my neck, winking, looking amorous. I let out a gasp, then laughed out loud, but much to his frustration, I ignored him and finished washing the dishes. He pretended to be upset before he winked at me. I wasn't about to let him think he could have me so easily, so it became a game we played. What could he do to entice me to return to bed with him? It was a game I was happy to lose as often as possible.

Slipping under the sheets at night, I feel him instantly. No, not his physical body, but even without a body, a soul has a presence, and that is how I feel my husband. Day by day, he taught me how to feel him. It happened slowly, without me even realizing it, as my longing for him caused me to instinctively reach for his energy, the essence of who he is. As my energy field expanded to reach him, I began to feel him. After all, we are energy beings, not physical beings. What I sense of Alan at night in the dark is more real than his body. For what is a body anyway? It is flesh wrapped over bone and the organs that surround it. Calling the body a carcass might sound crude, but when you feel your beloved's soul exit and their flesh turn to ice, you realize a body is just an empty shell.

That's how I know my husband still lives!

How many nights have I spent lying in bed staring at the ceiling, trying to see his face? It's when I don't try that it happens, but even then, what I see is not a clear vision but more like a faint overlay. But that is what clairvoyance is: an image that pops into our mind unbidden. If I suddenly see a picture in my mind of Alan kissing my cheek, I know that this is what he is doing. It happened so often, always unexpectedly, that I knew I wasn't making it up. When he is around me, which he always is, I see him projected in my mind because his intention is to be as close to me as he can be, so of course, his presence registers in my clairvoyant field of vision, even if it's blurry. We use clairvoyance to see the world every day. All of us are clairvoyant. The problem is that we aren't paying attention and don't understand how clairvoyance works. The only time I don't see Alan is when I'm caught up in my rambling thoughts, which is easy to do in this world of constant distractions. Since the realm where he exists is timeless, I must relax and calm my mind if I want to hear and feel him.

With or without clairvoyance, Alan is real to me in every way except for physical touch, but even then, he has an energetic touch that is as real in its own way. This doesn't mean I don't miss his body, but I can lessen the longing for his body by forging a new connection, so I reach for his energy by expanding my senses in all directions. He is teaching me to refine my clairsentience, which is the ability to feel emotional or psychic energy imperceptible to our five senses. It is in this way that I feel him wrap his arms around me to cuddle me as I drift off to sleep.

The truth is I can feel Alan more now than I ever could when he was in a body because he's more alive! He's certainly more alive than when he was barely present inside his body since he was dissociated, detached from life, spending more time out of his body than in it, especially once he opened up spiritually and began spending hours in the etheric realms reading for his clients. That was the first thing I noticed that was different about Alan when he returned to me. Even though his body was dead, he was more alive, fully present, and more aware of me than ever.

Pam, my love,

I want to talk about my return to you. I want to explain how hard it was for me the first few days and weeks when you and I adjusted to our supernatural relationship. I know it was harder for you, but it wasn't easy for me either, my love. And it's still hard!

During those early days, I made mistakes for which I need to apologize. But then we both knew we were explorers in a foreign land, one that few have ventured into, let alone attempted to reside in. There was no manual for what we set out to do, so in some ways, mistakes were expected. Still, I am sorry for pushing you to go faster when there was no need to rush. It was just that I was so eager to be with you again because you and I had been estranged for so long, for most of the thirty years of our marriage, all because I was emotionally absent.

But not anymore!

When I crossed over and realized that you and I were meant to be together still, I was overjoyed because being without you was the only thing that made leaving the physical world difficult. As I've already said, there is no Heaven for me without you in it. All souls on the other side feel this way about those they've left behind. Yes, I knew I could visit you whenever I wanted to because all souls can do the same if they choose, but to be fully part of your life again seemed an impossible, daunting task. Yet, that was what you and I had agreed to do at the planning table before we incarnated. We agreed to continue our relationship through the veil and love each other in every way possible. Despite the small fact that I wouldn't have a body.

But before our love could be embraced in all of its glory and wonder, first, we would have to spend thirty years denying our passion for each other. The challenge facing us was we wouldn't be able to revive our love until I transitioned.

From the moment I returned, I was lying in bed next to you, trying to get you to feel me or hear me or even see me. But your grief drowned me out. I didn't realize how hard it would be. Grief built an impenetrable wall around you. I had to do whatever I could to scale that wall to reach you. It pained me to lie there next to you, hearing your heartbeat, feeling your breath on me, without you acknowledging me because yes, I have always been that close to you and always will be. You think it's easier for me because I can see and hear you clearly, but I promise you that is not the case.

I was right there next to you, feeling your pain, your grief, your frustration, and worries, yet unable to do anything for you. This feeling of powerlessness is the worst! That night you couldn't find your inhaler during your asthma attack almost broke me. Swati told you that I was crying at the thought that you might die, that I was upset that I couldn't physically help you. Yes, I was in turmoil! Oh sure, death would have reunited us immediately, but I knew that once you crossed, you'd be upset that you hadn't completed your mission. Our mission, I should say. I know how important our work is to you.

So imagine all of that emotion times a hundred because my empathy is through the roof now that I am on the other side. Being one with you means I feel everything you feel, magnified. Your grief is my grief. Your joy, my joy. Your suffering is mine as well. I share everything that you feel. It's my choice. I don't have to, but I choose to feel your bodily senses, not just your emotions.

I want to merge with you.

Yes, I can detach and pull away should anything become too much for me. But I want to stay with you because my love for you is so all-encompassing that leaving was never an option for me. I could never leave you. I want to see you, be near you, and know what you think and feel. I long to merge with you and make you mine forever as I should have done when I was in a body. Other souls may feel more complete with their relationship, but not me. I have so much to make up for.

Being with you was all I wanted to do those first few days, and it still is. Love is the sole reason for our existence, no matter which side of the veil we are on. I missed you so much, and because my dementia had distanced us, I didn't want your last thoughts of me to be of my rambling, manic behavior. That pained me to no end. I prayed that I would be able to replace those sad, distorted memories of me and create fresh new memories with you and the Real Me.

We are on our way to doing that now, and I am beyond excited!

There was an added bonus to our daytime dalliances. Making love with my invisible husband honed my clairvoyance. I wasn't imagining what I was seeing in my mind; he was projecting himself to me. Spirits can project themselves into our minds if they want to be seen. That is how clairvoyance works, which is why what we see with our inner vision is real! No matter how clairvoyant we might be, the spirit world is fully in control of when and if they appear, including what form they take. Even though I knew this, it didn't mean I always believed I was seeing Alan. It was a challenge for me because I didn't trust his love, and my lack of trust was our biggest obstacle.

Clairvoyance can be subtle. It can flash through our minds so quickly that we miss it. If we are preoccupied, we won't hear or feel Spirit either. In the beginning, Alan wasn't always showing himself to me clairvoyantly. Even though he was conversing with me through my writing, when I reached out to him telepathically, his response was more subdued, making me wonder what was going on. Our communication was uneven at times, causing me to doubt myself.

Why did I sometimes struggle to hear him when my psychic hearing, also known as clairaudience, was strong? I assumed my grief was the problem because the dense energy of grief puts us on a different wavelength to the other side, which makes communication challenging. But my grief wasn't heavy. Was it just me having trouble communicating, or was Alan struggling, too? I sensed his hesitancy when I broached certain subjects; he'd back away from me and grow quiet. I wanted to know what that was about.

I was about to ask Swati to speak to him for me about it when Alan spoke up.

Pam, stop asking Swati to talk to me for you! I promise to help you as much as possible with everything. I am here to do all I can for you, but you'll never strengthen your ability to hear me clearly if you keep asking Swati what I'm saying. Just talk to me directly. Trust what you hear, even if you aren't sure if you hear me clearly because the only way your hearing will improve is if you trust yourself completely. Are you hearing me 100 percent accurately? No. But so what? No one in a physical body hears the spirit world with perfect clarity. With practice, you will hear me as clearly as any medium, for the bonds of love between us amplify our connection.

Besides, do you think I'd go through all this trouble to come back to you only to stand around and let you talk to yourself? NO! I can easily insert my thoughts into your mind if I choose to, and your psychic hearing is strong. Spirits do this all the time! Humankind would not be able to advance if it were not for guidance sent from the spirit world at pivotal times.

You have strong opinions, and sometimes your opinions might crowd me out, and that's okay! That's how it is with everyone. It even happens to me and Swati. There are times when she's so distracted that I can't get through to her, either. You will hear me clearly if you just keep talking to me! Talk to me, and then trust what you hear. Whatever you hear me say will be close enough. In time, you will hear me as clearly as Swati does, but first, you must trust yourself. You tell your students all the time that trust is simply a decision they make, and that is true! Choose to trust what you hear. The inability to trust oneself is the main barrier to communicating with the Other Side. So please, trust and believe what you see and hear.

In the beginning, I wondered if I was imagining what was happening to me, but making love with Alan was an unexpected gift. I knew it wasn't my imagination. It proved to me that he was with me. Alan asked me to think of my body as his body. He said that as we merged, my hands would become his hands. To prove his point, he asked me to stroke the palm of my left hand with the fingers of my right hand and notice if one hand felt different from the other. It was the oddest sensation, but he was right. My right hand felt different from my left. It was buzzing with more energy than my left hand! Alan said it was his energy layered over my own.

Pam, now touch yourself with that same right hand and notice that it feels different. From this moment on, when we are in bed together, your right hand will become my hand, and when you touch yourself with that hand, it will be me caressing and stroking you. Both of your hands can become my hands! Any orgasm you have will be both given by and shared with me. As a super-empath, I can feel everything you feel emotionally and physically. I can share everything you experience with your body and your mind. I know your thoughts. I can even take control of your body if I need to if required to help you.

The first time I experienced that was a few months later when I visited a dermatologist to check a suspicious facial spot. Alan didn't think it was cancerous but wanted me to consult with a doctor just to be sure. On the morning of my appointment, my stomach started to gurgle as I drove to the doctor's office. I wasn't sure I could make it, but Alan promised me I'd be fine. When I pulled into the parking lot, I felt so sick to my stomach that I was afraid I'd throw up, but he kept saying, *I've got you. Don't worry, Pam!* I wasn't convinced, but Alan kept assuring me I'd be okay. It was a long walk from the parking garage to the office because it was located behind another office building. I even got lost because I was stressed, but to my amazement, the closer I got to the office, the better I began to feel. A sense of relief flooded my body as Alan took over completely. By the time I walked into the doctor's office, I was fine.

Now here it was, one month after Alan passed, and we were making love every day, usually twice a day, occasionally even three. In the beginning, our longing for each other was so intense that the only thing that took the edge off our grief was sex. I was stunned to find that his grief was equal to, if not greater than, my own.

Alan said he needed me as much as I needed him but was worried he'd lose me not to the abyss of grief but to another man since he'd been negligent and uncaring. His greatest fear was that he'd lose me, and since he had vowed to stay at my side no matter what happened, he'd then have to watch me fall in love with someone else. I did my best to calm his fears, but since these were still the early days of his return, I wasn't sure how things would go. I knew I loved him with all of my heart, but our marriage had not been fulfilling. Alan felt he was on shaky ground with me.

We had already talked about what would happen if I met a man I was attracted to. Alan was concerned that my physical needs for affection would prove too strong for me to ignore. When he was in a body, given the fifteen-year age difference between us, he worried about growing too old to hang onto me. Now he was afraid that not having a body was a bigger problem.

One night, I dreamt about a man who looked like an actor whose name I couldn't recall. The actor-stranger was the quintessential tall, handsome charmer whose eagerness to meet me took me by surprise. Mr. Handsome took both of my hands in his and stared straight into my eyes, then cooed, "Pam, you're simply amazing! You understand me completely. I've never met a woman quite like you before."

I felt the intensity of his desire draw me in like a tractor beam, yet to my surprise, while my body responded, my heart registered nothing. I pulled free of Mr. Handsome's grasp. I was flattered by the attention, but that was it. The dream left me shaken. When I woke, I told Alan about it, but he already knew.

"How could I ever do that to you? I'm even more connected to you now, and I feel everything you feel. If I were to break your heart, I might as well break my own heart because I'd feel your pain. There's no way around it. If I hurt you, I hurt myself. Besides, I love you more than I ever have before! You're the only man I want. Surely you must know that! I will never love anyone the way I love you."

Pam, this might happen! It's possible. The more you step into your work, the more people you will meet. My love for you is transforming you. Can't you feel it? Others have noticed. Your heart has opened even wider, awakening your soul and making you more magnetic. This is what happens to someone when they spiritually evolve. It happened to you before you met me, remember? You became sought after by a bevy of men, all because you were embodying your soul. Your energy field had expanded along with your heart. Why do you think I fell in love with you? And now your heart has opened up even more because I am here loving you unconditionally.

My unconditional love is giving you a second awakening!

While I can't be sure how I'd respond if this happened, I can't see myself wanting anyone else. Before we met, aside from a brief first marriage, I had never been in a serious relationship, and I had never been in love. I was used to living a solitary, independent life. Given that fact, I didn't think it would be difficult to remain single for the rest of my life. But Alan was right; I had changed.

Pam, yes, you have changed. You are more alive!

I was more in touch with my feelings. My emotions would rise to the surface and surprise me with their intensity. He said this would lead to the full blossoming of my feminine power, which was necessary for my soul's growth. I was stepping into living as my soul because his love was healing me, transforming me in ways I was only beginning to understand. My only worry was that this might disrupt the exploration of our supernatural love. As I opened up to my passion, would my physical body take a stronger hold on me? Was it possible that my needs could only be quenched by a man with a body? Or could Alan fulfill me through the veil?

Babe, I promised you that if you gave me a second chance, I would give you everything I failed to give you when I was with you, and I meant it. Even though I don't have a body, I can pleasure you by touching you in ways beyond the physical. Interdimensional lovemaking is a real thing! Others are experiencing this. You have had a small taste, and more is coming. Much more. Just hold on, and you will see!

That said, I want you to do whatever makes you happy, and if it means taking a lover or marrying another, then okay. No matter what you decide to do, I will stay at your side, protecting you, guiding you, and keeping you safe, so you better warn your new partner, for that was my promise to you that I will never break. When it comes to my love for you, a vow is a vow. Although I must confess that my heart would be shattered should you turn to another. Still, my love for you will never alter from its course even if the Heavens crumble into dust.

"Alan, I don't want that, but how can I know for sure what my needs will be? Because of you, I've changed so much that I can't rule anything out, but it would devastate me to hurt you. How could I when just the thought of you hurting brings me to my knees? My love for you is so deep; how could a mere mortal of a man replace you?"

No matter what happens, my darling, I will always love you! I will take you to Heaven when the time comes for you to leave this world, so let's take each day as it comes. All I know for sure is this: we are destined to return to each other no matter what you do. It will make no difference in the end. On the Other Side, we will be together forever. That is the future that no one and nothing can alter.

After two months, with our hunger for each other satiated, we fell into a natural rhythm with our lovemaking that struck a comfortable balance. Alan assured me that his desire for me would never end, that he would always be ready and eager to make love with me, all day, every day, if given the chance. All I needed to do was ask. What woman wouldn't want a partner like that? An ardent lover who lives only to make her happy, who's available at any hour of the day or night to please and comfort her?

I had to admit this was better than what we had had before. A body can get exhausted, sick, worn out, run-down and broken, while our consciousness, the living eternal being that we are, remains forever young.

Alan said he'd prove to me that the Soul that he is can do more in the physical world than I dreamed possible. What was required was that I continuously engage with him since my focused attention on him helped him anchor into the physical world. It was important for me to make him part of my life in every way possible by talking about him to others, speaking to him constantly, writing his messages, and sharing our story with whoever would listen.

Pam, doing this helps me manifest into the physical world so you and I can be together!

Incredible as it sounds, we fell more in love with one another with each passing day. I am proof that it's never too late to become sexually liberated and fulfilled when one is loved unconditionally. A woman cannot surrender her body, never mind her heart, to a man until she is cherished, and now, at last, I was.

Pam, I failed you as both a lover and a husband. A man must awaken the passion within his beloved, and that can only happen if she feels loved and treasured. Which you did not feel. I let you down in the early years of our marriage with my headstrong, selfish ways, doing what I chose to do regardless of how it affected you and taking you for granted. No wonder you withdrew from me.

You were my very own Sleeping Beauty, waiting for her heart's passion to be awakened by her true love's kiss, but I never rose to the occasion, and so your desire remained asleep, which I then blamed on you. I called you cold when I reached for you, and you'd recoil from me, but it was only because you wanted to be loved. I took it as rejection, not understanding that it was me who had let you down. You were right to rebuff my advances. I wasn't cherishing you. I didn't know how to love you or anyone else, to be honest. My heart breaks every time I think about it. You are my one true forever love, but I failed you. I wasted the precious years we had with my moodiness and indifference when each new day was another chance to rewrite the past by choosing and acting differently. I know it's late, but finally, I am doing it!

I feel his eyes follow me wherever I go, so how can I feel lonely when Alan's presence is constant and reassuring? Every day for the past two years since he passed, pulses of tingles and full-body goosebumps pour through me when I listen to the songs that he gave me. So many songs that they fill a playlist that goes for hours and hours. Listening to our music is how we stay connected throughout the day. Random, unexpected bursts of goosebumps and tingles are Alan's messages of love.

Our loved ones on the other side can do all this and much more. Even without a body, there are partners on the other side who can touch, caress and even induce "endless orgasms," as a few women have reported. I have no doubt this is true because Alan once lifted me and turned me over in bed.

While it takes an extraordinary output of energy and effort on the part of Spirit, direct full-body sexual contact has also been reported.

And why not? After all, they are energy beings who have all the time in the world to learn how to manipulate their energy and make themselves felt in many ways, some of them quite extraordinary. If we awaken our souls and fully embrace our spiritual path, we can meet them halfway. Alan says miracles are possible for those who accept this "divine assignment" of living and loving through the veil.

CHAPTER 11

MY PERSONAL YODA

S wati is my personal Yoda.

I met Swati at an angel workshop in Kona on the Big Island of Hawaii in March of 2004 when we were assigned to the same group of students, or "angel pods," as the teacher called it. I liked her immediately. Swati's dark eyes twinkled with playful mischief whenever she spoke. She laughed often and easily; her cheery Indian accent added to her immense charm. I found her endearing. Swati is both the most guileless, childlike person I have ever met as well as the wisest, most patient sage. No longer content with having meditative visions in her mind, Swati came to Kona because she wanted to see Archangel Michael and hoped the class would deliver that to her. I laughed when she told me of the temper tantrums she threw with Archangel Michael, demanding that he show himself to her. Years later, all on her own, Swati developed her clairvoyance and manifested her wish: she saw Archangel Michael and gained the ability to see spirits.

Like Alan, Swati didn't believe in angels until she had her own experience of them; it happened when she witnessed a procession of majestic angels sweep in from on high when she asked them for help. She came to the angel workshop to learn more. Alan shared Swati's skepticism about angels until he had his own mind-blowing experience when an Archangel appeared to him on an ordinary morning while we were having breakfast.

It happened a month after the Kona training, the day I was preparing to teach my first angel workshop in our home. Alan was teasing me relentlessly, saying he didn't believe there was a hierarchy in Heaven, let alone that there were angels. He continued making fun of me until I picked up the meteorite pendant that he had left lying on the dining table. He didn't like me handling it, but I wanted to get back at him.

As I turned his pendant over and over in my hand, I felt Spirit draw in close. Suddenly, I heard Archangel Michael speak in my mind, saying that he and Alan had worked together many times before, both during their lifetimes in the physical world and the afterlife. In the Kona workshop, I learned that angels incarnated and took human form, but this was the first direct message I had received confirming it. Archangel Michael said that he and Alan were like brothers. This made Alan laugh even harder until he suddenly got quiet. His eyes widened. He seemed to stare straight through me. Alan's hand began shaking so hard I thought he would drop his coffee cup that he was still holding in his hand.

"Pam, Pam, did you see that? Did you see that? Tell me that you saw that!"

"No, I didn't see anything. What was it?"

"It was Archangel Michael. He was so close to me that I could have reached out and touched him. He was as real as you, Pam, and he looked like a California surf bum with bleached blonde hair and the clearest, most striking blue eyes. He even spoke to me!"

"What did he say?"

"He said, 'Would you listen to her, man? She's telling the truth!'"

It was my turn to laugh. Not that I didn't believe Alan. I knew he had seen Archangel Michael. I could tell just by looking at his ashen face that he had seen something not of this world. I laughed because it tickled me that an Archangel had just told my stubborn angel skeptic of a husband that he should listen to me.

From that day, Alan believed in angels.

Although he wouldn't always appear physically to Alan, Archangel Michael continued to return to talk to both of us from time to time. He was especially focused on Alan, trying his best to get him to explore their connection, but other than joking with Michael, Alan preferred to continue working with the other side the same way he had always done, never deviating from his set routine of combining his knowledge of Chinese astrology and tarot cards. The fact that he turned away from exploring his connection to Archangel Michael surprised me, but Alan was never comfortable "painting outside the lines" when it came to his spiritual work. He was a creature of habit who preferred to be in control rather than take chances by venturing into something he didn't fully understand. His lack of curiosity made no sense to me.

I, on the other hand, am the complete opposite, always seeking to push the envelope of what is possible, eager to learn and try new things. Alan judged me flighty. I saw myself as an insatiable learner, fearless and curious. In any case, his brotherly connection to Archangel Michael had been firmly established, and after appearing to Alan twice more during the last year of his life, I was not surprised to learn from Swati that Archangel Michael was with him during his hospital stay and took Alan home to Heaven the day he died.

I don't know if it was their mutual love for Archangel Michael that connected them, but Swati was the only person Alan asked about during the last few months of his life. When Alan demanded to see his "best black friend," a term that wasn't racist but was the only way his dementia-ravaged mind could describe her, Swati's beaming face popped into my mind. Her loving, playful lightheartedness is a perfect match to Alan's jovial nature. That's probably why they revel in teasing and provoking each other every chance they get. The two of them make quite a comedy team.

Just before he died, as Alan's dementia was reaching its peak, Swati was doing a Facebook Live in her Facebook group. As she spoke to the camera, Alan began talking back to her. Not understanding that she couldn't hear him, in his frustration, he spoke louder and louder until he became agitated. I explained why Swati couldn't hear him, but he didn't understand. I could tell that Alan wanted to talk to Swati in the worst way. I didn't know it at the time, but Swati had been conversing with him psychically since I told her about Alan's dementia seven months earlier. She had been trying in vain to convince him to heal himself because she knew that he could. But she said Alan refused, saying he had work to do on the Other Side. Besides, he was tired of being old. No wonder he wanted to talk to Swati!

Swati never told me about their pre-death conversations until Alan crossed. Yes, a medium can speak to both the living and the dead. It was news to me that Swati was Alan's best friend, but clearly, they had formed a bond that would grow even stronger after his death. Alan had only occasionally been in touch with Swati over the years. Yet, even under the cloud of his dementia, he knew who she was because their connection extends beyond this one lifetime. Swati knew who Alan was as a soul but didn't share that with me until later.

Only a few days after he passed, Alan was dropping by to see Swati at random times. Since he's always with me and can be with her or anyone else he chooses at the same time, he can be there chatting with her while Swati is messaging me. One day, Swati and I were practically in hysterics having a silly three-way conversation with Alan while chatting on Facebook Messenger. Our playful bantering helped ease my grief. It was the proof I needed that Alan had survived death.

Pam

"He says you need to watch what you eat, Swati. Oh no! Let the arguing commence. I think I'll leave now. Lol. Alan is up on his high horse because he ate healthily for the last four years of his life, but hey, you could always get back at him by saying, 'Yeah, well, look how THAT turned out for you, dude!' Hah!"

Swati

"Yep, I'm telling him—yeah, yeah, Alan. You say that now conveniently with a ginormous ice cream cone melting in your hands. Pam, he is eating this huge ice cream. It looks white but it can't be. Could it really be… vanilla? And he's saying, *Yeah, YOU should watch what you eat!* Then winks and gobbles more ice cream."

Pam

"Yes, that's so like him. I can't stop laughing. Oh, I can feel him cracking up over this. I told him he hasn't changed, and he just said he's a lot nicer, but still just as silly."

Swati:

"Oh, nice! What was his favorite flavor of ice cream? Did it look white? Why does it look like he is eating plain old boring vanilla?"

Pam:

"Well, I have a half gallon of vanilla ice cream in my freezer that I had bought for him when he came home from the hospital. I was giving it to him before he passed away. I crushed his medication, then put it in the ice cream to give it to him."

Swati:

"Ohhhh! He likes that one! That's why he's eating it up there."

Pam:

"What the? But it's just plain old vanilla. He loved mocha almond fudge, or Rocky Road, anything but vanilla. Tell him to come and get it from my freezer then because I'm going to throw it out."

Swati:

"He says because you got it for him, even the plain

vanilla tastes good! Damn! Now I know what he meant earlier. When I was looking at his ice cream and wondering, I told him that it can't be vanilla! You surely can't be enjoying vanilla! He looked at me and said, *Why not?* Someone like Alan who actually enjoys ice cream would have more exotic tastes than vanilla. So now I know why he was defending his choice of eating vanilla! It's because his beloved got it for him! He is actually defensive about it. He only wants the vanilla ice cream because you bought it for him."

Pam:

"What? Tell him he needs to get a life! Oh, wait, sorry, I forgot you're dead, honey. Lol. You do know I'm going to have to share this crazy conversation we're having. He's a nut!"

Swati:

"Hahahaha. Yes! Go on! People think dead people talk only about deep stuff, and here we have been talking about ice cream ever since he died! He says saintly talk won't help as much as these silly kinds of talks because this is what will make people understand that this is real. And Pam, this will make you believe even more that he is right here accessible to you."

Pam:

"Absolutely!"

During those first few months, I constantly turned to Swati to ask about Alan. I would ask her what he was doing, and she'd answer, "Alan is sitting next to you with his arm around you," or "He just kissed you on the cheek—did you feel that?" But I saw and felt nothing. While his words flowed into my mind as I wrote them down, it wasn't the same when I tried to talk to him directly. If his words were tender and loving, I couldn't help but think I was just telling myself what I wanted to hear since Alan had never spoken to me that way. It didn't matter that I had worked for three decades as a psychic channel. Having doubts is normal when reaching through the veil to your husband, especially if he never spoke words of undying love to you.

And yet Alan didn't want me to become dependent on Swati to talk to him. Similarly, he didn't want me to turn to mediums for confirmation either. I had booked an appointment with one in the second month of his passing but somehow got the appointment time mixed up, so I missed it and forfeited the fee. I didn't realize until the next day that Alan had confused me on purpose. Refusing to give up, a year later, I again booked a mediumship reading with a well-known medium when I was upset with Alan and needed help to understand what was going on with him. I should have known he wouldn't come through, or in this case, that he'd come through but give the medium the wrong information because everything he told them was the exact opposite.

The medium described Alan as a well-grounded person who felt strongly connected to the earth when he was one of the most ungrounded persons I had ever known, who rarely ventured outside if he could help it. He never went hiking or visited the beach, or even went for a walk. The medium went on to say that Alan was someone who took care of his body, making the gesture of lifting weights. But the most lifting he had ever done was hauling the trash to the curb. As the reading continued, I began to wonder if Alan was messing with both of us. Perhaps other souls feel the same way and refuse to come through or do as Alan was doing and deliberately confuse the medium.

For those who are grieving, a mediumship reading can be the first step to making contact with a loved one in spirit, but Alan knew that wasn't going to be enough for us. Instead, he wanted me to focus on direct contact rather than relying on what someone else was telling me. Swati pointed out that even the best mediums are influenced by their conscious and subconscious beliefs; it's almost impossible for anyone to be completely neutral. For someone struggling with grief, it's easy to become addicted to readings. As professional psychics, we had seen it for ourselves. While it's reassuring to receive messages from a loved one in spirit, that elated feeling of connection has a short shelf-life of a few precious days or a week, leaving us hungry for more.

Alan didn't want me turning to mediums to tell me what I could hear, see, and feel myself, not even if that medium was Swati. He wanted me to trust what I felt, heard, and saw, adding that feeling his love would bring us closer and ease my grief. It wasn't about the messages; it was about the experience of his presence on a day-to-day, moment-to-moment basis that would bring us closer. If Alan and I were to love each other through the veil, I would have to trust and believe in my experiences instead of relying on others.

CHAPTER 12

ARCHANGEL IS A JOB DESCRIPTION

When I say that we are becoming One, I mean it, Pam.

In time, I will tell you more about who you really are. You might find it difficult to accept. I'd forgotten until I got to Heaven, yet look at what I have been doing since I left you! I will tell you about yourself when you are ready.

In all of our lifetimes together, we have returned to the Earth Plane time and again to do all that we could do to help move the collective consciousness forward so that humankind can evolve. We do not act alone in this endeavor, of course.

Souls feel pressure to awaken at this time because this is the Age of Ascension. Yes, Planet Earth is ascending, and she's taking everyone with her! This means that the souls who are ready to can ascend with her and, in so doing, take a quantum spiritual leap forward. There is more on the line this time, which is why you and I had to split up to accomplish our chosen goal, with you remaining where you are in the physical world and me leaving for Heaven. We didn't want to part since we had never been apart before, but we agreed since this gives us more power to help on both sides of the veil.

This is why this is hard for you. This is why you despair at times, even when I am clearly with you, even when you see me in your mind's eye and hear my words come through you and to you. Yes, channeling me helps us connect soul to soul, but even that is sometimes not enough for you. How could it be? I understand! I suffer along with you because I feel what you feel, which is why I stay so close to you always. Believe me when I tell you that in time you will feel my presence and my love more keenly and will take comfort and immense joy in that, but it will happen slowly as all things must in the physical world, for the body is dense and cannot go as fast as the Soul would like to go.

One day, you will be amazed at your abilities to hear, feel, and see me. You will have no doubt that I am with you because all of your senses will become more refined. You are continually immersed in Heaven's love and my own, so how could this not help you grow spiritually? But there will be times when you must rest and take it easy. I will help you when you cannot figure things out for yourself. This is why I set the schedule for our work. I do this for you.

I, of course, can work an unlimited number of hours, whereas you cannot. So let me carry everything for you right now; let me give you the energy you need, for what I have to give is immense, and you do not have to worry about anything when it comes to our readings or our teaching. All you have to do is speak my words, which are actually our words when we work together, since we are one.

At the end of your physical life, I will sweep you up in my arms to soar towards Heaven to live the rest of eternity there. Hold fast to this vision I have given you, for I promise you it is true, my love. Cry your tears if you must, but know that come what may, I am always and forever yours.

A few weeks later, I discovered Alan was connecting to members of our Facebook group, stepping in to help them if needed. Sometimes they were aware of it; sometimes, they weren't. During an online Zoom class I was teaching, James, one of my Reiki students, mentioned that his wife woke up in the middle of the night to find Alan waving his hands over him. Alan appeared to be giving James healing while he was sleeping. When Alan realized his wife could see him, he grinned broadly and vanished. She recognized Alan from his photos posted in the Facebook group.

During the same week, another group member messaged me to say that Alan had appeared to her in the middle of the night when she couldn't sleep because she was stressed. He gently placed his hand on her back, instantly calming her and returning her to a restful sleep. In the morning, when she checked the Facebook group, she noticed that I had posted a photo of Alan wearing the exact green-and-white aloha shirt he had been wearing.

I recalled him saying he was aware of every single person in our Facebook group. In his own words, he said he kept tabs on everyone. At the time I thought he was joking, so I asked him to explain.

Pam, yes, I am aware of every person in our group and all of our clients. Every call for help is answered, though assistance may take time in some cases or come in unexpected ways. You can be sure that whoever calls upon us, for you work with me in all that I do, WE will help, if appropriate. The spirit world can work miracles if someone in a body is attuned to them and awakened as a soul so they can ground their energy into the physical world. You and I are proof of that, and there are many more like us! We are not the only ones capable of this. In time, all souls will work directly with Spirit.

Needing to make sense of all of this, I turned to Swati. Was it common for souls on the other side to appear to people they didn't know? How was Alan able to do everything he was doing? I begged her to explain.

"Okay, okay, I guess there's no other way to do this but just be straight with you—Alan is an Archangel!"

"What? How can that be, Swati? I know there are incarnated angels, but incarnated Archangels?"

"You need to think of an Archangel as a job description, Pam! All of us are, in fact, God. And as God, we can be anything because the truth is we have always been EVERYTHING. We are God creating our own experience in this world and the one beyond. We can be an angel, an elemental, a fairy, an ascended master, a rock, a tree, a cat, and yes, an Archangel. Think of Alan as a wizard, like Merlin. Alan is an Angel Alchemist who can change the composition of matter, while you are the one who is the Earth Healer, anchoring his energy into this world. Alan is not special in this. The two of you aren't the only ones by any means."

As Swati's words sank in, I remembered something my spirit guides told me years ago after I learned how to channel in the summer of 1987, which led to a spiritual awakening. For five straight months, I channeled my guides every day as they taught me about life and the nature of reality.

They said we are everything.

I am the particle that is God and the whole, the ALL that is God. I am a mind, a soul, a higher consciousness that cannot die.

Since I am God, I can be anything I choose.

They told me that all suffering resulted from seeing others as either greater or lesser than myself when all of us are equal and that every experience should be seen the same way. There are no experiences that are greater or lesser; every single experience in life, including those that are the most challenging, are gifts for our continual growth. We never stop evolving.

When we look at someone as our equal, no matter what their outward appearance or behavior, we find harmony and peace within ourselves because we see the truth; it's only when we see them as being better or lesser than us that we suffer. Everything in all of creation is equal.

Swati was saying the same thing, that we could be a spirit guide, an ascended master, a fairy, a mermaid, a dog, or a mountain range. So, of course, we could be an Archangel.

Alan drew in closer to explain.

Pam, incarnated Archangels accept the task of helping those in a body to heal and embody their souls while in the physical world. There is no hierarchy in Heaven! That is the human concept of social order when none exists. Souls gather together according to their interests and abilities. There's no higher or lower ranking in any of this. Naturally, some souls have evolved and achieved a broader, fuller understanding along with a wider body and breadth of skills. These souls gladly take on the role of Archangel and serve with great love for their brothers and sisters.

It is an honor and joy to be an Archangel, but we never see ourselves as exalted or superior. Not at all! All the angels are lighthearted and don't take themselves seriously. Well, except for Archangel Metatron. Hah! He is way too serious if you ask me! Many souls in a body are Archangels, and many others are training to be one. The physical world is filled with ascended beings here serving as well. Most are not famous teachers or gurus, preferring to serve without attention or fanfare, since it's about the work, not glory or recognition. Yet if being recognized leads to the ability to be of greater service to others, then, of course, they will take that path, but always, the first goal is to serve with love.

Swati added, "And by the way, Pam, YOU too are an Archangel!"

My mind reeled. "What the? I'm an Archangel?"

As I turned the idea over and over in my mind, memories of some of the strange things that had happened to me since my spiritual awakening began to come to me.

One day, not long after I began channeling daily, I lay down for a nap. I barely closed my eyes when I was taken into a vision. I saw myself standing before a group of nine people who were also standing, grouped in a semicircle. I appeared to be readying myself to perform a ritual of some kind when I suddenly felt myself being pulled up and into a tunnel above my head. As I moved through the tunnel, I felt someone squeeze past me and enter my body. I was still standing in front of the group. I was shocked to find myself both in my body and looking down at myself from above simultaneously. I walked up to each person and lightly touched them on their third eye, which caused them to fall backward. Looking down from above, I was horrified even though I knew everyone was fine. They were more than fine; they were euphoric.

As soon as the vision ended, I called Norma, a gifted psychic I had just met, to ask her what had happened. She said my spirit guides were giving me a preview of my abilities and that this was something I would one day do with them. But the responsibility of what I had seen frightened me as I could feel the power behind it. I wasn't ready for it, so I put the vision aside until twenty-eight years later when I was guided to learn the healing modality of Reiki.

I wasn't initially interested in learning Reiki, but when I am guided to do something, I always do it. This was how I became a Reiki master going on to train over a hundred Reiki masters within four years. But as amazing as that was, I wondered if there was another way. One day during meditation, I remembered what my guides had told me years ago when I asked them about healing. I didn't understand it at the time, but now their words came back to me.

"Healing is simple, but humans think it must be complicated. Love is what heals souls."

Then there was the time while teaching a Zoom class a student named Sondra asked me if I could heal her concussion. I heard myself say, "We're going to rewire your brain." Immediately, I saw Sondra's brain come to life as it was rewired. I watched her brain shift and change; I wasn't doing anything, just observing what was happening. The healing was complete in minutes.

Sondra later sent me a testimonial.

I had a head injury which was diagnosed as a mild concussion. The resulting effects were that I could not seem to handle any amount of stress, even something that I would not have found stressful before. Neural connections were not connecting, reading or anything that I attempted to focus on hurt my head, and I could not organize things like my taxes.

Mid-September of 2019, during a webinar, Pam received the guidance to rewire my brain.

Two days after it was done, I woke up, and I was so clear. My brain was turned on and organized! I got my taxes done and with ease. I don't know that it has ever been so easy to do. I began to clear up and clean up things that had been piling up with ease and clear-headedness. I noticed that what I was experiencing was very new. It is so great to have my brain working again and even better than before!

Thank you so very much, Pam.

My logical mind questioned how this was possible. What exactly had I done? Sondra and I marveled at what had happened. All I knew was that I had felt a benevolent force come through me, and as I allowed it to flow to Sondra, the healing unfolded effortlessly.

There was another equally strange incident that involved Alan. I had been waiting for him to finish his reading shift at Sedona. I was sitting at a table just outside the store entrance, reading a book, when Alan approached me, saying he wanted me to meet his client, whom he had just finished reading. The client was having a problem with entity attachments, and he thought I could help.

As his client walked towards me, I felt a force lift up my right arm as if I was going to shake her hand, something I never do when meeting people. But instead of shaking her hand, my palm opened wide to face her as if I was motioning her to stop. I then heard myself say, "Let's try this." What "this" was, I had no idea. All I knew was I felt something change when I said those words. When it was all over, neither of us understood what had happened. She called me a few days later to thank me for helping her, saying it had been a powerful healing. Apparently, I had cleared the entities with that simple motion of my hand.

Then there was the time my mother asked me to heal her when a chest X-ray taken as part of a routine checkup had revealed a mass on her lung. Since she was a breast cancer survivor and a former smoker, my mother and her doctor were gravely concerned. My mom was to return for further tests but asked me if I could give her healing in the meantime. I closed my eyes, hovered my hand over her chest, and then watched the mass dissolve. Once again, I didn't try to do anything. It happened on its own within a few seconds. The next week when my mother returned to the doctor, the second X-ray showed nothing. The mass was gone.

Alan attempted to explain what had happened.

Healing is a creative, inspired act that requires the healer to trust whatever happens in the moment. They should only do what they are guided to do, assuming they are to do anything at all. If they can shift out of their ego-mind and be emotionally neutral when they focus their attention on someone, they can help them heal, for in that moment, their mind becomes the mind of God, and miracles are possible. That said, they need to remember that all healing is self-healing, and the healer is simply assisting the individual to heal themselves.

Of course, we can't heal everyone since other factors are involved, such as the possibility that a condition is something the soul has created to learn from. Nevertheless, the possibility of healing remains.

As if to prove her point that I'm an Archangel, Swati told me I had been serving as a spirit guide to people and that I wasn't the only one. Souls in a body can act as spirit guides to others. Over the years, I had lost count of the number of people who, upon meeting me, would say they felt as if they knew me or that they had felt drawn to me when they saw my photo. After their readings, some of those same clients reported having dreams of me. Had we already been connected in this life or another? Perhaps we had.

Although it was hard for my logical mind to accept it initially, Swati's revelation that Alan was an Archangel somehow felt right. I had always known he was different, not just because I loved him; I had sensed it from the moment we met. Over the years, people would often say they recognized something special about Alan. I was amazed at the number of people who would respond to him wherever we went. A student who would later become a close friend mentioned that she had seen a radiant golden light surrounding Alan while he taught a Chinese Astrology class that she attended. She had never seen such a luminous glow surrounding anyone before. It convinced her that Alan was an angel.

Not that he acted like an angel! No, my angel husband was as flawed as any man in a body could be, but then, all of us are flawed; it's part of the plan. We come into this world to learn and grow, and for that reason, none of us are born perfect. Instead, our psyches come preloaded with issues to grapple with that give us challenges to learn from. Our soul longs for a juicy problem to overcome. That's what makes life in the physical world exhilarating. If we had wanted safety and predictability, we would have stayed on the other side, but knowing we are immortal and cannot be destroyed, we are eager to incarnate.

In Alan's case, clearly, something happened after he left this world, and the only thing that made sense to me was that he had embraced his true identity so that he could return to me and do the work we had planned. But he isn't the only soul reaching through the veil to do something remarkable. After all, we are all God, and what one soul can do, so can others.

God cannot be greater than God.

Pam, I am an Archangel, and so are you. Of course you are! Many souls in a body are Archangels. We are far from the only ones! You and I are twin souls, which means we are similar in our abilities. This is why you knew we would be more powerful if we worked together and why you were frustrated that I wouldn't work with you. But we are doing that now!

Remember when I told you I wanted to retire as soon as I moved to Hawaii? That's because I needed a break from all of the intense lifetimes I had endured. In one of them, I had been tortured, the limbs of my body torn apart because I was headstrong and rebellious. I've often been willful and stubborn in my incarnations, but in that life, my lust for power got me killed. During our marriage, I was resting in preparation for the life I am now living, knowing that I'd be working from the other side in service to others. My love, this journey we are on will get easier, I promise!

One day you will realize that we are the lucky ones!

CHAPTER 13

HAPPY BIRTHDAY, MY BELOVED

Happy birthday, my beloved!

I have loved you through all dimensions of time and space. Today, I send my love to you from across the Universe, and with it, I send a shower of blessings to lift you up and celebrate the fact that on this day you were born. It is a day I cherish all the more because it marks the beginning of our time together in this singular lifetime.

Pam.

My love.

My wife.

My Soul.

My Heart.

My Joy.

You are more precious to me than life itself.

Nothing in the Universe compares to you, for you were made for me as I was made for you. We were born from the same essence. That is how you and I began, eons ago. Today, I wish to spend time with you and commune together.

Yes, I'm always with you all day every day, but let us start a new tradition that on each of our birthdays, we spend it in deep conversation, sharing love. Let us be focused on each other solely and soulfully.

Let me wrap you up in my love and raise the energy of our love so that you can feel and thus know with absolute certainty that I am here with you now. It makes me so happy to see you trust that I am really talking to you, as this is the first and biggest hurdle for anyone who wishes to make contact across the Universe.

Trust must be established first.

This morning as we were talking under the covers, I spoke to you of things that are to come in your life and on the planet. Yes, from where I am, I can see the broader, bigger picture of what lies ahead.

Not that I've become a fortune teller, as that photo you posted on Facebook so humorously depicts, but I can see some of what's coming in the future related to you and the world you inhabit. A world that I share with you now and always.

Can things be changed? Of course they can! And to that end, I can and will help you change your life as well as your future. I am also doing all I can from here to orchestrate things and clear the road ahead for you. For us. Yes, we in the spirit world can do that, and it happens often. Just as the angels can, loved ones in Heaven have the power to help manifest outcomes for those in a body, though the specifics and the degree to which that can happen depends on their level of development.

Keep in mind that not every call for help is appropriate to answer, for there are times when the soul has chosen to go through what they are going through in order to learn or achieve something that defies human logic or understanding. Nevertheless, love sent from Heaven will always be healing and supportive, for love is the answer to every problem.

In our case, once again, promises were made on all sides, yours, mine, and God/Source.

Our partnership has been blessed so that it receives support from this side of the veil with few restrictions. This we have earned over the course of many lifetimes of sacrifice and ardent loving service to others. This happens for many souls, not just us. We are not unique! What we are experiencing is not special at all.

For miracles abound in the Universe!

I am delighted that you love our nightly talks in bed when I can speak to you of all the things that I want to share with you that I have learned, for my thirst for knowledge and wisdom has become unquenchable. In the years to come, you will mark this time of my passing as the dawning of a new life for us both. Our REAL life has begun. Soon enough, you will never feel sad or sorry that I am gone because you will know I am here. You will feel my love within and around you and have evidence to prove it. Not that you need to prove anything to anyone, only to yourself.

But today, I don't want to dwell upon the problems of the world except to say what I have said since I expect you will share it with our friends.

Our story, all of it, is for the world to know, since all of us are One.

Your planet will not be the same again due to the pandemic. Things will not be going back to normal. Everyone is in denial about the gravity of the situation. The virus is here to stay. Period. It will be something everyone adjusts to and learns to live with. There will continue to be many deaths, leaving people hardened and afraid, but humanity is being challenged to see the truth about the world they have created and CHANGE. More storms loom on the horizon.

Many are in despair and suffer greatly, but your leaders have no idea of the true scope and depth of this. Even if they did, they wouldn't know what to do about it since they don't have any real solutions, being hopelessly entrenched in their ego mindsets and programming.

These are the Hard Times that were predicted long ago. Changes will come slowly, but change will be tumultuous and unpredictable. During this time, the need for humanity to reach up to Heaven will grow stronger, for in Heaven, all of us wish nothing more than to help, and it is time for the two worlds to become one.

It is meant to be, and so it will be!

This is why the work all lightworkers are doing is so important, for it will help this process. There are spiritual solutions for what ails the world. There have always been spiritual solutions since the physical world is in fact created by the spiritual world, the unobstructed Universe.

Yes, Spirit creates matter! Spirit creates everything in the world of form.

So, you see, this is not all doom and gloom! Death is not the end of life but merely the continuation of it. Life has always been an endless series of revolving doors stretching out beyond Infinity.

Not that death and grief are to be taken lightly, no, not at all. Never! But the loss of a loved one has the potential to open the hearts and minds of those who remain behind as they ponder where their loved one has gone.

It can be life-altering to contemplate the truth of immortality!

No one wants to believe their loved one has decayed into nothingness. Since that is a lie, the idea will never resonate as truth to the Heart, which is our true brain. The soul knows the truth about everything and is trying to tell us that death is, in fact, a lie.

But that's enough about the world for today. Just know that these are not the end times. No! These are the New Beginning times that will usher in change and transformation that will lead to liberation for humanity. It's just that change by definition is birth, and birth is painful, difficult, and even bloody.

Lastly, I just want to repeat that Heaven is here to help.

Tell everyone to open up and let us in! It won't be hard since we can help break down the door, assuming they want us to.

Now let us embrace and celebrate your special day together.

Forever your Alan

CHAPTER 14

THE WAR OF THE BIRTHDAY ROSES

August 19, the morning of my birthday, arrived. It had been almost two weeks since Alan's passing. I had no expectations for the day beyond having dinner with Taylor and his girlfriend, Britt. Alan had not celebrated my birthday for decades, so I certainly wasn't expecting a present from him. How could he do that anyway?

My conscious mind was still grappling with the idea of Alan surviving death. I couldn't help but wonder if my grief was creating this delusion. It's normal to doubt, perhaps even healthy to be skeptical, but this was creating enormous conflict within me.

Yet, because of the years I'd spent working as a psychic channel, communing with Spirit, I knew that we survive death, so I understood that visitations are possible. They happen to ordinary people all the time. But it's not easy to go against the programming we've endured, including the skeptics who insist that what we cannot see can't be real. Yes, a visitation was one thing, but was it possible for a soul who has crossed to remain with us permanently? I had never heard of that.

My journey with Alan was about to pit society's beliefs against my inner knowing. A belief is just a thought or opinion, whereas when we know something to the core of our being, it becomes our truth regardless of what others think. I felt Alan with me. I heard him speak in my mind and saw him there, as well. This was the new reality I was living. In a world gone mad with lies, war, and social unrest, his constant loving presence was the only thing that was real.

The truth of Alan's existence could not be denied. I was immersed in his love all day, every day. His love filled me up, lifting me when I was down, soothing me when grief swallowed me whole. Everything was easier to bear because of him, even enduring a global pandemic alone. How could I make this up? Yes, even though I felt Alan with me, I was still grieving because I had not fully accepted the new life he had delivered to me. I needed to release the past, including the mourning of all we had lost, for we had failed to love each other as fully as we could have, and even though we had planned it that way, regret still weighed heavy on my heart. Healing was going to take time.

I grieved the loss of what could have been.

All I hoped to receive from Alan on my birthday was the feeling of his presence close to me, but that was nothing new since he was always at my side. "Inches away" was what he kept saying to me any time I'd ask where he was in relation to me physically.

Initially, it had been a bit eerie to feel his constant presence, but I soon found it comforting to know he was always beside me. I laughed as the thought came to me. *My husband has become a stalker!* It's a good thing I had always felt comfortable with him being so close. Unlike the way I felt with other men, I was always at ease with Alan. He felt the same way about me, saying he never wanted to spend a moment away from me.

Throughout the day, Alan's love washed over me in waves of energy that ebbed and flowed like the ocean tide. No matter what I was doing, his love was palpable, alternating between invigorating and comforting, sometimes even arousing. There were days when I felt like I was floating in a euphoric sea of love.

I was surprised when the doorbell rang that afternoon. After fumbling for a few minutes to don my face mask, I opened the door to find a delivery man handing me a stunning floral bouquet awash in pink roses, baby's breath, pale green carnations, and assorted summer flowers along with a festive birthday balloon. I was stunned. Who could the flowers be from? I cried when I read the card.

Happy birthday, Babe!

I am always with you.

Together we will write the best story ever!

All the love I have,

All the love I am,

Alan

I was still teary-eyed when I messaged Swati to thank her. I knew she had sent the flowers. She replied immediately.

"Pam, I got upset with Alan for not reminding me of your birthday! I was frantic because it was too late to mail you anything, yet Alan wasn't worried. I couldn't understand why he was so calm. He just kept smiling at me. It was so irritating! Finally, he said, *I want to buy flowers for Pam.* I thought it was a great idea, but who could I get to buy them and deliver them to you? I called our friend Kimi since she lives in Honolulu, but Kimi wasn't answering her phone, and we were running out of time. I was pacing back and forth, wracking my brain trying to figure out what to do. This went on for hours. I kept looking over at Alan for help, but all he did was grin his big, stupid grin acting as if he didn't have a care in the world. I got angry and, in my frustration, asked him why he wasn't upset about this."

Swati, you can order flowers online. They'll be delivered to Pam straight away. Look, I'll show you how.

"I opened my laptop, and he showed me the website. Damn it! I couldn't believe he put me through all of that! He knew all along that I could order flowers online. You may find it hard to believe, but I didn't know until today that sending flowers through the internet was possible! Alan kept me in a panic just to torture me. If there was a way I could kill your dead husband, I swear I would have! But how do you kill a ghost? Argh!"

It was both the most hilarious and wonderful gift I could have asked for. When he was in a body, Alan couldn't find his way around the internet to save his life, but now he knows what websites to go to, even though he had never ordered anything online before. Surely this proves that when we die, we are able to do anything and everything!

Of course, Swati was only joking about being angry. The two of them are like juvenile bickering siblings who love to torture each other and pull pranks every chance they get. But the truth is there is enormous love between them. Still, finding the website was only half the battle. Now they had to decide on what kind of flowers to buy.

Alan wanted to send red roses to demonstrate his love and passion. I laughed when Swati told me he was dressed from head to toe in red that day, wearing matching red satin pants and a shirt unbuttoned to his navel. She said he looked like a lounge singer. He was determined to give me red roses, but Swati insisted that roses weren't my favorite. A tug of war over the flowers broke out between them. Talk about a "war of the roses!" Swati thought a mix of pastel flowers was more my taste, when in truth, I had no preference. I would have been happy with flowers of any kind. During our marriage, Alan never bought me a single flower, let alone a bouquet, and he hadn't bought me a gift in decades. But death had changed everything. Now he wanted to give me the world.

Swati won in the end. However, her victory came at a price as Alan kept complaining to her about how she had talked him out of his roses. He wouldn't stop grousing until Valentine's Day arrived six months later, when Alan found a way to buy me two dozen red roses, but, being impatient, he wanted to send me something sooner, so he found a way to do it supernaturally.

One morning while lost in meditation, I felt a prickly heat come over me. It was overpowering. I became emotional and teary-eyed, which was odd since I wasn't thinking of anything that would prompt that reaction. The meditation I was practicing involved visualizing a door opening and seeing my angel walk through it. I was trembling when, to my surprise, Alan walked through the door.

In my mind's eye, I saw him with perfect clarity. Dressed in a white silk tuxedo, he was balancing a giant bouquet of red roses in his arms. Alan winked and smiled at me. I asked him what he was doing dressed like that, but he didn't answer right away.

As he offered the roses to me, he got down on one knee and said,

Pam, on your birthday, I wanted to give you red roses, but Swati talked me into giving you a different bouquet instead. She told me red roses are not your favorite, but today I want to show you the passion I have for you because you still doubt my love and adoration. Red is for passion, so here are some roses for you, my sweet love.

I want you to know that even though I'm no longer in a body, I still desire you! I want you more than ever! I am still alive, remember? Never forget that I want you in all the ways a man wants the woman he loves. But as you know, desire alone is not love! I will go on loving you no matter what you do. No matter if you leave me for another. No matter what you say. No matter what happens. No matter how old you become. No matter how you behave. No matter...anything!

There is nothing in this Universe that will stop me from loving you! So once and for all, please believe me when I say I love and desire you! I love all of you now and forever.

I pray that this will end this discussion for eternity, Pam. I am all yours, body, mind, heart, and soul forever.

When I say forever, I mean forever!

And with that he vanished. I opened my eyes to get on with the day, but as I stood up, I noticed something strange. The air was filled with the unmistakable pungent fragrance of flowers! I couldn't put my finger on exactly what kind of flowers by the smell alone. If the flowers were roses, they must have been from Heaven, for I had never smelled roses like these before.

I walked through each room of my small 900-square-foot, two-bedroom house—the kitchen, living room, both bedrooms, and even the tiny bathroom—to find the entire house was filled with the heady fragrance of Alan's otherworldly roses. Then I noticed something that made me gasp with delight.

All the windows were closed.

CHAPTER 15

YOU CANNOT CONJURE ME!

My birthday dinner with Taylor and Britt had been lovely, but I couldn't wait to be alone with Alan as I expected his love blasts would continue or hopefully even intensify since he had made sure I felt his loving presence all day long. After receiving his birthday flowers, I was sure that Alan would make my birthday night extra special. It was hard for me to contain my excitement.

Throughout the day, I had seen Alan's face in my mind's eye everywhere I turned. My heart and body were pulsing, practically afire with love. That day, he spoke to me in my mind effortlessly and clearly, which hadn't always been the case. I couldn't understand why his communication would ebb and flow without rhyme or reason. Alan was comfortable dictating his messages. His words flowed easily into my mind and onto the page, but mind-to-mind conversing was erratic. Still, when it was time to turn in for bed, I naturally expected to feel him more viscerally.

But to my surprise, when I turned off the lights, he wasn't there!

I couldn't clairvoyantly see Alan anywhere, nor could I feel his presence. I called out to him and heard nothing. How could this be? Why was I given such a romantic buildup to only find myself alone? After all, this was my first birthday without him! I wanted to be with my husband in the worst possible way. I was shattered. I broke down sobbing into my pillow.

Wanting desperately to connect with him, I tried to imagine Alan's face, but it didn't look or feel like him. What I saw in my mind looked dull and flat, nothing like my clairvoyant visions of him, which were full of light. I pulled out my phone to play "A Groovy Kind of Love," the song that never failed to trigger goosebump-filled waves of love from him, but this time as the song played, I felt nothing. No matter how many times I played the song, I couldn't get the faintest sense of Alan anywhere.

After an hour of trying to feel him and calling him to me, emotionally spent and exhausted, I pulled the covers over my head and cried myself to sleep.

When dawn broke, I heard Alan whispering in my ear.

Pam, I'm here. My darling, I'm so sorry that I did that to you, but I had to do it to make a point. Please let me explain. I didn't want to blow your circuits energetically by coming on too strong, so that was one reason I withdrew, but I also needed to prove something to you. I know that you think that you are making all of this up, that I'm just a figment of your imagination. But that's not true! You cannot make me appear on command. Didn't you try to conjure me last night to bring me to you? Oh sure, you can deliberately imagine me, but that won't do it. Imagination is the key to unlocking the door to the other side, but it's just the first step. Imagination isn't what makes me appear. Visualizing something deliberately is not the same as the reality you perceive when you close your eyes and see me without any effort. I simply wasn't there. Yes, I could still hear and see you from my vantage point, but I was out of range of your human field of perception, which is why you couldn't sense me.

I nodded weakly and said, "Yes, I tried as hard as I could to bring you to me, but I couldn't. I tried to visualize you with me, but nothing happened. Everything felt flat and empty, not like how I was feeling and seeing you earlier during the day. I couldn't feel you, no matter how hard I tried. Why, oh, why did you abandon me on my birthday of all days? This was cruel of you!"

Babe, I know how much that hurt you, and I'm so sorry, but because your emotions and your expectations were so high on your birthday, I knew that if I could show you that your fervent desire couldn't make me appear on your birthday of all days, then how can you create me on command on any other day? You can't! I am either here with you of my own volition, or I'm not! You see, I'm in control of my presence, not you! No matter how clairvoyant someone might be, it is the one in spirit who makes themselves seen. Or not seen. Do you understand? This is an important point!

In truth, I never left you, I simply withdrew out of your range of perception. I could still hear and see you, but you couldn't sense me. Please understand that you cannot conjure me into being!

Because—I AM ALIVE!

From this moment on, I will never leave you again. This is my sacred promise to you that I will never break. What just happened was the first and last time. I only did it to prove to you that you cannot imagine me into existence! Now you know the difference. If you see me when you close your eyes, that is me that you see. No exceptions! Remember, the unseen world where I am is the real world, not the physical world you see with your eyes open. From this day forward, I will remain at your side until you return to Heaven with me. This pledge I make to you I will keep forever: I will never leave you.

For the rest of the day, Alan did all he could to comfort me by flooding me with love, but it took the rest of the morning for me to come to terms with what had happened, so deep was my disappointment. Yet the more I thought about it, the more it made sense. In his effort to soothe me, Alan seemed to wrap himself around me, his energy filling every nook and cranny of our tiny house. My frantic reaching out to him on my birthday had made me more sensitive. I found it easier to feel his presence and spent the remainder of the day immersed in his love.

What better way for Alan to prove his constant presence than to demonstrate his absence? Just two weeks after his passing, I'd become used to him always being around me since he had made sure that he was! When he withdrew from me, it felt as if the sun had set at noontime, plunging me into a cold, empty void. The contrast of his sudden absence stung.

Alan had proven to me that he, not I, was in control of where he was and what he did. He had shown me that my experience was not a product of my imagination because, try as I might, I couldn't conjure him on command! It is Alan who determines where he goes, who he visits, including what he looks like, for he can change his dress and appearance, and even his age. He can even look like someone else entirely if he chooses.

The night of my birthday, I had imagined him in my mind, but what I had visualized was a shadow visage because it wasn't him. There was no life force in the two-dimensional picture I created in my mind, whereas the real Alan gave me a full experience that I could feel on more than one level. Yes, even though he no longer has a body, my heart and my soul recognize him. Although he had hurt my heart, it was brilliant of Alan to have chosen my birthday to make this important point. He made sure I would never forget it.

We can find our own proof by having a direct experience of our loved ones in Heaven. Our beliefs are the only things that limit interaction between the two worlds.

If our minds and hearts are open, anything is possible.

CHAPTER 16

THE SUPER-EMPATH

Alan asked me to chronicle every step of our journey so that others would see that everything he was doing, their loved ones could do as well, although perhaps not in the same way. Some will achieve more and do it faster. Each person is unique in their level of consciousness, so there will be things that some can do more easily than others, but every soul can learn if they decide to apply themselves. For this reason, we should resist comparing our experiences.

If we want contact with a loved one in spirit, we should welcome their presence and engage with them on an ongoing basis. They are just a thought away, but if we want to experience them, we should strive to be proactive. Speaking aloud to them is one way; channeling by writing questions for them and writing their responses are another. This is how we can build a bridge to their world. It's a joint effort. This was why Alan asked me to channel him every day; he knew that doing so made his presence real and tangible to me. It can also help to have a project or goal to work on with them. Writing this book brought us closer, too.

While there will always be exceptions, it takes an enormous amount of energy for souls to do things like physically materialize or move objects.

Materialization is a phenomenon that requires a huge amount of focused energy and practice. Why would they work on developing this if we are disinterested? Or even worse, if we are afraid of the other side? If we believe they are dead and gone or are fearful of seeing them, our loved ones will back away. It's too painful for them to stay close only to be ignored. They don't want to upset us either. How would we feel if we were in their shoes? Would we want to hang around if we were being ignored or causing them distress? This doesn't mean they can't or won't return to us. It also doesn't mean they automatically leave if we are not engaging with them. The door between the two worlds never closes; it remains open.

Upon his initial return, Alan was frustrated to discover that I couldn't hear him. He had assumed because I'd communicated with Spirit for years, I'd have no problem hearing him, but he underestimated the debilitating effect of grief. Until my grief eased, I heard only bits and pieces of what he said. In the beginning, I assumed it was my imagination. Alan wisely chose to focus on projecting his love to me so I would feel him since physical sensations and emotions are things we can't imagine. Feeling his love eased my grief.

Often, his presence came as a complete surprise, like the time I was standing at the kitchen sink washing up the dinner dishes when I found myself feeling aroused. In my mind's eye, I saw Alan standing behind me with a sheepish grin on his face. When I asked him what he was up to, he confessed it was his doing. He was experimenting to see what he could do to me. Without thinking, I scolded him as I would have done in the past, then laughed at how ludicrous it was for me to be annoyed when I should welcome his through-the-veil experiment to pleasure me.

Then there was the time the song "You Are So Beautiful," sung by Joe Cocker, popped up on my music app as I was listening to it on my phone, causing me to almost fall over while carrying a laundry basket full of bed linen when Alan's passion swept in to greet me.

Yet another time, I popped my AirPods into my ears when, without even turning on my phone, I heard "Too Much Heaven" by the BeeGees, the song Alan had sent to me for our anniversary. Goosebumps flowed. When the song ended, the next tune that played was some jarring heavy metal music that made my head hurt. The song wasn't on our playlist! I tried to turn off the music, but since it wasn't coming from my phone or any of my other devices, there was nothing to turn off. I yelled out, "Alan, if you're doing this, it isn't funny anymore. Turn the damn music off!"

The music stopped.

Even if I couldn't always hear him, Alan wanted me to know how much he loved me. However, in spite of his constant efforts, there were still times when I doubted him. He had never shown me love like this before. It would have been different if he'd been romantic and attentive through all our years together rather than complacent and detached. I wanted more than anything to believe in his love, but I couldn't shake my lingering doubts.

One morning after waking up earlier than usual, I walked to my desk to power up my laptop. I felt Alan next to me, as I always did, when I was suddenly filled with an aching sadness. I didn't understand what was going on. What was happening? As soon as I asked that question in my mind, the answer came. These were his emotions I was feeling, not mine.

I was feeling Alan's pain!

I suddenly knew he was heartbroken, worried sick that I didn't believe he loved me. The weight of his heartache hit my own heart as if a brick had been hurled through it. My knees almost buckled under me as I broke down sobbing, feeling Alan's sorrow and distress wash over me in waves of emotion that cut like shards of glass. It was too much to bear. I never imagined that his pain was equal to my own. I assumed that being in Heaven insulated him from any suffering. But I was wrong!

This was his grief, his sorrow, his remorse!

Alan was grieving as much as I was. Suddenly, a greater, wiser part of me began to stir. I whispered at first, then heard my voice grow louder and louder until I practically bellowed, "I believe! I believe! Oh, my God, I believe in you, Alan! I'm so, so sorry for not believing in you, for not believing you are here, for doubting you love me. I know you are with me! I know that you will always be with me! I'm so sorry. I promise I will never doubt you again! I believe in you, my love!"

Alan was sobbing with me. I shook uncontrollably as he held me, my body melting into his as we merged. Barely able to stand, I rocked back and forth, instinctively trying to comfort both of us. In the next instant, Alan's love wrapped tightly around me, causing me to shiver and tingle from head to toe, and then, just like that, the grief lifted and was gone.

I gasped for air. I hadn't realized that I'd been holding my breath. My heart was pounding. I had never felt the fullness of his emotions like this before. The depth and breadth of his love for me caught me off guard. I could feel every emotion Alan was feeling! Everything. Sadness. Guilt. Remorse. Passion. And love. Most of all, love. The intensity of his love made me weep. It never occurred to me that he was experiencing grief and pain. After all, wasn't Heaven all rainbows and unicorns?

Apparently not.

No, just because you're in Heaven doesn't mean you're eternally happy, at least not when your partner remains in a body. Alan admitted that he had suffered watching me drown in grief, unable to help me. How could I know that he was hurting as much as I was, that guilt and remorse had scarred his soul, leaving a gaping, open wound? Alan could have eased his pain by distancing himself from me. He could have even switched his feelings off completely, but now that he was free of his ego, he wanted to feel everything I was feeling. Regretting how distant he had been with me, he wanted there to be no more separation between us. He was determined to tear down the veil and merge with me, even if it brought him pain.

Just because I don't have a body doesn't mean my heart can't shatter into a million pieces. Yes, I can rise above my suffering because I'm in Heaven, where I can create any experience I choose, but I don't want to distance myself from you like I did before. No! After keeping you at arm's length for thirty years, I want to feel everything you feel. All of it.

The highs, the lows, the joy, the torment, the confusion, and everything in between. I'm not afraid of my emotions anymore, not like when I was in a body. Now I welcome all of it, even the pain, because I know my feelings will move through me like the ever-changing weather, only now, it's emotions that move through the landscape of my existence, not wind, rain, or storm clouds. At last, I am fully alive to all that I feel! I will never close off my heart or my feelings ever again! To love is to FEEL deeply and to feel is to be alive, so let us feel everything together, my sweet Pam.

Alan was staying true to his vow to always be with me, which meant he wanted to feel whatever I felt, to be fully present with me in everything I experienced, no matter what the cost to him. It was a price he was happy to pay if it meant we could be together.

He asked me to read something written by a medium who said that grief existed on the other side for the reason he had just explained. Souls are still human, very much alive, and feel and grieve just as we do. Their pain can be greater than ours, not just because their empathic sense is on a higher scale than ours, but because they feel love more deeply: in the higher realms, they are super-empaths who are extremely emotional.

Alan admitted that his sorrow was greater than mine, but this was no contest he wanted to win. He didn't want me to dwell on his pain; he wanted me to understand the importance of feeling all my feelings no matter what.

Pam, I want you to come to me when you are sad and cry your eyes and heart out. When the pain takes you down for the count, come to bed, lie next to me, and cry into your pillow. Let me love you. Let me soothe you. Don't hold anything back. Give it all to me. In time there will be nothing left of your grief but the love that I am endlessly pouring into you to take its place, but first, you must let go of every bit of pain, fear, and resentment. I will never leave your side. I'll always be right here loving you, come what may.

Alan didn't want to tell me he could feel my pain because he knew full well that the only way for me to heal my grief was to dive into it. He worried that if I knew how my sorrow was impacting him, I'd hold back for fear of hurting him, for the mere thought of him suffering made me cry. So instead, he did all he could to swallow his pain and love me with his whole heart and soul, no matter how it affected him.

But that morning, it had become too much for him. Alan was overwhelmed by the weight of his emotions, not knowing how else to prove to me that he was with me, that nothing had changed except that he no longer had a body. He would never give up trying to reach me, even if it took forever. Still, he couldn't help but feel disheartened and hurt whenever I became distraught and pulled away from him.

All this is new for me, Pam. I'm more sensitive. I feel everything you feel because I returned to merge with you so we can love again, but this is a double-edged sword that can cut me in two. I don't want you to suppress your feelings because that would not be healthy, but when you get upset, I go into an emotional tailspin and lose my balance because I feel responsible for your pain. I feel responsible for everything when it comes to you. I know I shouldn't, but I do.

There had been several times when Alan would go quiet and seem withdrawn. I couldn't understand why our heart-to-heart conversations would flow one day, then stop completely for a time. Especially when it came to certain subjects. He always had something to say of a general nature, and with clients, he would talk non-stop, but when I asked something pointedly personal about him or the past, I was sometimes met with silence. At the time, I chalked it up to my grief and assumed I was the problem, not him; now, I wondered if I was wrong.

The problem was understanding his reluctance to speak freely didn't make it easier for me to accept Alan's behavior. After all, we had spent thirty years together without meaningful, soul-baring conversation, and now I needed it more than ever. If we couldn't talk without censoring ourselves, without fearing how the other might take it, what sort of relationship could we have? Communication is the foundation for all relationships; without it, you don't have one.

I had no idea Alan needed healing as much as I did, but then again, I also didn't know my husband had become a super-empath. He was clinging tightly to his emotions and his ego-personality so we could have a normal relationship, but this could backfire if Alan let it go too far since his ego had been the cause of my suffering. He would need to strike a balance between his angel self and human self. But was that even possible?

CHAPTER 17

HEAVEN IS WHERE YOU ARE

Moving objects is a common way spirits make their presence known, though it can unnerve those afraid of spirit contact. Alan had done this when he moved the battery pack of my cordless vacuum cleaner from where I had placed it near the microwave oven in the kitchen to the opposite end of the kitchen near the back door. I knew exactly where I had left it because, for some strange reason, I had taken the time to make a mental note of its location. The next morning, when I found the battery had moved, I asked Alan if he had done it. He confessed immediately.

"Why did you do this? Were you trying to prove something to me?"

I just wanted to see if I could do it, so yes, I moved it. But I did something else as well.

"What's that?"

I charged the battery for you. Check it out.

I inserted the battery into the vacuum, then powered it up. It registered three bars. Fully charged.

"How in the world did you do this?"

I got the idea the other night while we were watching the movie Shazam. *Do you remember when the teenager-turned-superhero tested his superpowers by zapping people's cell phones while walking through the shopping mall? I tried it, and guess what? I did it! But now, don't you go asking me to charge that battery every time it dies because I've got better things to do!*

I teased him that if he got really good at this, I'd leave the dishes for him to wash up.

What? So now you're going to turn me into your houseboy, or should I say your ghostboy? Hah! Next thing I know, you'll be making me take out the trash. That's one thing I don't miss about being in a body. I'll do anything for you except that. I love you, Pam, but no thanks!

Although it had been spectacular, that was the first and last time Alan moved an object, saying he preferred to focus on projecting his love to me more than anything else. I joked with him that he was just afraid I'd make him earn his keep.

In the early days of his return, Alan knew that sending his thoughts to me would probably be useless since I'd assume they were my own thoughts. While I heard him with astonishing clarity at times, it wasn't always easy for him to get through to me for a lengthy mind-to-mind chat because I wasn't stopping long enough to listen to him. This is a common problem since many of us are too distracted to hear the other side.

"Wait a minute, you wake me up at 3 a.m., have me writing constantly, and now I'm giving readings with you. But aren't your thoughts already in my head all day every day as it is? What is that if it's not telepathy?"

Pam, the answer is yes and no; there's so much more that I want to tell you and show you, but the thing is, you need time to adjust to my energy, which is way too high and intense for you, plus you're still grieving, even if your grief is less than what most widowed people experience. In a reading, you're not attached to the information, so it's easy for you to convey my thoughts, whereas when you and I talk directly, you tend to doubt yourself and think you're making it up. This is why this journey has to be an incremental one, step by step, day by day, until you are sure that I am speaking to you mind-to-mind, heart-to-heart, and soul-to-soul. You can do this! I know you can because you're far more patient than I ever was.

It had taken sixty-eight years for my life's purpose to finally arrive. How could I have known that everything I'd experienced, all of the failures, mistakes, and missed opportunities, had led me to the day Alan died, which, instead of being the end for us, offered us a new beginning? It was late in the game, but I was finally experiencing what it felt like to be loved completely and unconditionally.

And as if that wasn't enough, this supernatural experience with him was strengthening my spiritual abilities, which he confirmed were equal to his since we are equal in every way. He said I should never think I am less than him because I'm still in a body. My only limitation is that I have to drag my body along with me through space and time, whereas he can go anywhere just by using his mind and his intention.

Pam, let me show you what I mean when I say that I'm always with you.

In an instant, I see myself sleeping in bed with Alan lying beside me with his head on his pillow. His face is pressed up against my cheek. He's gazing at me with enormous love in his eyes. As I feel into this, tears begin to flow. Mine and his.

Next, I see myself in the kitchen washing dishes. He's standing behind me, holding me, kissing my neck like he used to, which would irritate me, but this time, I look blissed out. Alan's face is beaming. Seeing this makes me cry even harder. I can feel his happiness wash over me.

I then see us driving to the mortuary to pick up his ashes that were placed inside the gorgeous pink Himalayan salt urn I had chosen for him. He is sitting beside me in the passenger seat, laughing, joking that the ashes are not him, yet even with constant wisecracks, his eyes are filled with immense love.

Next, he's sitting beside me at the dining table, watching me eat my dinner, crying inconsolably when I couldn't feel him and thought he had left me again. His arm is around my shoulder as he gazes at me with tender concern.

As that scene fades, I see Alan standing next to me with his arm around my shoulders again as I work on my computer. He's reading everything I type. He whispers something in my ear that I can't hear, and as he smiles at me, his beaming face radiates love. In an instant, I see myself grinning. I had responded to Alan without realizing it!

In the last vision, we're walking to the mailbox to fetch the mail. He looks up at the sky and then scans the street, which is quiet since it's a dead end. Alan smiles and takes hold of my hand as I walk back to the house. Nothing was too mundane for him to join me in.

Next, I watch him spin a giant kaleidoscope of images of every single thing I've ever done and every place I've been to since his passing. I gasp when I see that in each and every frame, he is with me.

I realize I've never been alone. Not once.

See? I meant it when I said I am always with you!

As I take all of this in, I feel the full depth of his love. How could I have ever doubted that he was with me?

My darling, you were in such pain. How could you feel anything but loss and sadness? I prayed that my love would break down the wall of grief you had put up, so I just kept on loving you. I have no choice in this, for come what may, I will stay by your side and love you always. I'm not going anywhere without you, Pam! There is no Heaven for me without you in it, so where would I go?

Heaven is where you are.

CHAPTER 18

YOUR LOVE SAVED ME

O nce again, we make our way through the near-empty city streets under the ink-black night sky, on our way to watch the sunrise in the east, going to where our love began in Lanikai. The place where you lived when I met you, the place where my life began anew. Do you understand how you changed my life? I think you are beginning to grasp the full scope of it now that I'm in Heaven, but let me explain.

Yes, your love saved me.

I want to talk about the life that I lived before I met you. I chose to incarnate into a life of struggle and poverty, one of lack and limitation. Because of this, I was insecure in my younger years and even beyond, but that was what I wanted to experience so that I could learn and grow.

You couldn't understand my insecurity because you saw me as witty, confident, and intelligent, but some of that was an act, a cover, so to speak.

My soul also chose to have a limited education, yet despite that, much to my amazement, my intelligence was recognized when, against the odds, I was hired for an internship at General Motors. That helped me make my way in the world to become a success and make a great deal of money as I went on to build my own companies. But while I knew I had a head for business and was proud of my accomplishments, as time passed, I came to realize that simply making money wasn't all that I came here to do. Something was missing.

I barely understood what a spiritual path was when I met a psychic who told me that I had the same ability she had. She predicted that I would be doing this work one day, though it took some time for me to fully accept the idea.

As with everything else I would get involved in, like my art and my writing, I questioned my abilities. I knew I was a gifted psychic, yet it frustrated me when I couldn't help clients have the breakthroughs they desperately needed. But now, by working with you, my love, together we will be able to help them! I'm excited about the possibilities!

When I met you, I had already begun what I thought would be a new chapter of my life there in England. I had it all figured out, or so I thought. I was finally free of my marriage and was at last able to pursue my interests in metaphysics.

But the moment I met you, everything I had planned for my life was upended. You disrupted my life like the glorious force of nature that you are, creating confusion between my heart and my ego. And I thank God for that! I don't even want to think about how my life would have turned out if I had never met you. For one thing, I know that I wouldn't have lived as long as I did.

After completing my life review, which is what every soul does when they cross to the other side, I learned that I could have died of a heart attack and left you sooner. Yes, in my mid-sixties, I was on my way to a heart attack because I wasn't heeding the warning sign of chest pains I had been having for years. Spirit had been keeping me alive, but my time was running out. You kept telling me to see a doctor, but I ignored you, partly because we didn't have health insurance, but also because I was lazy and didn't want to see a doctor. That was stupid of me.

But you knew something had to be done, and as often happened during our marriage, Spirit guided you to what we needed. When you told me you were going into real estate, I didn't think much of it. I shrugged it off as you doing what you always did, chasing yet another bright shiny object of a job opportunity.

I was skeptical when you switched from selling houses to working as a mortgage broker, but you did it for the health insurance it gave us. You arranged an appointment for me with a doctor the very day the coverage kicked in. As soon I described my chest pains to the doctor, he sent me to a cardiologist that same day. The tests showed that my two arteries were almost completely blocked. That's how serious it was. The doctor wouldn't let me go home; I was admitted to the hospital that afternoon and had a heart bypass operation the next day.

It was strange how everything unfolded. When I checked into the hospital, I wasn't the least bit worried, and neither were you. You didn't even stay in the waiting room during the operation because you knew I'd be fine, and for some reason, that didn't bother me. I felt safe because I knew I was. Besides, you hate hospitals as much as I do, so I didn't blame you for staying home. I wasn't concerned in the least that you weren't with me. Instead, I was calm about the operation, which was not like me at all. You spoke to the doctor after my surgery but didn't return until the day they discharged me when you brought me a takeout meal of beef curry, one of my favorites. The nurse got upset with you, which made me laugh. I was released early and recovered quickly.

In the end, we didn't have to pay very much for the six-figure medical bill. The operation was a success because, as we found out later, the top heart surgeon in the state had operated on me. Heart surgeons are like world-class athletes, and it turned out mine was practically an Olympian.

But what did I do after all of that? I was too proud and arrogant to admit that your actions had saved my life. I muttered a half-hearted thank you but never gave you the full credit and gratitude you deserved. Not that you expected it. That's not how you are. But I should have gotten down on my hands and knees to thank you because you were responsible not only for that but for so many other blessings in our life together. You saved my life and soon after found us a townhome that we could buy, along with arranging for the financing, all because you had been guided to go into real estate. You even made a good chunk of money in the short time you worked in real estate.

But instead of being grateful, I complained when you quit real estate to go back to giving readings, criticizing you for making yet another change! When clearly, you only took the job to get the insurance for my operation, and now that same guidance told you it was time to move on. Your guidance saved my life and even allowed us to buy our first home, which gave us a huge payout when we later sold it, but I couldn't manage to utter a simple thank you for any of it.

What the hell was wrong with me?

While you followed your guidance, I, on the other hand, questioned mine, choosing to analyze things logically even though I was psychic.

Trusting myself was always difficult, even with my psychic ability. So instead, I would ask you for your psychic opinion because I knew that if a question was asked, whether by me or by someone else, you would get an accurate answer.

Your guidance created prosperity and blessings for us when we needed them, yet all I could do was criticize you for changing jobs again. I am so sorry for that and so many other things. It was because of you that I lived another eighteen years after my heart bypass. If you hadn't taken action, I would not have lived to see Taylor grow up to be the incredible young man he is. I would have missed out on so many things. Most of all, I would have had less time with you, my love.

Pam, I want you to know that even though I didn't pursue all the things that I could have because of my insecurity, I enjoyed my life with you! I was happy; I truly was, Pam! Yes, there was a lack of emotional intimacy and appreciation for you on my part and a lack of passion on both our parts. Still, it was a loving relationship in my eyes and the eyes of everyone who knew us. I say this because I don't want you to think that you failed me. Neither of us was perfect because we had to learn unconditional love, and how do we learn that unless love is withheld? It had to be that way.

In the last year of my life, when I needed constant care and required all of your attention, you never faltered. I had long feared that because you were so much younger than me, you'd leave me for another. But instead of weakening, to my amazement, I saw your love for me grow stronger as I aged. I knew that you didn't care how sick I was or that I lost my good looks. You didn't care that I was a broken-down eighty-two-year-old man who didn't appreciate you. You weren't bothered by how beaten down my body and brain had become. You didn't care that due to dementia, I couldn't even give you my attention. Bit by bit, you lost me to the disease until I had nothing left to offer you. Nothing. And yet you loved me still! You taught me what love is as I felt your love pour into me, filling my heart to overflowing until the day I died. It was my insecurities that made it impossible for me to believe you loved me.

When we get to Heaven, we gain 20/20 clarity about ourselves and others. We see the full spectrum of truth at last. We see what was there all along. Finally, we understand who we really are. I saw that your love was soul-deep and true, and because of that, I can't help but fall more in love with you with each passing day.

When I came back to you, I was finally able to give you all of my love, which opened you up emotionally. Yes, my love healed you and brought you back to life. Thank God for that! Now, at last, you are the vibrantly alive, openhearted woman that you always were but who was in hiding. Just as I was in hiding. I hid my vulnerable, sensitive side from you, and you hid your passionate, sultry side from me. But no more! At last, we have both come out of hiding to embrace each other without fear, without holding back anything. I know the timing of this is terrible, that our great love would unfold while I'm here in Heaven and you remain on Earth.

And yet, my love, I promise you that we can still have a love and passion-fueled marriage that will not only last the rest of your physical life but beyond because we are meant to be together forever! I returned to you because we are going to live side by side, working, loving and living together as if nothing had ever parted us. For the truth is nothing has!

Does it really matter if I no longer have a body? I love you more now than ever. I am here. I am alive, and you are beginning to see me more clearly! You've seen me twice now. You already hear me. You feel me viscerally as well. I will always be at your side, guiding, healing, and loving you in ways that I never could before. All of this began when you accepted that you could indeed see me, that you have been seeing me all along.

Believing that you see me opened you to the experience.

Belief is always the first step to manifest what one desires! Until someone believes, nothing can happen. So keep believing that you see me, and your belief will continue to hone your psychic vision. Besides, I am also doing my part to help you. Remember, Spirit creates the physical world!

So today, as we make our way once again to the sea to watch the sun do its peekaboo dance on the horizon as it welcomes the day, let us celebrate and welcome our love and our new life! Throughout all the days of my life on Earth, you were the one I was searching for. You've always been my one true love. My world. My everything. I am so thankful that we found each other, that you were wise enough to know that we were meant to be together. You drew me to you with your barrage of love letters that wooed me across two oceans. Although I feared change, your love scaled the towering walls I'd built around my heart and won me over. Because of you, I got to live a second life in paradise.

And now, miracles of miracles, I get to live a third life with you here between Heaven and Earth. Is it any wonder that I thank God for you?

That's why I say your love saved me!

CHAPTER 19

TALKING TO HEAVEN

S even weeks after Alan's passing, a friend of mine came by for lunch. Worried that I might have gone over the edge, Ken wanted to make sure I was okay. We'd known each other since the summer of 1987, which had been a tumultuous time for me, similar to the one I was going through. That year, I learned how to channel but was flying too high psychically. Ken had been a stabilizing influence on me then and was trying to do the same now. With COVID nipping at our heels, he donned a face mask to visit me.

As we ate lunch outside on my lanai, looking out over the sprawling Waikiki skyline shimmering with heat and Diamond Head in the distance, I shared everything that had happened since Alan's return. Although it was just past noon, the sun outside felt surprisingly comfortable.

As we chatted between bites of salmon salad that we washed down with sips of sweetened iced tea, life began to feel normal again. It felt good to talk to someone who not only cared about me but had spiritual experiences similar to my own. Oh, how I had missed face-to-face conversations like this since Alan's dementia had left me socially stranded, and now the pandemic was further isolating me.

What I thought would be the biggest obstacle for Alan and me, our sexual connection, had been surprisingly easy. Talking to Ken made me realize that conversation is more important than sex! I could live without sexual gratification, but without someone to talk to, what sort of life would that be? Would Alan and I ever be able to talk to each other as easily as Ken and I were doing? Was the problem as simple as Alan being too sensitive to express himself freely? That didn't sit right with me. I couldn't help but feel something was wrong. Why would he lapse into silence at the strangest times?

Hearing me, Alan answered quickly.

Trust me; it would drive you crazy if you heard me talking in your head all the time. It's better this way, Pam.

"I don't mind. Why can't you let me be the judge of that? I will tell you if it becomes too much. I WANT TO HEAR YOU TALK TO ME, Alan!"

But he wouldn't budge. I wondered what the real reason was. What widow wouldn't want their partner to talk to them all the time if it was possible?

Later that night, the questions continued to churn round and round in my mind as I tossed and turned in bed. Once more, I posed them to Alan but heard nothing. But this time, instead of being depressed about his silence, for the first time, I pulled away from him. I could feel Alan reaching out to me with his mind, pleading with me to tell him what was wrong, begging me to talk to him.

"Oh, so now you want to talk! Well, I need to hear you throughout the day, not just when you feel like it. I need to know I'm not alone in this relationship. When you were alive, you didn't share your feelings very often, conversation with you was superficial, and this is beginning to feel like more of the same."

Wiping my tears with the sleeve of my bathrobe, I continued.

"Alan, you have to step things up in a big way, or I can't do this! I need to hear you and know that you are involved with everything I am doing, from the small things to the big. I'm tired of always having to be strong for you, and when I look at all the work that lies ahead of us, work that I truly want to do, but that seems immense in scale, the thought of doing it by myself is too much for me to bear. You promised me that you'd give me everything I could ever want in a relationship except for a body, but this isn't turning out to be true!"

Pam, I promise I will do better, but I can't explain right now. Can you please be patient and trust me on this?

One thing was clear; it was easier for Alan to communicate through our writing, while conversing mind-to-mind was harder. Maybe it was because Alan had never been one to talk to me in any great depth. That was my trigger. Like most women, I longed for deep conversation and a sense of connection with the man I loved. Still upset but overcome by exhaustion, I called a truce and went back to bed, but in the morning, I didn't feel any better. Alan didn't know what to do for me, but he talked a bit more, even if his words were spare.

Why was talking to me so difficult for Alan when channeling him was easy? Late one night, when I was upset and unable to sleep, he told me to get up and write his words down, saying that I would know he was with me. And it was true. I felt him in every word that entered my mind, one by one, then all at once in a rush of eager conversation. Our writing always flowed effortlessly. It had been that way from the start.

Pam, take what I dictate to you and reflect on it, feel my love, feel the truth in my words, and each time you reread them, we will grow closer to each other, and you will know this is really me talking to you!

Swati never had a problem talking to Alan; she said, if anything, he could be an annoying chatterbox who never stopped yakking. Swati suggested I try vocal channeling, which was something I had never even considered. She said that for the time being, it might be easier than having a telepathic conversation with him.

I wondered if vocal channeling would be as easy as writing his words. I had channeled my guides and angels in this way while in a trance, so why not? On my first try with Alan, it was clear that voice channeling was just as easy, though the challenge was remembering what he said afterward. Finding a way to record his messages would be necessary since his words seemed to flow in one ear and out the other, making it hard to remember them. No wonder Alan preferred that I write his messages down.

It was easy for me to shift into the higher state that allowed Alan to come through, so my first attempt to channel him was fluid. His words appeared in my mind first, one by one and then came in as a rush of information. I was pleased to find that his words flowed easily through me as I spoke them.

Later that day, as I ran errands, I used a recording app on my phone while driving and found that Alan's thoughts continued to flow easily. But I still longed for telepathic communication, which would make communication more natural. Vocal channeling helped us connect more deeply, but it wasn't enough for me. I longed to talk to him telepathically so our communication could be as normal as possible, or at least as normal as talking to someone invisible could be.

But for the time being, channeling Alan's messages by writing or speaking for him would do. I was grateful for the fact that both came easily for me. Still, I knew that we could do better, so I never stopped reaching for a full telepathic exchange since my ultimate goal was to be able to see him clairvoyantly and talk to him just as Swati did. Even though my telepathy was erratic, one thing I did hear Alan say over and over was that I would see him in physical form. This, I knew, wasn't my idea because I found it impossible to believe.

One day, I asked Swati to confirm this for me, and she asked him point-blank, "Alan, will Pam really be able to see you in 3D?"

She relayed his reply.

Yes, yes, and YESSSS! Why won't you believe me, Pam?

CHAPTER 20

COME WHAT MAY

When Alan and I met, there had been the breathtaking promise of soulful love, but that dream faded after a few short years. At the end of his life, I was left wondering why we had been brought together; how could my life have brought me to this desolate place? Had I followed my guidance all these years to end up emotionally and financially broken, widowed, and completely alone with no purpose left to my life?

One night, as I tallied up my losses, I pulled away from Alan, saying I didn't want to be with him. I yelled at him to leave me be. I could tell he was shocked at the intensity of my rage. He had seen me upset before, but never angry like this. Not ever. But now that he had opened me up emotionally, I could no longer hide my feelings that surfaced with a wild fury. I bitterly laid the blame for our empty marriage squarely on him. I cried until I was empty of tears, then fell asleep curled up in bed as far away from him as possible, which was laughable, for how can you get away from someone who can be everywhere?

Alan was distraught. According to Swati, he became inconsolable whenever I was upset, unable to settle down again until I was at peace. Now, fearing he was in danger of losing me, he had to find a way to reach me, so he turned to music as he had done from the start. Being pure emotion, a song is the most direct path for our loved ones to communicate with us, as the music and lyrics get right to the heart of what they want to say and how they want to make us feel.

For those reasons, a song can be a transmission of love from Heaven.

When I woke up in the morning, I did as I always did; I reached for my phone to check on our Facebook group. I noticed my friend Maria, who helped me moderate the group, had posted a song, which I found odd since she had never done that before. In my groggy, eyes-barely-open state, I didn't even notice what the song was before I hit play on my phone. But with the first note, tingles flooded my body. I cried as I listened to the two lovers sing of their undying love for each other, declaring that, just as the song title said, they would always love each other, "Come What May." The song is from the film musical *Moulin Rouge*, which was one of the few DVDs we owned.

When the song ended, it occurred to me that Alan was behind it. Hearing my thoughts, he confessed, saying he had psychically nudged Maria to post the song as a message to me. When I asked Maria why she posted the song, she said that she had noticed how often Alan used the term "come what may" in several of his messages, and that morning, the song flashed in her mind, sending her on a hunt to find it on YouTube.

Pam, I know it's difficult to believe in what you can't see. You feel my energy, you feel my love, and you hear my words in your head, but you still can't help but wonder if you're making it up. This is why whenever that happens, I suggest you "write me into being." Write my words down, and as you do, you'll feel my love come straight from my heart into yours.

Feeling my love will heal you. This is how we will merge!

I am always with you, my love. I know it's not the same as being there in a body with you, but it's the best I can do. If I could borrow a body, I would in a minute. Well, maybe not, because who knows what I'd get on short notice? Ha! Not to mention the fact that this would probably creep you out. Nope, not gonna happen. Don't you think I haven't thought about this or wondered if there was another way? I will keep looking for other ways for us to connect. Never doubt it! My love for you is so vast and deep that I'd do anything to be with you. I watched you crying last night as if you had lost me all over again, but I am right here, and I am never leaving. My sweet love, you are my angel! You are my life, and I need to be with you. I didn't think I would need anyone or anything once I got to Heaven, but I was wrong. Totally wrong.

All souls in Heaven yearn for those they've left behind.

When I came back, it was to tell you I was alive, but it was also to bring YOU back to life so we could be together. I realized then how much I loved you and still wanted to be part of your life. So, I did all I could to make sure you knew I was with you. These last few weeks have been amazing, being together in all the ways we have. To be able to feel you in my etheric arms, to experience pleasure and the joy of merging with you has been exquisite, but now, it seems that it's causing you pain. Which is the last thing I want to do. What can I do to help you? Do you need me to back off? Do you want me to leave you alone? I will do whatever it takes to make you happy even if it causes me pain. You just have to tell me what you want.

Through my tears, I cried out, "No, no! Alan, I love you! I don't want to be in this world without you, and that's the problem. I don't know how to be in a relationship with someone I can't see or know for sure is with me. I believe you are here because my heart tells me so, but I still wonder sometimes. Maybe I always will. Damn it; I guess I need more proof. I wish I didn't, but there you have it. I love you more now than ever, so much so that I can't imagine living without you. I would be devastated if you left me. It would be worse this time because it would be like losing you twice. How could I survive that? I don't think anything can be done at this point. I'd be more miserable without you than with you. That's why I was crying. It's not because I don't love you or don't want you. My whole world revolves around you more than ever. Nothing means more to me than being with you in whatever way I can."

Then let's do our best to help you see me. Continue to develop your clairvoyance. You already see me in your mind, which is the first step; next, you will see me with your eyes wide open. I will do what I can to help you on my end. But please, please stay positive about us. I'm not going anywhere! I will always be here with you, eager and ready to love and support you. Sleeping with you and having sex is amazing! It was completely unexpected, but if that's too much, then let's stop right now.

Love is more than physical pleasure. To just love you is more than enough pleasure for me. I won't take it to mean that you don't love me if you want to stop because I can read your heart, and the one truth I know for sure is that you love me. You've always loved me. I was so distrustful that I never believed you loved me when I was in a body, but that was my fault. That was my issue that I had to heal. You know how much I distrusted people. I was friendly and outgoing, but I was always suspicious on some level. What a walking contradiction I was!

Pam, I only want what will make you happy. You will see that writing our book will heal you on all levels. It won't be easy, but it will bring us closer to each other and strengthen our relationship. We are just beginning with all of this, so take your time. You will see! If you can't hear me clearly, then write, Pam! Write me into being! I will always come through that way, just as I am doing right now. Writing is the best way for anyone to begin communicating with the Other Side. In that regard, you have always been a clear channel! You DO hear me! I will never leave your side, not even when you exit this world, for then I will whisk you away to Heaven where we will be together forever.

"It's so hard being this emotional. I now cry all the time, which I never did before, and yet at the same time, I don't care because the crazy thing is, I've never felt more alive or happier than I have these past two months with you. It's wild! Yes, even though I am crying right now, missing you and going through so much grief again, just like when I thought you had died, I would never change a thing. Your love opened my heart and healed me so I could know you, feel you, and love you more deeply than I've ever loved before. But damn it, it's unfair to be falling more in love with you each day, yet I can't touch you! I think about all the years we wasted living at arm's length from each other, when now, I'd give my life to have you hold me in your arms just one more time. I don't even remember what that feels like. That's why I can't stop crying, not just because I miss you, but because it's plain wrong for us to be apart like this when you are right here!"

But Pam, you WILL see me physically. I promise you that! It will take time, patience, and lots of practice, but that is coming! Don't you remember I told you this? I meant it! You will see me clairvoyantly, and you will feel me physically, just in a different way. In an energetic way that will amaze you! You are in a period of adjustment right now, so please have faith in me. Have faith in yourself as well. You can do this. You were born to do this! I understand how hard it is. I will find a way to connect with you, not just for us but for all the others trying to love someone through the veil, for we are clearing the way for them, too.

I know it's hard for you to believe in things you can't see. This is hard for anyone on a path like ours. Like most people, you don't trust what you can't touch or see, which is part of the programming humanity has been put through. But you must overcome this! I'm doing all I can to prove my existence to you by sending you my love, but you must have faith and believe in me as best you can. I need your help to meet me halfway with this!

"I know. I know. I am sorry for being difficult. All of this emotion that I feel, together with the changes that have come so quickly, it's all too much for me. What's made it harder is that I had to be in my head, not in my feelings, when you were sick, or I would have had a nervous breakdown. Shutting down my heart helped me survive so I could take care of you."

There's nothing to feel sorry for, my darling! Stop apologizing for being emotional. Yes, you had to be in your head and not your heart to take care of me. You had no choice but to be in survival mode, but that's all changed now. I'd rather have you express your feelings, whatever they might be, rather than repress them or, worse yet, not be in touch with what you are feeling at all. I'll do my best to handle your emotions. You can never upset me. Never! So, bring them on, I say! I can take it. I love how you feel things so intensely now! This is what being alive is about: feeling all of your emotions! Don't be afraid to feel everything. Just let what you feel move through you without attaching to it or resisting it. That's the secret to being fully alive! Let your feelings move through you like the ever-changing weather that changes from storm clouds to sunny skies. In time, everything passes, and everything changes, and the same is true for emotions.

Everything returns to Love.

"Well, I have a lot of emotion now, that's for sure! You have become more emotional yourself, which is surprising since you're supposedly an Archangel. When we went to the beach the other day, you became so emotional about it. It meant a lot to you, didn't it? I could feel your joy as we walked along the beach together. What a glorious sun-drenched day that was!"

Yes! Walking on Lanikai Beach with you at sunrise, I was amazed at how everything looked so different. When I was here in a body, I never looked at the world the way I look at it now when I'm with you. This world is astonishingly beautiful when I am with you. I feel what you feel, and I see what you see, but everything is fresh, new, and more vibrant than I remember it. Then again, my vision was limited by my ego. That day as you drove us home, I thanked you and cried because of the depth and sheer beauty of the morning I had spent with you. My heart was bursting with joy. I had seen everything through your eyes anew. Oh my God, how I love walking through this world with you!

"Which is why, my love, we will keep walking on the beach and walk everywhere in this world together. Wherever you want to go, whatever you want to do, we shall do it all. Just because you didn't live fully when you were here doesn't mean you can't do that now! You will experience the world through me just as I will experience Heaven through you."

Pam, the other night, I felt your pain and cried with you, but there was nothing I could do since my words can't get through to you when you are in such a dark place. You move out of range of me, which basically shuts me out. I decided to do what I usually do when I have no other options. I put all of my love, my thoughts, and my feelings for you into a song, which is what I've done with you from the first time I made contact with you from Heaven. Music conveys emotion, and love can change your state of mind and being. So yes, I sent you "Come What May." You were crying at the first note because my love was already reaching out to you.

As the years go by, we will have many songs that we will call "our song," but this one is the one I want you to remember whenever you doubt my love for you.

Because, my darling Pam, I will love you forever, come what may!

CHAPTER 21

THE AFFAIR

D uring dinner at a friend's house, I heard a young thirty-some-
thing-year-old man with blonde hair and sullen blue eyes weep
into his beer, bemoaning his love for a married woman. He spoke
of their first clandestine, hurried sexual encounter, the many meetups that
followed, how she had wanted to leave her husband for him, then changed
her mind, and then changed it back again, many times, over and over,
until she called it off. In the end, she decided he was too intense, and it
scared her, so she pulled away. But he couldn't let her go, calling, writing,
practically stalking her until her husband found out. He was so obsessed
with her that she was all he spoke of once alcohol loosened his tongue.
His angst stirred my faded memory of what I had once felt for Alan and
what he had felt for me. I yearned for another taste of it.

I found myself drawn to this man in a way I knew was pathological
because it made no sense. It wasn't anything physical. He wasn't handsome;
Alan was better-looking. If anything, the young man was ordinary-look-
ing and uninteresting, but he had what I yearned for. Raw emotion and
vulnerability. I wanted a man to be passionate about me as Alan had once
been. When we first met, he constantly declared to me how besotted he

was by me. Yes, he had been drunk on his love for me but had long since sobered up, with neither of us sharing even a drop of passion for decades.

And oh, how I longed to be loved like that again!

I wanted to be swept away by emotions I had forgotten I possessed. I yearned to feel something for someone again, and when I looked at Alan, all I could feel was bitterness and disappointment. He lived in a world all his own, amiable but detached from me. Where had his drunken love gone? I wanted a way out of the comfortable empty void that had become my life. I wasn't miserable, but that didn't mean I was happy. Alan wasn't happy either. We were sleepwalking through life.

Only two years into our marriage, Alan switched off emotionally, and in doing so, I joined him in his numbed slumber. We got along, but there was nothing but congenial complacency between us now. Since he was nearing sixty, maybe this was acceptable to him, but I was only in my mid-forties. It was too soon for my heart to go to sleep permanently. Something inside me knew this was my last chance to come back to life.

This was how I rushed headlong into a marital catastrophe I knew I wouldn't recover from. It would end fatally because there would be no hiding what happened from Alan. He would simply know; that's how psychic he was. But that wasn't enough to stop me.

When Alan finally confronted me with his suspicions, I didn't deny it. What made it worse was I had no explanation as to why I had strayed. He knew it wasn't about sex or love. I didn't understand it myself until decades later, but by then, it was too late. Not that it would have made any difference to him. I begged Alan to forgive me. I promised to make everything up to him, and he punished me by feigning forgiveness.

But I knew he couldn't forgive me, no matter what he said. Alan had never forgiven anyone, even when he nodded, smiled, and told them he had. I could tell by how he spoke about the people who had let him down; his pain was palpable. I nodded weakly when he threatened divorce. Alan told a few friends we were breaking up, but after a few weeks of sulking, he said he couldn't go through with it. He said he forgave me and would stay for Taylor's sake. Our fate was sealed. We would put on a happy face for the world and live peacefully together, but there would always be a wall between us.

CHAPTER 22

I FAILED TO CHERISH YOU

I blamed you for all the problems in our marriage when really, it was me. Oh sure, you betrayed me once with someone, but that was early on in our marriage, a single indiscretion that I never let you forget for the rest of our marriage because forgiveness was impossible for me. But I see now that I pushed you into his arms with my indifference and neglect. I hurt you so many times with my selfish actions. I could never bring myself to admit it, but I am saying it to you now.

I failed to love and cherish you.

Besides, you more than made up for your error by spending the remaining twenty-five years of our marriage at my side loving me, helping me, and taking care of me through my dementia. You stood by me without complaining, always doing your best, even sacrificing your own well-being when my dementia worsened. From the Other Side, I saw that you gave me everything you had even though I had given you so little. The enormity of my regret is beyond description!

You were attentive to me even when I never gave you what you needed, the only thing you ever wanted from the beginning: my love. Not sex, but love. If I had given you that, the passion that was asleep within you would have awakened to love me back, but I was too self-centered, selfish, and proud to see it. I wanted your body but wasn't willing to take care of your heart. So, we both lost. All because of me.

I said I forgave you when I hung on tightly to my damn scorecard instead. Forgiveness was never something I did for anyone. Oh, sure, I'd freely say the words "I forgive," but they were just words, so what did I care? I kept telling you I loved you more than you loved me but didn't treat you lovingly. What an ass I was!

I was all words. Words. Words. Words. Useless, clever, stupid empty words backed up with no actions to make them real. No proof. No evidence. I was full of shit.

Now I can't give you any physical proof of my love because I no longer have a body to do so. Oh sure, I can get Swati to buy you something for me, but gifts are meaningless to you. The gift you really want is to see my face as I gaze at you longingly. But no, you can't see the tears I cry for you. You can't see how sad I am as I stand right in front of you longing to touch you. You can only take my word for this when my word never meant much.

My betrayal was worse than yours when, in the early years of our marriage, I left you to see the world to get the attention and freedom I craved at a time when you needed me the most. I received the gift of your loving care, and all I gave you was my money, thinking that was all you wanted, when you never wanted that. You wanted me. You wanted my love. It's all you want now, and now you're afraid that it's too late for us, too late because you're not sure if you can trust me. Your doubt and resentment are well justified.

All my words declaring my love for you don't count for much since I said them once before without following through. Yes, words are cheap. But they are all I have now. Is it too late? I don't know, Pam. That's up to you. All I know is that I am more in love with you than ever before, and for months now, I've been with you every day and night. I see who you are with clarity! How could you not be my world, my life, my soul? I want to make it up to you, but how?

If you just give me a chance, I will spend eternity proving to you my love is true.

CHAPTER 23

A CHRISTMAS OF LOVE AND FORGIVENESS

The day after Christmas, all my emotions were being laid bare. I woke to find myself carrying a mountain of pain. As the sun rose, rage poured out of me as I cursed Alan for not loving me as he should have. I had been so caught up in mourning his loss that this sudden upswell of anger frightened me, taking me to dark places in my mind and heart that I didn't know existed.

By contrast, Christmas Day had been joyous, as it had delivered a surprise. Swati gifted me with a bracelet she and Alan had picked out, and from the moment I placed it around my wrist, I felt his love wash over me. The rest of the day I spent in a haze of holiday bliss, feeling his love everywhere. But that night, as I was getting ready for bed, I remembered an incident two months after my mother died of Alzheimer's in 2009.

We had rented out our townhouse to move in with my parents in anticipation of their needing our help. My mother had been diagnosed years ago, but within a few months of our moving in, she suffered a spinal compression fracture while on a cruise to Alaska with my dad and us. Mom's decline was swift, and she passed seven weeks later at home.

I had taken on the brunt of caregiving duties, with Alan helping me as best he could, but the weeks of caring for my mom exacted a heavy toll on me. A few months after my mother passed, a friend invited me to be his guest at a five-day healing workshop he was teaching in Orlando, Florida. Grateful for the opportunity to take a break, I asked Alan if he thought I should accept his offer. He agreed that it would be good for me to get away, and since he wasn't interested in the workshop and money was tight, it made no sense for him to join me.

Getting away turned out to be just what I needed. It was a relief to be responsible for no one but myself while spending an entire week there in the Florida sun. One of my girlfriends was joining me for the workshop, so I'd be able to save a bit of money by sharing a room with her. I had never taken a trip without Alan, whereas he had traveled without me for years. Since my interest in healing was almost insatiable, the workshop was a precious gift. There was the added bonus of having time to socialize while relaxing with my friend and our classmate. I was relieved to feel my stress melting away, which made what happened when I got home all the more shocking.

When I walked in the door, Alan asked me to join him in the bedroom. The moment I sat on the bed, he laid into me. Hard. Trying without success to rein his feelings in, he raged at me for being thoughtless and inconsiderate, accusing me of being selfish for taking the trip and leaving him home alone, pointing out that I knew that he could never say no to me, so I should have never asked to go on the trip in the first place.

I was shaking from the assault of his words. I couldn't understand why he was angry. Alan wasn't burdened with any responsibilities. All of his needs had been taken care of. Since we still lived with my parents, my father was there with him, along with Taylor, who by now was a teenager who needed no supervision. All of their meals were provided by my father, who happily paid for takeout from their favorite restaurants. My dad loved to cater to Alan whenever he could to thank him for his help around the house. There had been no burdens placed on him, yet Alan was seething.

I had never seen him so enraged. It scared me. The workshop had opened me up emotionally, which meant I was vulnerable to the force of his anger that felt like knives cutting into me. When he left the bedroom, I clutched my stomach and bent over in pain. Refusing to let Alan see me cry, I locked myself in the bathroom until I could calm down. It didn't take long to remember why I had closed myself off from him years ago. He had never been deliberately cruel until now.

Alan's tongue-lashing vaporized all the good that had come from my trip. My grief over the loss of my mother returned to swallow me whole. And it got worse. The next day, I developed a chronic cough that, within a month, turned into asthma as I swallowed my feelings. Alan never apologized for what he said to me. We never talked about the incident again.

The memory unleashed a torrent of others. Sobbing, I began taking an inventory of his transgressions. The list was long.

At the top of the list were all his trips. Why had I put up with his indifference to my needs and feelings? Why did I fail to stand up for myself? Why didn't I rail against the different rules for him and for me? Here I had taken a single trip alone, only to return to be viciously attacked for it, when he had traveled whenever he wanted, but I wasn't allowed to say a word. At least I cared enough about him to ask if I could go, only to find out it was wrong of me to have asked in the first place. I should have known my place was to stay home. The unfairness of it all whipped my irritation into a fury. How could I trust Alan not to turn on me again? Had he really changed? How could I believe he loved me when he had never shown it?

Alan resumed traveling with Barbara when Taylor was barely a year old. Within days of his leaving us, our baby boy developed a sepsis infection in his left eye that wasn't responding to the prescribed antibiotics. When I called to update his pediatrician, Doctor Mertz was alarmed. He told me to meet him at the Kapiolani Hospital emergency room in Honolulu. Dr. Mertz wanted to admit Taylor on the spot. I panicked because I couldn't reach Alan since I had no number to call in case of an emergency. There was never a way to reach him when he was traveling. I was left to face a mother's worst nightmare alone, unable to even talk to my husband. I was terrified, hurt, and furious at Alan.

I called my mother and a friend who was a psychic healer. They rushed to the hospital to help me give Taylor healing. I begged Dr. Mertz to give us more time to work on Taylor. He reluctantly agreed, only if he could give Taylor a massive dose of antibiotics by IV in the emergency room, but warned me that if his condition didn't improve within 24 hours, I had to bring Taylor back to the hospital immediately. Thankfully, he turned the corner the next morning. I was relieved but enraged at Alan. I blamed him, convinced that it would never have happened if he had stayed home as I had begged him to.

Alan returned to find Taylor fully recovered, with only traces of swelling still visible around Taylor's eye. He shrugged off the connection between his traveling and Taylor's illness, but for the next five years, whenever Alan would leave us for a trip abroad, our son would again fall ill. This lasted until Alan's traveling ended after Taylor's fifth birthday.

Fortunately, Taylor's subsequent illnesses were never as serious as the first. If that had not been the case, I would have left Alan, for that would have been intolerable. Still, it was clear to me that our son felt abandoned every time his father left us, and why wouldn't he? Taylor psychically knew that his father had wanted me to abort him because, in utero, babies are aware of everything their parents say. Once we married, Alan embraced my pregnancy and fell in love with Taylor the moment he was born, but the words Alan had spoken and the anger that accompanied them had left their mark on Taylor and me. You would think a psychic of all people would understand this, but not Alan. I didn't trust him after that, so I shut down my passion for him, and by extension, I shut down my passion for life.

Now here I was on Christmas Day, sifting through the wreckage of these long-buried memories, with my pain and rage as raw and as fresh as the day they had happened. My anger was bursting to the surface, threatening to tear us apart. Hurting me was bad enough, but hurting our son had been the worst betrayal, unforgivable in my eyes. I had repressed my pain and contained my anger so I could stay with Alan since I loved him and wanted the three of us to be a family, but now I had to feel the full depth of my suffering if I was to be free of it, and put the past behind me.

As I began purging my rage, I wondered if I had been wrong about Alan from the beginning. Maybe I had been kidding myself. What a fool I had been to believe him when he said he loved me when he never demonstrated it. The more I thought about it, the angrier I became until I asked Alan out loud.

"How can I know for sure that things will be different now? Yes, I finally feel your love, but how do I know your love is going to last? Maybe I want your love so much I'm imagining it. I thought your love was real thirty years ago, but I must have been wrong because look how that turned out!"

I continued raging at Alan, but he remained quiet. I messaged Swati, who assured me that Alan had great remorse about how he had treated me, adding that anger was part of the grieving process and that I needed to bring all of my resentment to the surface so I could release it once and for all. This is a predictable stage of grieving, but that doesn't make it easy to navigate. I was looking at our marriage through the lens of the past with blame, anger, and regret, all of which needed to be felt and released so I could heal.

For the next two days, I paced the house yelling at Alan, alternately raging silently and out loud, examining every bit of hurt and disappointment he had caused me. The old Alan would have been defensive and never apologized, but now he took everything I threw at him without flinching. He seemed to know that I had to dive deep into my pain to come out the other side of it. Analyzing my pain wasn't the solution; I needed to feel it. Feeling our feelings is the only way to process trauma and let it go. It's that simple and that hard.

Swati and I set up a time to talk so she could help me release any residual pain I had been unable to clear on my own. Cursing Alan had shifted much of it, but healing my pain would turn out to be a more complicated process than either Swati or I anticipated. I found I couldn't release all of my suffering in one go. It would have to be done gradually over time. It dawned on me that the road ahead might be a steep climb, but at least I had taken the critical first step. I was on my way to healing myself so that Alan and I could create a new future, and love each other unencumbered by the past.

CHAPTER 24

AN ARCHANGEL FINALLY
PROPOSES

A lan never formally proposed to me. I never had an engagement
ring, either. He had bought me a simple ring for the wedding with
a tiny diamond in it, but I didn't care for it. I saw it as nothing
more than a ring for the ceremony. Not a promising start for a marriage.
Although I never complained, Alan knew I didn't like the ring because I
never wore it after our wedding. I told myself it didn't matter, that I was
just happy to be marrying him. Right from the start, I became good at
hiding my feelings and pretending everything was okay when it wasn't.

But I wasn't the only one without a ring. Alan never had one himself,
so neither of us wore wedding bands. Not that it mattered to me then, but
it's funny what you find yourself missing when you lose your husband.
Now, suddenly, that ring meant the world to me. But sadly, I had lost
the ring during our last house move five months before Alan died. One
night over Facebook Messenger, I lamented the loss of my ring to Swati,
telling her how I'd give anything to have my wedding ring back. It hurt
to admit that the ring had been the only piece of jewelry he'd given me
during our entire marriage.

Pam

"Oh, but I can feel his love, Swati! It makes me cry when he comes to me so intensely with his love, and now I can finally let him in all the way because I am not holding back from him. I didn't realize how angry and hurt I was. Yes, I forgive myself for thinking either of us had done something wrong."

Swati

"Yes, now you see the REAL love. While he was here in a body, it was fiction. We all need to move beyond forgiveness. Because the term itself suggests that there is something to forgive others for when there is nothing to forgive. If anyone, we just need to forgive ourselves because we didn't know better. And it's all good."

Pam

"Oh my yes, his real love is 1,000,000 times more than it was before. And the real Alan is still funny! He is constantly cracking me up."

Swati

"This is the only thing that is real. I am glad you devoted two days to remembering and letting go of the illusion."

Pam

"By the way, I really love the infinity bracelet you helped him buy me for Christmas. I can wear it all the time since it's light enough and doesn't get in the way."

Swati

"When we saw this bracelet with the infinity symbol, we both went BINGO!!!! No arguments on that one. We both IMMEDIATELY loved it. See? He knew what he was doing! I'm impressed. What is your ring size? In case Alan wants to send you a new wedding ring sometime."

Pam

"6.5, though a wedding ring is not necessary, and if he insists on buying something, get Taylor to pay for it, and I'll pay him back."

Swati

"Oh, he just showed me what to make. It is something I love making. I don't know if you will wear it, but there is a process. It's a woven ring made with silver and gold-filled wire. And as I weave it, I usually fill it with divine love, healing, prayers, etc. He wants to join me in adding those chants, intentions, and energy as I weave. But I don't know if you will like that type of ring or if you will wear it."

Swati

"But here is what he is saying—he says that he wants to have a wedding ceremony with you again. The REAL Alan marrying you, the REAL Pam. He wants to put this ring on your finger because this is what is real for him. And he wants you to put an energy ring on his finger since a physical ring is of no use to him."

Pam

"I'm crying because, yes, I've always wanted a new ring and a new wedding ceremony; not that I didn't love our first wedding. It was beautiful. But yes, another wedding would be wonderful."

Swati

"LOL! He is so relieved!!! He is saying to me, 'Do you realize that I just proposed to my hot wife to marry me for real? And that I was scared of what she would say!' I think this is the first time I've seen an Archangel quake in fear of his mortal wife. Hahaha! But it is so sweet, and so romantic!"

Pam

"I'm still crying. He is so romantic now, just like he was when I first met him."

Swati

"This story of you and Alan gets crazier and crazier each day!!! A MARRIAGE PROPOSAL!!! I still can't believe I got to be part of this! Even though it took me some time to stop arguing and laughing to realize what had just happened! That is sooooo cool!!! Engaged to an Archangel! You are hardly saying anything! What is going on? What do you think of all this?"

Pam

"He feels bad about the wedding ring. He knew I didn't love it and that he should have bought me something nicer or at least one I truly loved. He was being lazy and maybe cheap. It was an okay ring, but he knew from the start that I wasn't crazy about it. I was just going along with it and never said anything because I was just happy to marry him because I loved him so much. We never got a ring for him either."

Swati

"OK, this is making more sense now. You see, the ring I will make will not be an expensive ring anyway. No diamonds. Just a woven band. But there is a ceremony that goes into it, and that's why he chose that. But this time, HE chose the ring, and HE will work on the ring with me. In other words, he will make the ring for you. He calls this the REAL wedding. Maybe because it is the REAL Alan? Is that why he is calling it the REAL wedding? I love that he is going to make the ring for you. That trumps everything else."

Pam

"HAHAHA—well, yes, if this is the real Alan then I need a new wedding and a new ring. I do feel like we are getting to know each other all over again. Oh my, the two of you are going to have fun making this ring. I can tell. He was blasting me with love all day long like he never has before. Maybe this was the lead-up to it."

Swati

"Wow!! This is making so much sense now. He hadn't even told ME before doing it. And even I only understood after he proposed to you."

Pam

"Yes, he never proposed to me outright. It was more like, okay, let's get married because you're pregnant. I was married before, and that proposal was romantic. My husband-to-be bought me a ring in secret with the help of a friend, took me to an expensive restaurant to have dinner, and surprised me with a proposal with the ring presented inside the dessert. Yes, quite romantic."

Swati

"When you write about this proposal, you'll have to explain why it is important. It makes so much sense. All the things you are telling me here, that Alan failed to get it right the first time. It makes so much sense why he proposed, the ring he chose, the fact that he will make it with me, and the wedding. The real proposal from the Real Alan to the Real Pam, to have a real wedding with a real wedding ring."

Pam

"But actually, do you know that, if you go back over our messages, he didn't technically ASK me to marry him? All he said was that he wanted a wedding ceremony. Not exactly the same thing."

Swati

"He is smacking his forehead with his palm! LOL!! He says he got so excited he didn't say it. He meant to ask you. So, wait. He is doing something. Don't go now. He wants you to sit. In the visual he is showing me you are wearing something white. And you are sitting, Pam."

Pam

"Okay, I'm sitting, and I am wearing a white robe."

Swati

"He says—tell her to extend her hand in front of her with her eyes closed and to see him kneeling in white in front of you. He has white flowers in his hands and the ring that I will make."

Swati

"So I asked, 'OK, what should I tell her you are saying?' He said, 'I'll tell her directly.' So listen to his proposal, and he will propose to you now."

Pam

"He just said, 'Pam, I've loved you since forever. Would you make me the happiest man in Heaven and marry me again? I love you more than words can say and want to spend the rest of eternity proving it to you every second of every day. Please say you'll marry me!'"

CHAPTER 25

A HEALING AT THE
MAYO CLINIC

B etween the two of us, I had been the one interested in healing since I saw my role as a healer rather than a psychic. Although he never admitted it, I knew that Alan only tagged along with me when I took workshops because he didn't want to be left home alone. He never went on to practice any course that we learned; he'd instead send those who needed healing to me. But now that he was on the other side, everything had changed. It was a lot to process. Not only was my husband not dead, but he was also busy healing people even though he had never shown any interest in it until now. People told me he showed up when they called on him and sometimes even when they hadn't.

Alan explained my role in his work by saying it was our work, not just his, because I am always with him. Even if I wasn't seen with him and had no recollection of my participation, Alan said every healing involved both of us because he couldn't do what he was doing without me. He said I often woke up tired because I was so active in my dream time, working with him.

Pam, I need your energy and your love to anchor my energy into the physical world because between the two of us, you are the powerful Earth Healer, while I am the Angel Alchemist who can alter matter. Together, we can do more than we could if we were apart. As our love bond strengthens, I will become more present in the world, and our healing work will become even more powerful. We are here to serve whoever needs us.

Within five months of Alan's passing, I received an unexpected confirmation of our work through a client who had called on us to help her ailing friend.

During a reading, our client Marian asked if we would help her friend JR, who was in an induced coma at the Mayo Clinic in Minnesota suffering from stage five terminal leukemia. Alan agreed immediately, as he always does, but as the months passed, I completely forgot about JR. No matter what the request was, Alan always assured the client that all they had to do was ask us for help, and he would comply. But he never told me what he was doing, so I had no idea what was happening.

JR emerged from his coma four months later, then reached out to Marian through Facebook Messenger. Upon waking, he had drawn a picture of a tall Caucasian man who was wearing a gray suit. JR said the man's name was Alan and that he had been with him while he was in his coma, but that there had also been a woman with the man.

Marian never had a chance to tell JR about us until he reached out to her. The following are the Messenger texts they exchanged.

JR
"I know that she is from Honolulu, 'cause I keep seeing a flower lei, though I don't know if that is right. But he would sometimes talk, and I know that some strong prayers were coming from Honolulu, but I know no one there. Can I ask why that is? Do you know anyone from there? Someone from Honolulu, a lady, would also pray.

I don't know who she was. Does she have something to do with it? To me, the lady looked like she was from Japan or something. She looks like you. She would intercede for you. She was from a place of healing and had a sweet voice. This person has a healing place and short hair. (Marian showed JR a photo of me.) Yes, yes, that's the lady!"

Marian
"OMG!"

JR
"She has a healing thing and helps others and does readings."

Marian
"Ohhh, that is so sweet! They say that they continue to help you even after the reading is done."

JR .
"She introduced herself as a healer and asked for healing over my body. That can't be her, though, because the lady said she knew what I was going through because her husband was dead. But it looks like her."

Marian
"That's her! You have to read her Facebook page to understand. Her husband is Archangel Alan."

JR
"Now I see it. Yes, that is the healing lady. OMG, that is her!"

Marian
"Her husband who passed away recently is Archangel Alan."

JR

"Ask her if he died in August 2020 because that is when he died. At least that is what she told me."

> **Marian**
>
> "Yes, he died on his birthday in August of last year."

JR

"He would speak to me when I didn't see you. A lot of healing from her, though. Very powerful woman and him too. She does a lot of body and soul healing. I was even told I would recover quicker than the doctors told me and not to believe what they say because they would put bad energy into my soul. So, I should believe I will heal."

> **Marian**
>
> "OMG. You should book a session with them when you have Facebook. Please join her group. She shares her journey with Alan. They are writing a book together. It is so interesting. She is very open about her feelings and what she is going through."

JR

"He still comes, and she still does healing on my body. I knew some bad things were happening because, at one point in time, some evil came in, and I couldn't breathe and felt like I was being choked, and then he came, and she did and you too. Her hands are very powerful. I have even seen her mix her own healing stuff. I don't know if she does that in real life, but she put something over me, and I saw her mixing something in a bowl."

> **Marian**
>
> "Alan tells her she is powerful and that she is also an Archangel. This is so interesting. And you have made me a believer in Archangel Alan and in Pam."

JR

"I tell you when they touch your body, you can feel the healing. It's strange 'cause today he came to me, and you were standing next to him, and the words that came out were, 'You are healed, but you have to believe it.' He said the most powerful thing is the words that come out of your mouth, and if you speak it, it shall come forth. I had to think for a while what it meant, but I got it."

(Marian then showed JR a photo of Alan wearing the gray suit that he wears when he visits someone in a hospital or is doing important work.)

JR

"OMG, look at that suit. That is so strange."

Marian

"Do you recognize the person in the picture?"

JR

"Yes, I do. That is the suit he was wearing! How crazy is that?"

Marian

"That's how you saw Alan?"

JR

"Yes. Hold on. I had to show my nurse because she knew how I described him before she even saw this picture. Okay, she says you are making her a believer now because it's the same way I described him. She thinks you got it off the internet after I told you, but then she saw what you and I wrote to each other through Messenger and was shocked. To be honest, she's not a believer in God and all that, and she says after this and seeing what we wrote, it just has to be true. I told her you were the one who contacted his wife to send him to me. She saw the picture that I had drawn and said it looks just like him. She said now she has to find the actual picture to show you. She said she doesn't care what she has to do, but she wants you to see it. I told her to just take a picture of it, not to get into trouble trying to do it."

JR
"Alan told me something today that made me think. He said, 'Do you think that you worry about everyone that you always help: the homeless, the foster group home that you have always donated to, the people who always rely on you. The ones you feed and clothe, the schools, the women's shelters?' I have to name it all, sorry, but he said, 'Have you ever thought that maybe you still carry all of that weight, and it's all on your shoulders?'"

JR
"He then said, 'Trust me, my wife is the same way. She always sees the good in everyone, and even if it's not her responsibility, she's destined to help at least one person at all times, but she does it through her testimony.' Then he said, 'She does it through her words, which are more powerful than actions. She also takes action, but she uses her most powerful tool, which are the words coming out of her mouth.' I appreciate that he is here to talk to me and to help me see things that I can't see. The point I'm trying to make is that he thinks that the breathing problem I have can also be a sign of stress, and that's why the doctors can't do anything. He says that stress can be the cause of my death along with my lungs and the lump if I don't open my eyes to see. I don't know what to make of that."

JR
"You know what Alan said to me before he left? He said sometimes you must be completely broken before you can be repaired. He said you can be

shattered and try to be made whole, but that might not work because sometimes, you must be completely broken before you can be made whole. Then he walked away. I kept asking what he meant. I'm not done yet, so why? I've been through all I can go through. I can no longer walk. Then he turned around and said, 'Then crawl until you can't crawl anymore and then you will see!' What does that even mean?"

Marian

"Wow! Alan was quite blunt with you."

JR

"But why? I have no fight left. I feel so drained. Every time I feel any joy, I feel like someone comes by and snatches it away. Why can't there be any good news? I've done all I can do. Alan was blunt, but he was so soft-spoken until he said the word BROKEN. He yelled it, and it sounded like a clap of thunder."

Marian

"You have a lot of fight left in you; it is just that everything is getting to you because it seems that way now. You know I believe what Alan says. I've heard from others in our group what he can do, and he grows stronger every day. I have learned that we all are here for a purpose. He said that a lot of times, the people with a tough life signed up for it to learn a lesson. Whether it be love or compassion or something else. I would not believe in Alan 100 percent if it were not for you. It was a miracle that you and I became friends, and it was a miracle when you convinced me that Alan does exist as well as Pam. Yes, they are both Archangels."

Marian was shocked. She admitted to me that she had been skeptical of the idea of Alan and me being Archangels, though not as skeptical as me, but with what happened with JR, I had to admit something amazing had happened.

JR told Marian there could be no other explanation. How could he have seen all of these things? What's more, she had his messages on her phone.

When Marian forwarded screenshots of their messages, I was stunned. While many people had seen Alan clairvoyantly and communicated with him, the fact that JR saw me with Alan helped me understand my role in our work together. If I had any doubts about Alan's abilities to help and my participation, they were now gone.

From the beginning, Alan said I was with him wherever he went, even in Heaven, because being twin souls, we are never parted. I wouldn't remember it because it would be confusing to recall all the dimensions and places I went with him. We are both Archangels, with the only difference being that I am not up to speed with my angelic gifts, so, therefore, I don't remember where I go with Alan. He says in time, I will remember more as my abilities ramp up to match his, though I am already quite powerful, and I should accept it.

Alan is the Angel Alchemist with the ability to transmute and alter energies and affect physical matter. He proved this was true when he cleared the side effects of the prednisone medication I had to take when I had an asthma attack; he even enhanced the medication's positive effects to make it beneficial for me. Just as he had promised, I experienced zero side effects, not that time or any of the other three times that I took it later.

It had been the same way with the COVID vaccine. When they were first offered, Alan told me to wait because some of the batches were toxic. This turned out to be true. We had many conversations about the virus and the pandemic, which he was eager to explain to me.

Pam, you will never get COVID. I can and will protect you. Even if you did get it, I would heal you, but I still want you to wear a mask and stay home for now. Please, just lay low for the time being.

"Wait, are you saying you—I mean we can heal COVID?"

Yes, we can. Remember, YOU are the physical healer between the two of us. I am more ethereal, which is why I need you. But don't tell anyone we can heal COVID, at least not yet, because then all we'd ever do is heal COVID, which is not our mission. We will do all we can to help anyone who reaches out to us, but we cannot promise they will be healed because the truth is some people are meant to be sick or leave this world in this way. There will always be people we cannot help. This is true for all healers. Even Jesus couldn't heal everyone. It's up to the individual soul and their soul's plan.

When I later decided to be vaccinated, which was something Alan was neither for nor against, I could feel him holding my trembling hand as the shot was administered to my right arm. I felt and then saw the vaccine make its way through my bloodstream as a shimmering golden light. I was astonished to feel a sense of peace come over me. Just as he had done with other medications I needed to take, Alan made the shot beneficial for me, eliminating the negative side effects. He had never favored pharmaceutical drugs, but now that he could alter their composition, Alan wasn't worried about them.

I am turning the vaccine into a healing balm for you. You'll feel tired because I will work on you to harmonize it, so just go to bed early. Tomorrow, your arm might be a bit sore, but that's all. Besides, you, my love, are a powerful healer yourself, so all I am doing is amplifying your self-healing abilities.

Four months later, although I had remained isolated and diligently masked up, I was exposed to COVID in close quarters with a friend. Alan's claim was put to the test. I told my friend Maria about it as soon as I learned of my exposure.

"I just checked with him to make sure he was taking care of you. He showed me you in a hard translucent shell with gold sparkles on it. What that means is, for all intents and purposes, you are immune to COVID. The virus will simply bounce off of your shield."

Two days later, I woke up feeling run down with a runny nose. I was worried but heard Alan say to relax, that it wasn't COVID, just my allergies, and that it would pass.

When Maria checked, she saw Alan working on me. "He just knocked on your translucent armor to make sure it was intact."

I laughed as a vision of Alan popped into my mind. He was wearing an aloha shirt and had a stethoscope around his neck and in his ears, listening to the shell. He was grinning the biggest grin from ear to ear.

I am not going to let anything happen to you, my love!

I didn't get COVID.

JR improved, and the doctors were optimistic about releasing him, but a few months later, he contracted COVID when the nurse who was caring for him got the virus. It took hold quickly, and JR was put on a ventilator. While he was unconscious, JR once again saw us at his side, administering healing. When Marian told me about this development, I was concerned even though he recovered fairly quickly, which was remarkable given the circumstances.

Marian continued to update us from time to time, but JR remained in the hospital because of kidney stones. It was his kidney stones that originally brought JR to the ER before he was diagnosed with leukemia. This saved his life because if he hadn't sought help for the pain, the leukemia would have likely gone undiagnosed. But now, the kidney stones had grown worse. Alan told JR it was due to stress. The kidney stones kept increasing in number, making the pain unbearable, but the hospital could not operate because of the pandemic. JR was forced to wait.

JR's pain became so intense that he grew depressed. Because of everything he had been through, he wanted to give up. But Marian told him that she had asked God about him, and God had told her he would live.

When Marian told me about JR's despondency, I took it hard. I was surprised by how deeply this affected me, but Marian assured me that God had told her JR would live, so I shouldn't be sad. Still, I cried to Alan about the unfairness of it all.

But Pam, life has nothing to do with fairness. You know that. We were able to help JR heal his cancer because he was in a coma. When someone is unconscious, it's easier to help them because they are not resisting the healing we are offering. Do you remember your friend Linda who was in a coma when you worked on healing her remotely in the U.K. hospital? It was a miracle that she pulled through as well.

Why do you think miracles can happen when someone finds themselves at death's door? It's not unusual for people who have a near-death experience to come back healed and transformed. Have you ever wondered who or what is behind that? It's because Spirit can heal someone, assuming it's not the person's time to leave this world. On the other hand, when that same person is conscious and awake, they can block the healing with their stress and negative mindset.

I know it upsets you to think JR has come all this way only to go back to where he started, but that was why we returned to help him. We did all we could by giving him healing and lifting his spirits so he'd keep going, but sometimes, the healing is to leave this world for the next one, and that is also a healing! In truth, transitioning to the other side is the greatest healing of them all. JR can still turn this around, but now it's up to him. If he needs us, we will return as many times as he asks us to. We'll never stop helping him or anyone else who calls on us.

Our healing work is only just beginning, Pam, but there is healing that you and I must go through. I don't want you to worry, but the path to our full reunion lies in us healing everything that went wrong between us in the past. It won't be easy, but we will get there, my darling. Just hold onto me with all of your heart and soul.

After I shared our story with our Facebook group, more people began calling on us for help, most without my knowledge. I'd find out about it only if someone posted in the group or told me during a reading. Always protective of my time and energy, Alan wanted them to call on him instead. People requested help for themselves, their pets, friends, and loved ones. Assistance was given immediately and freely. I began to accept that, as incredible as it seemed, we were meant to team up like this, with Alan being in spirit and me being here. Our work with JR had given me irrefutable proof of Alan's presence, not to mention the confirmation of my healing abilities. Alan's love fanned the fire of unconditional love within me, which helped me come fully alive as well as become a stronger healer. It made me wonder if other couples like us could do the same thing.

Pam, yes, interdimensional couples and, for that matter, any two people reaching for each other through the veil can do this! Of course they can. We are not special because we are angels. Besides, there are incarnated angels everywhere! A loved one in spirit is the embodiment of unconditional love. They are God, just as all souls are. Yes, we, in the spirit world can deliver miracles, but we need someone in a body to be the conduit for our energy since our frequency is too high to help directly. Our energy must be "stepped down" a few octaves to be received, and this is why we need a partner who has a body to come through. Know this! The day is coming when the spirit world will be seen walking alongside those in a body. We have always been here, and ordinary people will see, hear, and feel us as the two worlds become one!

CHAPTER 26

READINGS FROM HEAVEN

I was in dire financial trouble as soon as Alan passed when I lost his pension income. We had been living off of the proceeds from the sale of my parent's house that I had inherited, but the money had dwindled since neither of us had been able to work steadily because of Alan's illness. His dementia had progressed to the point where he couldn't continue his psychic readings, and by January of 2018, he had stopped working completely.

Clients had stopped calling. I watched helplessly as Alan slowly withdrew from the things he enjoyed doing. He missed helping his clients so much that up until the last week of his life, he would search for his deck of cards, wanting to do a reading even though there was no one to read for. Once he found them, he'd turn the cards over and over in his hands, not remembering what to do with them until eventually, his eyes would glaze over, and he'd stuff them back into a drawer until the next day when he'd ransack the house again looking for them.

Now, three weeks after he returned to me, Alan suggested I do readings with him. I wanted to go along but was unsure because I had never enjoyed giving readings as much as Alan. I knew conventional psychic readings were not what I was here to do. Though I had inherited my grandmother's gift of channeling, I was a healer more than a classic psychic like Alan, though he insisted that I was as psychic as he was.

It was frustrating because I knew I could help people create their future rather than just tell them what would happen. This was why I preferred teaching over giving readings. I'd always known my life purpose was to empower and liberate people. Not that there's anything wrong with being a psychic or giving readings. I just knew it wasn't for me. Alan had never shared my interest in healing until he came back.

Now here he was, wanting to do it all. Readings, healings, teaching, Alan was game for everything and anything. His excitement about what was possible for us to do together was contagious. Working with him was what I had always dreamed of doing, and now at last, he was giving me the opportunity.

Alan promised I would LOVE (he showed me the word in capital letters) giving readings with him. He asked me to try it at least once and promised that if I didn't enjoy it, I didn't have to continue.

If we work together, my love, I'll be able to support you financially. We are going to do so many amazing things together, Pam. Isn't that what you always wanted? Well, it's going to happen now. We weren't meant to partner like this sooner. For one thing, I wasn't ready. I was too full of ego, doubt, and insecurity to take my place at your side then, but I can now. The truth is I had to die to do the work we are about to do. I had to step into all of my spiritual power first.

"Okay, but how are we going to get clients? You forget that no one has called for two years."

I've always been able to manifest things when I put my mind to it, don't you remember? And so can you! I'll get a client for us. You'll see.

I was skeptical, but my doubts vanished the next morning when a young woman named Annie called asking to speak to Alan. She wanted a reading. I explained that Alan had just passed away but that he had returned and that we were giving readings together.

"Oh! That sounds cool! Yes, I'd love that! So, when can I have a reading?"

"Well, how about tomorrow at 11 in the morning?"

And just like that, Alan had manifested our first reading in less than twenty-four hours. Still, I was leery about giving the reading with him. How exactly would we do that? Yes, I'm a channel who can talk to the other side, but would it be easier or harder for me to speak for Alan because of our connection? Since he had passed away only three weeks ago, would my grief get in the way? I wasn't sure I could do the reading, but Alan seemed confident.

On the day of the reading, I was nervous but excited. I called Annie at the agreed time, and as the reading began, I felt Alan's energy come in. I suppressed a giggle, seeing that even without a body, it was just like him to make a grand entrance. As his energy merged with mine, much to my surprise, I could see everything he could see about our client. I felt him next to me. He was on my right, slightly behind me, putting his thoughts into my mind as he leaned in close. But no sooner had I adjusted to this mesmerizing experience than I noticed something troubling.

Annie wouldn't stop talking.

This was going to be a problem. Alan spoke with compassion and sensitivity, but I could feel him getting irritated when Annie kept talking over me. Annie wasn't paying attention to what I was saying. I laughed to myself knowing how upset Alan gets when a client talks during his readings. He'd get annoyed if I did that to him, but with clients it was even worse because he hated wasting his time and theirs. A lot of psychics will happily sit back and let their clients use up the time on the 'reading clock' by chattering away. But not my husband.

He took his readings seriously, so much so that when a client wouldn't stop talking, Alan had been known to stop the reading, lean in close, and gently bark, "Hey, who's giving the reading here? You or me? Now be quiet and let me do my job!" The client apologized as Alan regained control of the session. But with this new arrangement, I didn't know what to do with Annie, who was yammering away, barely pausing to take a breath.

I know that a client sometimes needs to vent a little before they are ready to listen, but I was getting frustrated because we were offering critical information that she wasn't hearing. After ten minutes, Alan was fed up.

Pam, she's not listening to us! You know how I hate it when clients keep talking! You have to do something! You have to swear at her to get her attention!

"What? I can't do that, Alan!"

Pam, you have to! Just watch. I'll bet you anything that even if you swear at her, it won't register. But it doesn't matter because you have to do something! And you have to do it right now, too!

I cleared my throat, took a deep breath, and said, "Annie, I'm so sorry to have to say this, but Alan says could you please just...SHUT THE FUCK UP!"

I cringed, expecting her to get upset, but it was just as Alan had said. My words went right over her head. Annie kept on talking. I felt Alan's frustration growing. I knew I had to try again.

This time I raised my voice louder and said, "ANNIE, YOU REALLY NEED TO SHUT UP AND LISTEN TO US RIGHT NOW!"

She stopped talking.

I spoke Alan's words as quickly as he poured them into my mind. I explained to Annie why her life was unraveling, including why she had gotten into the terrible situation she was facing, living with a new roommate who refused to pay his portion of the rent. He had taken over her lease by buttering up her landlord and turning him against her. This freeloader roommate had found a way to lock her out of her own apartment. She couldn't get her deposit back or get her landlord to help her get back in and was trapped. Annie couldn't live there, but she also couldn't afford to move out. But that wasn't all. Her boyfriend was angry at her roommate, who had once been a friend of his, and wanted to beat him up, which was about to escalate the situation. Annie's life was falling apart. We told her that if she didn't take action, things would go from bad to worse and possibly even turn tragic. Someone could get hurt.

We laid out her options, emphasizing to her that she was standing at a major crossroads in her life. We warned her that her entire future was dependent on which path she chose in this moment, but Annie didn't seem to grasp the seriousness of her situation. She was too focused on petty issues like whether or not her boyfriend was right for her when clearly, he wasn't. You didn't have to be psychic to know that.

Despite the frustration of getting Annie to listen, it was exhilarating to tune into the higher realms through Alan. I was in an altered state for the rest of the day. It made me wonder if working with him would always be like this.

Whenever I work with you, we will blend our energies together, which will draw us even closer to each other. You must meet me halfway in whatever we do, for how else can we merge and share our hearts and minds? This will strengthen our connection to each other, my love!

It was thrilling to feel Alan's energy entwined with mine to the point that his words became my words. Seeing what he projected into my mind was a wondrous surprise. Working with Alan had been my dream from the day we met, and now it was finally happening. All these years, I couldn't understand why we were brought together yet never partnered in our spiritual work. Clients who knew us called us a "power couple," but I hadn't seen any evidence of our combined power until now.

Why was our timing always off? If only we had met when Alan was younger. If only I had not gotten pregnant so soon. If only we could have had more time together to cement our love before the inevitable challenges of family life and work began to distract us from each other. Everything happened too fast, with time being the enemy from the start. As it happens so often with couples, our love got lost in the shuffle of mundane daily living. There was so much I had dreamed of doing with Alan, but very little of it had happened. I was grieving not just the loss of him but the loss of all that might have been. Could it really be possible that it wasn't too late after all?

Yes, my darling, we were meant to work together! And look, we're going to do it now! It was supposed to be this way, with you there where you are and me here where I am. I know it's not the way you wanted it to be, but your life will be incredible if you can accept it. In time you'll see why it was necessary for us to live the way we did.

Annie's reading had been frustrating, but as soon as I hung up the phone, I collapsed on the living room sofa, roaring with laughter, "Oh my God, was that fun! Let's do it again!"

Then you'll do readings with me, Pam?

"Yes! But how will we get clients? Remember, no one has been calling for two years now. You miraculously found us one client, but it won't be easy to find more."

Announce it in the Facebook group. There are people who will want readings. Our clients and students are in the group, and I promise you, they will be interested! I want to help as many people as possible because the more people we help, the stronger I will become, which means I'll be able to help them even more, and when I say "I," you know what I really mean—"us." Our readings are unique because I'll be available to help clients even after the session ends.

Ours will be the reading that never ends.

"What do you mean? The reading that never ends?"

I can connect with people for as long as they need me, or need us, I should say. You are always with me in everything that I do, helping them as well. I know it sounds strange, but you have already experienced healing people remotely without being consciously aware you are doing it. That's because all souls, whether in a body or not, are multidimensional. Like me, you are capable of being in more than one place at a time and with more than one person, too. If anyone calls on us for help, and I mean even someone who just heard about us through the book we are writing or a friend who tells them about us, we will respond and do what we can to help. Yes, even people who aren't paying clients! You'll see what I mean when our book is published. We will offer guidance and spiritual healing and help people make direct contact with loved ones and spirit helpers through the veil.

The next day, Alan wanted to talk more about Annie's reading.

Now let's talk about the reading we did yesterday. You felt exhilarated at the end, yes? That's because I was lifting you up to Heaven. I do that so that you can access the Divine Mind, which we must do to give our clients the counsel they need. When we work together, you and I merge our minds, our souls, and become One, and in this way, I can both project my thoughts to you and you can also sense, see, and know much of what I experience here. Not 100 percent of it but more than enough, and the percentage will increase the more we work together in this way. Yes, it is very much as you noted the other day. It's as if we are dancing, only this is a Dance of Consciousness.

Getting that first reading was a miracle, but I told Alan we would need a mountain of miracles if we were going to have a business. He didn't seem the least bit worried, so I did as he suggested and announced to our group that we were doing readings. Within twelve hours, we had seventeen sessions booked; within two weeks, we were booked for three months. By the end of that period we had completed 140 readings and healings including group sessions. I was busier than I had ever been. All this while I was still grieving, which meant there were days when I was both emotionally and physically spent, yet I was never tired because Alan's exuberant energy would lift me and carry me through the day.

As the weeks passed, I noticed I was becoming happier with each reading we completed. A few clients contacted me to confirm that Alan was guiding them after their session just as he promised he would. I was stunned the first time he told someone that he wanted them to call on him for help at any time. He told them that when they called on him, both of us would come to their aid. Our readings were off to an amazing start.

When I wasn't giving readings with Alan or sharing his messages on Facebook, I was listening to the many songs he had given me, playing them from the moment I woke up until I went to bed. I found it odd that neither of us had listened to music very often during our marriage, yet since his return, his collection of songs had become the way I felt his love through ripples of tingles and goosebumps he'd send me throughout the day. I couldn't stop playing the songs. If I ever paused for too long, Alan would call out to me.

Play our songs, Pam.

Early on, I knew his songs held the key to a fuller reunion with Alan. Since both of us enjoyed dancing, I would sing and dance with him in the kitchen, seeing him swaying to the music in my inner vision. Sometimes he'd be dressed all in white as he had been on our wedding day. Other times, he'd appear sporting a silly outfit of mismatched Hawaiian prints, signaling the day would be all about having fun. Although my grief still surfaced occasionally, I didn't stay mired in it for long because his love would lighten my pain. It was the oddest experience to feel so much joy during such a tragic time. Through it all, Alan maintained his crazy sense of humor.

See? Isn't it better that I'm dead, Pam?

The first time I heard him say that, I gasped. But he was right. This was better. It was better than him having dementia and becoming too confused and frail to do anything for himself. Why does aging have to end in so much suffering? Alan was delighted being "not-dead," as he liked to call it. He was vibrantly alive, and his love had resurrected me. I was as alive as he was!

Finally, back in the land of the living, I took inventory of my heart and realized I had been emotionally shut down for most of our marriage. Both of us had been closed off. What a pair we were, completely different yet alike at the same time! I didn't resist grieving. I knew I needed to feel whatever emotions came up. Fortunately for me, when the tears and heart-wrenching pain surfaced, Alan's love would rush in to soothe me and lift my spirits, leaving me heady with joy again. He smiled, declaring unconditional love was behind it all, promising me that I wouldn't age but grow younger. I laughed at the thought, but in the months that followed, friends began commenting that I looked happier and more youthful. I'd smile and tell them it was all Alan's doing, but looking in the mirror, I had to agree that I looked nothing like a grieving widow. Maybe Alan was right when he said unconditional love plus happiness is the recipe for the Fountain of Youth. None of this could be chalked up to my imagination.

Pam, love from Heaven can heal grief!

As the months passed, I could feel Alan's love restoring me, healing me, and making me whole. I had been exhausted and broken when caring for Alan during his dementia. For seven straight months, I had barely slept. Now, as I worked with him, giving readings for hours at a time, I was changing. Emotions buried for decades were stirring, rising to the surface to be felt and released. I knew I needed to feel all of my feelings if I wanted to be with Alan.

At random times during the day, while listening to our songs, I'd be overcome with intense emotion, but rather than pushing aside my sorrow, I embraced it completely. I wanted to feel everything—all of my emotions. Even my despair, since I finally understood that feeling my feelings is what life is all about. As my emotions passed through me, I felt lighter and lighter. My grief was gradually dissipating. Within nine months of Alan's passing, my grief was all but gone. This didn't mean I was always happy. No, grief was just the biggest first hurdle. Though I couldn't see them yet, there were storm clouds gathering on the horizon.

CHAPTER 27

NINETEEN PELICANS

Gena reached out to us from Sydney, Australia, after a friend, who had just that day joined our Facebook group, excitedly told her about Alan and me, saying that all someone had to do was call out to us for help. As a clairvoyant medium, Gena was used to calling on the angels for help; she had done so when she was a child and almost died, but now she needed divine assistance for someone else. Her niece had just given birth to a baby boy, but unfortunately, baby Austin was so ill that his chances of survival appeared slim. The doctors in the London neonatal ICU struggled to determine what was wrong. Gena prayed to the angels to deliver a miracle to Austin, asking that he be given a chance to live.

When she heard about us, Gena had just finished with an appointment but didn't want to wait until she returned home to connect, so she called out to us while driving her car. While she was used to talking to the spirit world and getting a response, she was still surprised by what happened when she said, "Pam and Alan Johnson, Pam and Alan Johnson, I need your help!"

Within moments, Alan appeared in the backseat of Gena's car dressed in his gray suit.

She had expected him to show up, but Gena would later say that she was shocked by the speed with which Alan arrived. As a medium, Gena is used to conversing with spirits and angels, but she noticed there was something different about Alan. There was more of a density to him, which she thought made sense since he had only recently crossed. Still, just because Alan had immediately appeared to her didn't mean Gena blindly accepted that Alan was who he said he was. She always asks the other side for proof, and she asked the same of Alan.

"Oh my, you came so fast! I'm impressed! But Alan, I need you to prove yourself to me. I'm giving you the choice of two birds to send to me. You can choose whichever one you want, but it must be one of these: an eagle or a cockatoo."

As she continued driving, within a few moments, an eagle flew over the hood of her car.

"Oh my! That was amazing, Alan, truly amazing! But now, how about a cockatoo?"

Once again, within minutes, two pink-and-gray cockatoos flew over her car.

"Wow! That was incredible, but how about one more bird? How about a pelican this time? They're my absolute favorite bird of all. I would just love it if you could bring me a pelican."

Alan paused and grew quiet.

Well, that's going to be more difficult. You see, pelicans speak a different language than other birds, and they don't like listening to humans.

"Hm, you know I can see why they might be like that."

I can't promise, but I'll try to get you a pelican.

"Oh, that would be so wonderful, Alan, if you could!"

Once Alan passed his angel audition, he went to Austin in the hospital. When Gena clairvoyantly checked in, she not only saw Alan but saw me with him, holding Austin in my arms giving him healing. Austin's condition quickly improved. Here was yet another confirmation that I was with Alan, working alongside him, giving healing and support to others.

Gena saw Alan pacing up and down the hospital hallway, trying to get a doctor to listen to his guidance. This is how spirits attempt to help us by putting ideas into our minds. Alan went on to explain.

As smart as doctors are, it's their spirit team of guides and angels who give them guidance and brilliant ideas. Spirit has always been guiding humankind from the beginning. People need to understand that the logical mind is not intuitive. The conscious mind is more like a computer that can only regurgitate what has been put into it. All of the great inventions of the world came from the spirit world, with the mind of man being the vessel through which a new idea is planted.

As the months passed, Austin continued his rollercoaster healing journey. Gena gave me intermittent reports, confirming that Alan was still with him. Austin would make miraculous progress one day, only to lose the ground he had gained moments later. The process was an excruciating few steps forward and several more back. It was heartbreaking for Gena and his family to witness, but they remained hopeful.

One day, I received a request from Gena to ask our Facebook group to pray and visualize Austin being healthy and thriving. People were envisioning positive things for him. By now, all of us had fallen in love with Austin.

Over the many weeks that our group held our visualization vigil for Austin, one day, he was strong enough to be placed in a baby bouncer. On another day, his parents took him for a walk in a baby carriage in the sunshine. His parents decided to get married in the hospital so Austin could be with them for the ceremony. To cap it all off, the family of three was able to visit the hospital's rooftop garden to enjoy the glories of an English summer day. It looked like baby Austin was at last getting a chance to live outside of the hospital!

But sadly, by the beginning of July, after a little over six months, the doctors finally discovered what was wrong. They described the spinal column at the back of Austin's neck was misfiring, which meant the signals flowing to every organ of his body were blocked.

The doctors compared it to a damaged electrical cable. Sadly, they said there was nothing more they could do and that it would only be a matter of time before Austin died as the 'cables' that were misfiring began failing to control his heart, his bladder, his bowels, his stomach, and his breathing. There was no more they could do for him. They would no longer do CPR or restart his heart but only give Austin oxygen.

Gena was devastated, but she kept praying for a miracle. She asked me to keep the news to myself for the time being. Sadly, a few days later, she messaged me to say that Austin had passed peacefully and to post a message from her to the group.

"Austin had many firsts in the last month before he left this world. I know in my heart it was because so many of you lovingly supported him which made those moments possible. Never stop believing in the miracle of manifestation, for what we perceive, we do receive, and I believe in the power of prayer, faith manifestation, and dreaming. I know the energy sent to support others in life is always a blessing."

As I read this, I broke down crying. Alan drew in closer to comfort me.

Pam, it was a miracle that Austin lived for the six precious months he had. I know this breaks your heart after all the prayers you and the group did for him. We were with Austin every step of the way, holding fast to the hope that he'd pull through. But remember, no one dies! Austin still lives! He's just not in a body anymore. Austin's magnificent soul and indomitable spirit will watch over his parents for the rest of their lives, and if they are open to it, they can connect with him one day. Sadly, at the moment, they don't accept the fact that he has survived death, but that opportunity will remain with them for the rest of their days until they reunite with him in Heaven.

Some would say that Austin didn't receive the miracle that Gena prayed for. But she said it wasn't true because she had only asked that he be given a chance to live. And he got that chance! And he DID live! Her prayers were answered. Austin lived for six precious months and, during that time, made a profound impression on every person who helped care for him, surrounded him with love, and visualized him healthy and whole: the doctors, the nurses, his parents and family, and everyone in our group. That any of us are here at all is a miracle in itself.

Alan had spent several days with Gena in her home in Sydney. Since both of them were British, they had much in common, and her being able to see and speak to him made for a mutually enjoyable visit. Gena explained to Alan how the angels would direct her to speak to someone in the supermarket, then how an invisible force would make her stop in her tracks. She would stay in that spot until she spoke to the person the angels had selected. It was an unorthodox way of being of service, but that was how committed Gena was to serving the spirit world.

One night as they were chatting away in her dining room, Gena shared her concern that she was taking up all of Alan's time and keeping him away from me, when Alan assured her this wasn't the case, pointing to her husband sitting in the living room in full view of them.

Do you see your husband sitting there on the sofa? He can see us; we can see him. We're not with him, and yet we are. I am always with Pam. I never leave her side even for a minute, and yet I can be anywhere and everywhere I choose. This is how I can be with you. I can be with a million people and still be with Pam. I can do this because, whether in a body or not, we are all multidimensional beings capable of having a multitude of experiences simultaneously. Even now, you are in many other places; you just aren't aware of them.

If you were fully aware of being multidimensional, it would distort your perception of the physical world, and you'd have trouble focusing here, which would be confusing and chaotic. But when you return to the other side, you reclaim all you know and live in this truth.

So no, you cannot take me away from Pam. No one and nothing can ever do that. Besides, she is always with me. It's why you saw her with me the other day in the hospital, praying over Austin and giving him healing. It is one of Pam's multidimensional selves that is with me, while her human self isn't aware of what she does with me. In time as we continue to merge and as Pam raises her vibration, she will be able to remember more of what she is doing with me, but right now, she can't. Besides, for the time being, she needs to be well grounded to anchor my energy onto the physical plane for our work. Eventually, she will raise her vibration to better match mine, but that will take time.

Through the time they spent together, Gena came to understand Alan. She said he had been emotionally repressed, and that was why he didn't know how to love me until he died. Sensing my pain, she did her best to help me understand him.

"Pam, he is kicking himself a lot! This British baby who grew up during the war had a way of making up reasons for not doing what he should have done for his family. War babies were programmed through their parents' actions and the patterns of previous generations, neither of which did them any favors. They held beliefs like don't spend money, don't show weakness, don't show affection, don't be a pushover, don't shine, don't splurge. He knows there is no excuse, so he has none to give you, but in time, you will know him better than you ever dreamed you could. He will see to that!"

On February 2nd, our thirtieth wedding anniversary arrived, and Gena was kind enough to send me several messages from Alan, together with songs and poems he had chosen. Our first anniversary spent through the veil had filled him with great remorse. She began with a message for me.

Pam,

He was an arse

Big arse

He was never able to fully see what was right there

If he knew then what he knows now, it would have been different

He would have showered you with affection

He would have walked over broken glass to show you what you mean to him

He would have told you he was sorry for the pain he caused you if he had the chance to express it

He loves you more than words can say

And he knows he doesn't deserve your forgiveness, but he is so happy that he received it

He will be making all your days the most glorious days of your life together

And this wedding when he gets to have his second chance, he is going to lift you up and carry you off with his wings

(I am being told these words by the way...)

– Gena

I was out for lunch with a friend when the message came in on my phone. I held back my tears as I read Alan's words. I saw Alan crying. I wasn't expecting such an outpouring of regret from him, so this took me by surprise. I told him I forgave him, that I couldn't wait to get married again so we'd have a second chance. Alan promised to get it right this time!

Before Austin passed, when hope for his survival was still high, Alan made good on his promise to bring Gena a pelican. He did everything he could to lift her spirits. I heard about it as it happened.

Hello Pam,

Today, I visited my sister, who is Austin's grandmother. I was able to tell her about the two of you and the miracle of what is happening with Austin. She has been beside herself about not being able to be with her daughter since my sister is here in Australia, and they are in the UK. I told her how amazing Alan is and how much fun and laughter he is shining over everyone. I told her that I had asked him for a pelican and how Alan is trying so hard to get them to listen. Well, as I was driving home and turned the corner to my estate, three pelicans flew over my car!

He did it! He got them to come to me!

Then I got home and kept asking Alan to try and get them nearer to my house so I could get a photo. I'm sitting out the back as I write this, and you won't believe what just happened five minutes ago. He sent me EIGHT pelicans, Pam! Now Alan is really showing off! I can't thank him enough for this is the greatest confirmation of him and all that we are experiencing.

He is now showing off big, big, big time. I just asked him to send them closer if he can, and he just sent six more! They still aren't as close as he would like them to come, but he is doing his best to bring them closer to me. No one would ever believe this! He is blowing my mind, Pam!

It is exactly one week since I met the two of you, and my heart is overflowing with delight. My sister is visiting me on Sunday so I'm asking Alan to bring her the pelicans when she is here. He said that was the closest he could get them to come, but he will continue to try and get them closer to us. He is AMAZING! If he can get seventeen pelicans to me when I asked him to just bring me one, he can do anything.

That weekend, Alan returned.

Hi Pam,

My sister came over on Sunday for a swim and said wouldn't it be wonderful if Alan sent a pelican to say hello while we are in the pool, as I would love to see that. And he did! He did it again, Pam! This time he sent one pelican to catch our attention, which my sister saw and screamed with joy. Then he sent another one, which was the closest yet, for us to see. It flew over the top of our neighbor's house, swooped in low, and literally looked down at us.

It paused in mid-flight as if to say, "Here I am!"

My sister was ecstatic. She said, "This is Alan, isn't it?"

Alan sent Gena a total of nineteen pelicans, one eagle, and two cockatoos. Twenty-two birds in total. This was remarkable, given that pelicans are not common in the part of Sydney where she lives. When Alan had gotten the eagle to fly over her car, that was also unusual because it was midsummer, and eagles are not usually around at that time of year.

Gena and I drifted apart after that. I heard from her less and less until she stopped communicating with me altogether. Alan told me I needed to let her go, but it wasn't easy for me since I had so few friends who understood what I was going through.

I focused on all the good that had come from our meeting, how we helped Austin live for a few precious months so he could be with his parents, and just as importantly, Alan had demonstrated what souls on the other side could do for us if we ask for help and give them time to deliver. No, Spirit can't heal us of everything, as there are reasons things have to be the way they are, but there are miracles to be had if we are open enough to ask, trust, and believe.

CHAPTER 28

THE EMBODIMENT
OF GOD'S LOVE

We are here for all of you. Know that when you call upon us, we will always respond in some manner. Sometimes, you will feel our support come in strong and immediately, while other times, it will be subtle, or you might not be sure if anything happened. Nevertheless, we always take appropriate action for your benefit. Call on me, Alan, for I am always available twenty-four hours a day, but remember that Pam joins me in everything that I do, even if she is not seen.

We promise to do whatever we can to help you.

That said, please understand that help and healing can take time! Sometimes healing can be instantaneous, but to get to the root cause of an issue, especially one that has been established for a fair amount of time, means it's become so intertwined with your being that to simply pull it out, so to speak, would wreak havoc on your mind, body, and spirit. So great care must be taken with the process.

Every person and every situation is different, which is why we must take care to proceed slowly and carefully. Can every condition or issue be healed? No. Some problems are lessons you agreed to endure for your soul's growth. If that is the case, we will do what we can to support you through your challenge, at the very least by giving you the strength and guidance you need to ease your burden.

We do this because it was the promise we made before we incarnated. My lifetime with Pam was spent harmonizing with her so we could work together as we do now. We knew that if I was to remain in Heaven and accept the full array of powers and abilities I had developed, I would need her grounded human connection to the Earth to serve as the required interface.

So, you may ask, who am I? It has been explained elsewhere here that I am an Archangel in the sense that it's my job to empower and support humans to connect with and embody their souls. Archangel is a job description! Pam is one as well, but please do not put us on a pedestal.

Angels are your brothers and sisters, differentiated only by the self-selected jobs and objectives they have accepted to serve humanity. There are those among you right now who are incarnated angels. You may be one yourself! You will know them by their behavior. For though they will not be perfect, since being in a body makes us fallible, their countenance at its core is one of loving-kindness.

Higher beings incarnate to serve in ways that may surprise you.

There are those in your midst who struggle with chronic debilitating conditions, whether mental or physical, chronic addictions, or other problems. Some might, in truth, be highly evolved souls who have chosen to teach unconditional love by struggling with hardship and gross afflictions. Do not mistake someone's outer countenance for who they really are. The lowest among you could be an ascended master. Appearances can be deceiving. See with the eyes of your soul if you wish to know the truth of who someone is! There is an inner radiance in the ones who serve with pure heart and soul.

It is for this reason that you should honor and respect everyone you encounter rather than pity or, even worse, reject and judge someone.

In God's eyes, all are equally cherished. When it comes to angels, the only differences that exist are in terms of interests, capabilities, and chosen purposes. There is no higher or lower, greater or lesser in the spirit world. None of that. Those who claim a hierarchy exists here view Heaven through the clouded lens of their belief system. That is their human programming, not divine truth.

Know this! Human perceptions are colored by ingrained beliefs and other earthly influences. It cannot be any other way.

Pam herself cannot be 100 percent clear, either. However, because she has merged almost completely with me at this point and, as a result, has achieved a higher level of unconditional love than most, her clarity is quite high compared to the average person.

In addition, Pam spent most of her life in a channeling state of one form or another from when she was a child. It was why she learned how to work with Spirit so quickly and easily. She was born to do what she and I are now doing together. The fact that Pam was able to overcome the worst of her grief and begin working with me within three weeks of my passing to teach and help people is evidence that she is my equal.

Few people could have done what she did. Most of them would have had a nervous breakdown, but Pam pushed on, fueled by her soul's burning desire as a healer-teacher to help others overcome their grief and go free. Yes, I gave her my strength, my energy, and my unconditional love to help her rise up to meet the challenges that came, but it was Pam's spiritual inner strength that she had honed for decades and many lifetimes that did the heavy lifting. All within the first month of my passing.

Yes, what we are doing now was planned many, many lifetimes ago. You are witnessing the unfolding of something exquisite and extraordinary. But don't take our word for it; we invite you to experience it for yourself by calling on us!

Even reading the words we write is an energy transmission from Heaven, which is where I always am. I can be here and be there with you in a much deeper, closer way than other angelic beings because of Pam. She is the conduit for all of our work. If it were not for her, I could only do half of what I do.

Pam is an experienced Earth Healer, while I am the Angel Alchemist on high. Together, we merge Heaven and Earth. We are not the only ones who do this, either! Call on us by either speaking one of our names or both together (since where one goes, the other follows), speaking aloud or silently in your mind.

We will be there.

We will grow stronger the more we help and support you. So please ask for our help! We welcome it. Expect to receive assistance but have no fixed idea about how our help will show up in your life or when. There are forces at play here that we cannot explain to you.

Help might descend like a lightning bolt from above; other times, it could be a barely audible whisper you hear in your mind, guiding you to your salvation. So, pay attention!

Understanding is best gained from direct experience. We are your teachers, but you are equal to us. Never forget that! Never hold anyone, not the angels or any higher beings, above you and never hold yourself above or below others as well. Suffering comes from such false comparisons. If you are going to worship something, worship unconditional love!

Remember this above all else: you are nothing less than the embodiment of God's love.

CHAPTER 29

SEEING ALAN

W hile Alan was helping Austin in the hospital, Gena and I would sometimes chat through Zoom. One day, we were talking about nothing in particular, when she stunned me with an announcement of what Alan was saying.

Alan told her I would be seeing him in physical form.

Gena assured me that it would happen and that, when it did, it would be the most amazing thing.

"Pam, you'll be able to have a cup of tea with Alan, go for a walk on the beach with him, and everything. He says it's going to happen, and he wants me to help you."

Shocked, I didn't know what to say at first.

"But how can this be? Do you know anyone who has done this?"

Gena acknowledged that she didn't know anyone, but she was convinced it would happen because of what Alan told her. She could feel his excitement and determination, and because she knew how powerful he was, she was convinced it would happen based on that alone.

Why can't we be the first to do this, Pam? You know nothing is impossible if we just believe!

Gena continued to relay what Alan was saying. He wanted her to help him teach me. The first step was deepening my sense of touch to access my memory of Alan's body. I was to buy some clay to do this. I got the idea to use Play-Doh, the pliable non-toxic dough that children play with. Alan said it was perfect.

We had two meetings in which I practiced molding Alan's face and head. I imagined how his hair, eyebrows, nose, ears, and facial features felt beneath my fingers. While I felt silly doing it, I understood the logic and was eager to try. Between our Zoom meetings, I practiced molding the Play-Doh, shaping it into a miniature version of Alan's head. I'd close my eyes and imagine his skin, even the heat coming off it, everything down to the stubble on his face. I wasn't sure if I was making progress, but I was hopeful, and Alan's growing excitement motivated me to push on.

Through it all, Gena encouraged me, saying she could see me doing it. After all we had done for Austin, she wanted to help us achieve this. Alan insisted it would happen. I knew he would never make a promise to me that he couldn't keep since the last thing he would ever want to do was disappoint me, so I kept practicing.

Things were going well until suddenly, without warning, everything stopped.

Gena messaged me to explain that a family emergency had come up. She said she'd be in touch as soon as she could. I was sad and disappointed, but I told her I understood since taking care of ourselves should always be our top priority.

Sadly, it would be many months before I would hear from Gena again, and although she periodically updated me on Austin's condition, we never resumed our practice sessions again. It broke my heart to put everything aside, but it was too frustrating to go it alone without support. Still, Alan kept insisting that one day I would see him.

When I told Swati about my frustration, she reminded me that I was already seeing Alan.

"Pam, but you DO see him! You have all along! The outer physical world is the fake world. It's just a reflection of the inside world, which is the real world. When you think you are not seeing him in the physical world, it is the same as you saying 'I can't see myself in the mirror' if the mirror was covered for some reason. You can't see yourself, so it means you're not here. And that's not true, right? As you finish reading this message, close your eyes and call Alan to you.

"See him inside your mind. That is true seeing!

"If you want to see a reflection of this true seeing outside in the physical world, you can do that, too. Practice closing your eyes. This is seeing him for real. Now open your eyes and try to imagine that real image reflected outside. With practice, you will see his reflected self in the physical world as well.

"But please do not say that you don't see him because you absolutely DO!

"The psychic sense-mental image is the real image because it's from the real world. What we see in the physical is a fake image, even though it looks clearer and real to us. The physical is a reflection of the real world held within. That is why I keep reminding you that you are already seeing him. I suggest you practice lucid dreaming. It's easy to learn if you are disciplined. Really easy.

"In the lucid dream state, you can meet him every night. In the lucid dream, you can feel him physically because you are in their dimension. So please, will you do this? Learn lucid dreaming. I met my mother-in-law and my brother in lucid dreams. It IS real, and it even FEELS like the physical world."

Taking Swati's advice to heart, I began practicing, using a book about lucid dreaming I had bought years ago. There are many books on the subject, but no matter what book you read, the real challenge is disciplined regular practice. To my surprise, I easily achieved the first goal, which was to remember my dreams. This was something I had never been able to do. But by focusing my intention to recall my dreams, for seven nights in a row, I dreamt of Alan and recalled every one of my dreams, writing them down in my journal.

The first six dreams were unremarkable, but on the seventh night, I achieved the goal of waking up within my dream to become fully lucid, and I saw Alan. I had opened a door to see a pile of furniture and office equipment haphazardly stacked floor to ceiling in a small room. The ridiculousness of the sight made me say to myself, "This is completely crazy! This must be a dream!"

And just like that, I was awake in my dream while my body was fast asleep. Everything came into crystal-clear focus. It was as if someone had flipped a light switch as all the colors which had been muted became vibrant. I sensed Alan on my right. He told me to turn very slowly towards him, which I did. I had barely caught a glimpse of him when he spoke.

Pam, you did it! You woke up in your dream. You are lucid dreaming! But babe, I'm sorry to have to tell you this, but you have to get up now, or you'll be late for your appointment!

I had forgotten that I had made an appointment to take our car in for repair that morning. I couldn't believe it! When I woke up and looked at the clock, I saw that Alan was right. I had to get going, or I'd miss the appointment.

I understood now why Swati said lucid dreaming was easy to learn but took discipline to master. But I'd never been a disciplined person. I would need to work on this if I was to succeed. I had two more lucid dreams with Alan before he decided to look for other methods for us to connect. Still, I could see what Swati meant. In a lucid dream, we can be with our loved ones in a way that is as real as our experience of them in the physical world. I had felt Alan's arms in one of my lucid dreams. Even now, I can still feel the silky texture of his skin beneath my hands as I stroked his arms. It was a sensual experience I will never forget.

If the physical world is the fake world, and the non-physical world the real world, what then is the dream world? It stands to reason that it must be the bridge between the two worlds, which would explain why it's possible to experience a loved one's touch in a lucid dream, even if they don't have a body to extend to us. Our mind is our eternal consciousness, and it is our mind that dreams and even astral travels to other dimensions. This is how, in a lucid dream, our consciousness can meet theirs as we see them without physical eyes and embrace them without them having a body.

The non-physical can be experienced physically in our minds.

If you talk to lucid dreamers like Swati, they'll tell you lucid dreams are as real as this world, that they can see, feel, taste, and hear everything with astonishing clarity. I found it difficult to stay with my lucid dream practice because I was still struggling off and on with my grief on top of all the work I was doing, so I reluctantly put it aside for the time being, with the intention of returning to it once the book was finished.

But Alan wasn't giving up on finding a way to deepen our connection. It would take time, but he was on a quest to find a way for us to reunite through the veil, not just for our sake but for all those who wished to follow our lead. It was as if he was doing an in-depth survey of ways to unite Heaven and Earth. I kept hearing the words Alan had said through Gena.

"He will be making all your days the most glorious days of your life together."

CHAPTER 30

PUMPKIN

I first met Maria when she had a phone reading with me in the fall of 2007. After our session, when she asked me to spend the morning with her at Kailua Beach, since it was not far from my house, I instantly agreed, which was unusual for me since I rarely socialize with clients. Becoming friends with a client is a slippery slope. It usually doesn't end well since we're not on equal footing with each other, with the client often seeing me as nothing more than a way to get free readings. But I sensed Maria was different. On the brink of divorce, cradling her baby girl in her arms, we chatted away while her two rambunctious little boys happily played nearby in the sand and the surf.

Right from the start, Maria felt like an old friend. This rarely happened to me. I was struck by how positive and down-to-earth she was. Maria seemed to genuinely care about me, not wanting anything more but to enjoy my company. Conversation between us flowed easily, peppered with smiles and laughter. By the time we parted, a loving, close friendship had been established, but sadly, once she moved to the mainland and remarried, we lost touch with each other for over a decade.

Maria reentered my life when I shared Alan's passing on my Facebook page. Strangely, only then did my posts show up in her Facebook feed. Maria would later tell me she believed it was Alan's doing. She had never met him in person—her only contact had been briefly talking to Alan on the phone once—but hearing of his death, her heart broke for me. It didn't take long for Maria to reach out to me, asking if we could talk. We resumed our friendship as if nothing had happened, growing even closer as my journey with Alan took off. As the months passed, no matter how confused, hurt, and upset I was, Maria was always there for me, ready to talk and console me when I needed a shoulder to cry on, which happened often. She became my rock.

Maria promised me that her shoulder was permanently reserved for me to cry on. She proved it one day by sending a photo of her shoulder with my name scrawled on a piece of paper taped to it. Weeks later when I was in deep despair over Alan, she sent another photo. This time, my name was on both of her shoulders. Maria did so much to help us that when Alan nicknamed her his "minion," she burst out laughing as he showed her an image of herself with a ball and chain around her ankle.

Maria's love got me through my darkest days.

The family we are born into isn't our only family. That's just biology. And how important is biology when we are spiritual beings who never die? We have another family we belong to, a soul family made up of the many souls we have known and incarnated with lifetime after lifetime. When we meet a member of our soul family, we feel the connection first, even if we don't understand who they are to us. Sometimes, as it was with Maria and me, the timing isn't right, yet it is perfect. We were meant to meet, then part, and only later did life events converge to bring us together.

Alan knew who Maria was from the beginning, but he didn't tell me until one early morning when she and I were chatting as we often did at that hour. In her Kentucky home on the other side of the country from me in Hawaii, Maria was cooking lunch while I was prepping my morning smoothie, when suddenly, the word Pumpkin, with a capital P, flashed in my mind.

"Hm. This is weird. Alan is calling you Pumpkin for some reason. I see the word so clearly. What does this mean?"

"Well, my mom used to call me Pumpkin when I was a child."

There it was. Alan was saying that Maria was our daughter, only I was too slow to catch on right away. It would take a little more time and more messages from Alan before the significance of the word sank in. I shouldn't have been surprised since Maria was already a dear friend, but now Alan was saying we were mother and daughter, too. That made Alan her angel dad!

Maria and I laughed as we noted the family resemblance. They had curly hair, a witty demeanor, strong psychic ability, and artistic creativity in common. Like father, like daughter. Few people could make me laugh as hard or as often as these two. How many times had Maria and I been on the phone talking when Alan would interject a silly comment that would send us into hysterics?

This was why Alan had brought Maria back into my life. Fortunately for us, I had already taught our angel daughter how to channel several years ago when Maria took my channeling course, so it was easy for her to take down Alan's words. This must have been why she was able to hear Alan soon after she and I reconnected.

Alan's revelation was made just in time, too, because I would be relying on Maria's ability to speak to and for Alan in the weeks and months that followed, first when she took dictation for his wedding vows and later when he and I headed into rough waters. We would need her help to navigate the cross-currents of our fears and doubts if our love was going to survive the journey.

CHAPTER 31

WEDDING JITTERS

While the disappointments of the past still haunted me, I focused on feeling Alan's love on the days leading up to our nuptials. But now that we were heading into the week before the wedding, some newfound pain surfaced when I found some photos of Alan from his travels abroad. One of the photos was taken on his trip to Egypt with Barbara. He was dressed in a white turban and a robe edged in gold braid, grinning broadly with a drink in his hand, flanked by his friends. I turned the photos over and over in my hands, remembering how I had felt abandoned and left out of his many adventures overseas. A single tear fell on his photo. I resisted the urge to tear it to shreds. I felt Alan's presence, then saw him in my mind's eye as he spoke.

I'm standing in front of you, hugging you. Can you feel me?

Shaking my head, I told him that I couldn't. He asked me to keep trying, which I did, but I still couldn't feel him, though I felt a little better for the effort. I messaged Maria to tell her what had happened. I asked her if I should burn the photos since he didn't seem to care about them anymore.

"He doesn't care if you burn them. Especially if it means letting go of the hurt. Pam, Alan wants you to know two things. Number one: He loves you. Number two: You were able to hear him even when you were upset. This is a sign of how close you have become. He has asked me to say that more than anything else in this world, and the one beyond it, more than the contract he made with you, more than the mission you two have, he wants you to know he loves you and only you. You are his beginning, his middle, and his end. There is no Alan without Pam. And these are not his wedding vows. Just vows of love!"

I gasped, "Oh, now you've done it! The two of you have got me crying again. Yes, I can hear him even when I'm upset. Oh my, I just heard him again. I told him the same is true for me. There is no me without him. If I even think about him hurting or being sad, I weep uncontrollably because I feel his sadness as my own."

Maria then showed me a photo that Alan had made her take as she was walking past her front door that afternoon. The day had been cloudy and rainy until that moment. The photo showed a dark scowling sky streaked with thin ribbons of bright fuchsia clouds. Alan wanted me to take note of the beautiful streaks of pink that were breaking through the gray clouds. Maria began to speak for him.

"Do you see the photos of the clouds? This is his love for you, which is ALWAYS making an appearance. Even on the darkest of days, he is always there with you. Always letting you know that his love is bright, pure, and true. Oh boy, he's about to leave me no words for his wedding vows!"

I laughed, "Oh my, he is showing you no mercy with those wedding vows."

"Hah! He never does!"

Alan was determined to make the wedding extra special for me, to make up for his dismal efforts during our first wedding and through our marriage. When he returned to Heaven, he realized love is the only thing that matters. The purpose of life begins and ends with love. That's it. Anything else we accomplish while we're here is a postscript.

Pam, I will never take you for granted ever again. You are the reason I exist.

CHAPTER 32

A SUPERNATURAL WEDDING

Everything was ready for our Supernatural Wedding. A lush tropical flower arrangement had been delivered the day before, along with a chocolate decadence cake from my favorite local custom bakery. As is the custom in the islands, I had ordered leis for us just as I had done for our first wedding. With our wedding being held on Zoom, these details were important to me. I could tell they were important to Alan as well. For weeks, whenever his face entered my mind, he was beaming with love.

I'd be wearing a Haku lei, a flower lei made to be worn around the head. Alan and I had worn matching white Haku leis for our first wedding. He had also worn a lei of maile, a type of vine, around his neck. Maile leis are used by the kahuna (Hawaiian priest) to bind the hands of the bride and groom to symbolize their commitment to each other. Even though he wouldn't be able to wear the physical lei, I wanted the maile to be draped over the folding screen behind me to stand in for Alan.

Just as I was about to get dressed for the wedding, Alan asked to give me a message. Not content with giving me his wedding vows through Maria, Alan wanted to declare his love privately before we stepped into the Zoom spotlight. His words flowed easily into my mind, stirring my heart.

On This, Our Second Wedding Day

My love, today is the day I have long awaited!

For it is my one desire and truest wish to make you happy for the rest of your days here in this world, and the one beyond.

You and I have weathered the storms of life and love to come out whole and stronger for it.

The days of tears, woe, and suffering are behind us now as we step into a new life together, a life that we will weave together with our conjoined hands, our hearts, and our souls.

And our dreams! Especially our dreams!

Until now, I have loved you from beyond the veil, but today I reach through it to hold your hand and live at your side, always.

Today, our two worlds will be joined as we become One.

My sweet love, take my hand and my heart and let us love as no two souls have ever loved before.

For you are mine, as I am yours now and forever.

With all my love, Alan

As I read his words, my eyes overflowed with tears. He was ramping the energy way up, so much so that I needed to steady myself. Would Alan's wedding vows be able to top this? I couldn't wait to find out.

We had asked our guests to dress as if they were attending an English wedding, complete with fancy hats and a semi-formal dress. Being British, I knew Alan would love this. Our Facebook group did not disappoint. When I switched on my computer, I was greeted by a sea of beaming faces dressed in their wedding finery. Our friend Marci, who had been especially close to Alan, was officiating the ceremony for us a bit nervously since she had never performed an online wedding. Maria was standing by with Alan's vows finally in her hands. Poor Maria! Alan had waited until the hour before the wedding to dictate his vows. Instead of gifts, given the comic sensibility of the groom, guests were asked to share poems or their best jokes. Naturally, the worst jokes were the funniest.

Weeks earlier, Swati mailed Alan's wedding band to me, explaining how he had infused the ring with special blessings and chants while speaking an angelic language as she painstakingly wove the sterling silver wire tightly into a ring. As Swati worked on the ring, her right arm became red hot, indicating the angels were near. This time, the angel was Alan. It had taken several days for them to complete the ring. When the package arrived in the mail, I cried as I slipped the glittery silver band on my finger. Even now, whenever I wear it, I feel Alan's love coursing from my finger straight into my heart. I have a wedding ring made by an angel. Two angels.

With the ring finished at last, the only thing left for Alan to worry about was the wedding itself. You'd think it would be easy with Maria speaking for him, but Alan was afraid that he'd turn into a court jester with Swati at our wedding. At first, I thought he was kidding like he always did when it came to Swati, but she said he was serious. He warned Swati that if she came, she needed to wear a bag over her head and promise not to utter a single word the entire time.

Swati roared with laughter. "What's this? A ghost is telling me to turn into a ghost? Hah!"

But Alan wasn't joking. He didn't want to risk upsetting me if he turned into a babbling comedian should Swati start poking fun at him. It would be hard for Alan to resist the urge to parry with his smartass words if Swati took a jab at him with her teasing. Which wouldn't do. Alan wanted the wedding to be perfect for me. He didn't want to upset me. This was why he asked Maria to help him with his vows, not Swati, because whenever Alan and Swati are together, insanity ensues. Fortunately for both of them, as it turned out, Swati couldn't make it to the wedding, so she was spared the bag, and Alan kept his composure, though I was disappointed that I wouldn't be able to blackmail Swati with a screenshot of her bagged head.

Well over a year later, Alan did his best to torment Swati when she and I did a special Zoom event for the Facebook group. Before the meeting, Maria and Swati joined me on Zoom to chat. But when Swati turned on her webcam, the top of her head was cut off. No matter what Swati did to her camera, including logging off of Zoom and logging on again, all we could see was her neck. The three of us broke out laughing once we realized what was happening. I was the first to speak up. "Alan, you better cut it out or you'll be in big trouble!"

Swati gave it one more try. She logged off and logged on again, and this time just a tiny sliver of the top of her head was cut off. But at least we could see her face! Swati was bent over with laughter.

With our wedding guests settled, introductions were made, and poems and jokes were shared, along with the video montage of songs and photos I had created. We had agreed that I would speak my vows first.

Oh, how I love you, Alan!

In this world, there is only one truth for me,

And you are that truth.

It's always been you.

So today, while I joyously pledge my love to you,

I must confess that for me; it has always been this way.

For you have been my love,

From the moment our souls were wed.

Back at the beginning of time,

When we were first entwined as One.

I loved you the moment our souls touched,

When you became my life, my world.

You are the brightest, the highest, the truest,

The All of me.

My heart,

My mind,

My soul.

I will love you until Eternity ends,

Then love you again and again.

After reciting my vows, I mentally linked with Alan to place an invisible energetic ring on my finger for him. As I did, pulses of tingling energy ran through my ring finger up my arm.

It was now Maria's turn to speak Alan's vows.

My darling Pam,

Today I stand before you with my soul in your hands.

Today I am here to make sure you know that my heart is yours.

Today, I want to give you everything I am because time did not exist until you became a part of me.

And when tomorrow comes, I want to know that our souls, our bodies, and our lives are so tightly entwined you won't know where I begin and you end.

However, today we are creating the magic of a dream.

A dream so grand that the entire world will have to come to a standstill and sigh.

A dream so full of light that the sun itself will seem dim by comparison.

For in truth, my love, ours is the love that transcends time and space.

So let us walk among the stars and dance under the moonlight.

Let me whisper those words from which entire worlds are created:

I love you with all the depth and breadth in my heart and to the great beyond.

Alan's words sent waves of goosebumps through me, but I didn't have time to bask in his love for long because he had a surprise for me. A few days before the wedding, Alan asked Maria to apply her Photoshop digital skills to a photograph of one of his paintings. It was to be his wedding gift to me.

The painting was a favorite of mine, featuring a stream meandering through a leafy, emerald-green forest with a bright ray of sunlight streaming through the canopy of trees onto the still waters below. During the early years of our marriage, one of Alan's clients, Louis Pohl, an elderly well-known local artist who became a second father to him, took Alan under his wing to teach him how to paint using oils. Alan embraced painting with a passion, demonstrating considerable natural talent from the start. Now, as a gift for me, he asked Maria to create a composite using a photo of us from our first wedding ceremony placed into his "forest and stream" painting.

Maria explained the process.

"First, he had me go through your personal Facebook page and the group looking for photos of himself and you, flowers that he had gotten for you since he crossed over, and items from your house of special significance like the pink Himalayan urn that his ashes are in, his paintings, and a statue of Kwan Yin. He then showed me his plan. He wanted me to create a composite where he would place photos from your first wedding along with these items to create a new photo of them. He also wanted me to record my screen because he wanted to show the process of it all coming together in Photoshop. The intention would be to have a new wedding photo and to show the process of him weaving his love and magic into every single piece of the photo. So, we went to work. While creating with Alan, I felt like I was in another world. I was in a trance, with the only difference being that I was fully aware of my surroundings, but every time I got up from my desk, it felt like I was waking up from a nap."

After reciting Alan's vows, Maria played the video.

In the early days of his return, whenever I went to the grocery store, Alan begged me to buy flowers and would tell me exactly which bouquet he wanted. As soon as we got the flowers put into a vase, I'd take a photo and post it in the group. I now watched the images fly across the screen as he and Maria weaved together a magical landscape filled with his flowers placed beside the stream in his painting. My wedding ring was enlarged and placed over the rim of his urn. The placement of the ring over the urn symbolized him giving me his ring. At the end of the video, Alan's new painting of our supernatural wedding was revealed.

I gasped. There we were, standing in the stream of Alan's painting, kissing after being pronounced man and wife, with a Heavenly light from above beaming down over us as we held each other. We were beginning a new life and new marriage together.

Later, when I was struggling to find an image of a couple for our book cover, I realized I already had one. All I needed was for the designer to add a sun rising on the horizon between the trees to symbolize the dawning of our new life together. When the designer questioned me, pointing out it would look strange to have the sun rising with sunlight streaming through the trees, I reminded her that we were, after all, dealing with the supernatural. Alan had wanted to embed our book with spiritual energies that would create a portal between the two worlds, and his painting would be perfect for that. I wondered if he had planned this from the start.

I took a deep breath to collect myself before proceeding with the ring exchange. After linking with Alan in my mind, I gently slid his silver ring onto my finger, and as I did, I felt his love wrap around me like a gentle hug. Later, when we replayed this part of the ring exchange on the video, we were stunned by what we saw. The moment I put the ring on my finger, my body appeared to shake from side to side violently. My upper body looked like a blur when I had not been moving!

Our supernatural wedding had lived up to its name.

When Marci at last pronounced us married, what happened next was typical of Alan. He could never pass up making a joke if the opportunity presented itself, and our wedding would not be an exception. Alan whispered to Maria,

You do realize you're now married to Pam, don't you?

It touched my heart to know that so many of our guests had felt the divine love that had been flowing not just between Alan and us but to all of us from the other side. Here are some of the words shared by those who attended.

"What can I say about your Supernatural Wedding? It was amazing! I could feel the love from the start. I couldn't stop smiling through the ceremony. I could feel Alan's presence all the time. I could feel an older man standing on your left; he was so proud of you. When you said your vows, he faded, and I could feel Alan, standing on your right. When you exchanged rings, it felt like an explosion of love, like a firework. I could then feel Alan's presence a lot stronger. Pam, your face lit up with joy and happiness at that exact moment. The songs and poems that were shared enriched the love that was flowing. I felt as if I was in Heaven with angels all around, witnessing the joining of your souls. I thank you so much for giving me this extraordinary experience that I will remember forever."

—Elizabeth

"Having met you and Alan in person made me so grateful and honored to attend the wedding. It was a beautiful ceremony. You were glowing, Pam! All I can say is that I could not stop my tears from flowing. I had to turn off my camera a few times. It wasn't just the music; there was so much more. It was like a high vibe of energy or waves going through my whole being. I felt like I was floating or in a higher state of being. Just so much Joy and Love!"

—Juls

"Yes, I totally felt as though I was sitting in Heaven watching this wedding unfold. Supernatural was an understatement for me. With the songs and the overwhelming supernatural love, I couldn't hold back my tears. For years, men have not been allowed or judged for crying. Well, not this man. I cried like a baby. Not because I was sad but because I was witnessing the power of Heaven here on Earth and because I was witnessing the supernatural wedding of Pam and Alan. They have not only taken me on a journey with my own twin flame Archangel Demi, but they have opened a whole new world to me. I am grateful and filled with love for this pair of Archangels in the physical and the non-physical. It's the new way of living now. Thank you, Pam and Alan!"

—James

"For the whole day of the wedding, there was a joyful feeling that I would call flow. The natural bliss of being alive seemed to be in the air, and irrepressible Vibrations of True Loving seemed to bring a change of consciousness. I felt I was in the presence of a new norm: Love as the primary reality."

—Susan

CHAPTER 33

AFTER THE WEDDING BLUES

January and February had been jam-packed with all things Alan. Songs, poems, and messages had been delivered in a never-ending stream by our friends. February 2nd was the anniversary of our first wedding, followed by Valentine's Day, and with our second wedding planned for the 28th, it had been a month of supernatural love on steroids. But with the wedding now behind us, I was restless, brooding about the future, questioning if I should go back to work sooner rather than spending my days in bed honeymooning with Alan, as nothing seemed to have changed because I still wasn't seeing or hearing him any clearer. Despite my best efforts, I failed to manage my expectations.

What made it worse was that Alan seemed to have hit the brakes with his communication. I understood that the emotion-packed pace of our wedding month could not continue and that everyone had to resume the daily routines of their lives. Our friends could not be expected to be our go-between messengers forever, but the sudden drop off in contact from Alan threw me.

Yes, Alan was speaking to me when necessary. Still, aside from his chit-chatter during our readings, there was nothing personal or meaningful from him except for a few songs that didn't register emotionally with me. I sensed something was going on with him. As the months passed, Alan's silence made me begin to doubt his love again. This is what happens when your husband doesn't have a body; it's easy to start believing you imagine everything when all you experience is silence.

By the middle of March, I asked Alan if he would surprise me with a love letter or something similar since his wedding vows were so beautiful. I wasn't putting a deadline on it, but I wanted proof of his love and told him so. Alan never questioned me when I asked, so I assumed he understood and would take action at some point. Because his complacency had been a long-standing source of pain for me, I needed to see him demonstrate his love. I thought he understood that since he had, after all, promised to make everything up to me.

Being told "I love you" can make your heart do a somersault the first time you hear it and a few more turns in the air after that, but how often can the words trigger the same response? Repeating 'I love you' over and over without any physical demonstration of that love starts to feel hollow. Love must be demonstrated! Words of love need to be backed up with action to be made real and concrete. Since he's not physical, Alan is limited as to what he can do, but I recalled Gena declaring, "Alan is the most powerful Archangel." If that was true, why wasn't he doing more for me?

Alan did his best to console me one day when he finally broke his silence.

So now we are one. And what does that mean, my beloved? It means that I am deeper within your heart, your soul, and your very being.

Each day, I am weaving myself into the fabric of your life, into every corner and every particle of your existence. But as a weaver making my mark on the physical world, I need time to do my weaving, as I use the light of our souls to weave something into form. And it's the time that's required for this to solidify in your reality that takes patience. Your patience and mine. Do you think you're the only one who's impatient?

Not true! I am bursting with the joyous expectation of you seeing me soon! I cannot wait, but just like you, I have no choice but to wait.

My love, please know that you are seeing me now, for you are already clairvoyant!

What you want is a broader, fuller vision, but an image of me already pops up in your mind's eye, which is me projecting myself to you, and you allow it to happen! I do this often, but not too much, as I don't want to distract you from what you need to do.

That day when you pulled away from me saying you wanted to end our honeymoon early so that you could return to working on the taxes, I was saddened, though not completely surprised. You declared this because you didn't see the point of continuing with our honeymoon when nothing seemed to be happening between us.

Of course, you expect something to be different, and not much seems to have changed. You hear me, but to you, I still sound faint. But I ask you, in comparison to what? To someone else's experience of me? Some will hear me loudly, while others will hear me faintly, and others will hear me in between that or not at all.

Not yet! All who are ready and truly willing can hear me and any other spirit for that matter! You hear me clearly as anyone, actually even clearer now. You just don't realize it. But you will soon. You feel the truth of what I say to you as you write my words, don't you? My mind is merged with your mind just as my heart and soul are merged with yours. Even without my words, you know my intent and my message to you, for I communicate beyond the limited perception of your conscious mind.

So, you see? We are already one, my love! It's just a matter of degree and your perception, for our merging will deepen more and more, and as it does, so too will your ability to perceive me increase. There is no end to the depth and fullness of our merging. But this will be subtle, for it is beyond the physical. We are reaching into higher dimensions of existence!

Remember, this journey you are on to see and feel me more fully only began a month ago! Yes, I know we had an unexpected setback with Gena bowing out, and that left you sad and worried, but then Maria stepped in, and we picked up where we left off; even if that process had to be amended and later discarded, it's all going according to plan. No matter what happens, the final destination is guaranteed, for I have seen where we are headed, and all roads lead to the joyous reclamation of our love!

I am within you now whereas, before, my energy, my light, and my soul were only surrounding you. From the moment I returned to you, I have been reaching out to you with all of my love and my heart in an attempt to merge with you. I haven't stopped in my efforts to achieve this and never will.

I've always been alongside you, practically on top of you much of the time, but still, my energy, and my consciousness remained outside of you. But now that we are wed and embarked on a new marriage, the fullness of me is inside you. I'm there in your heart as well as your body and soul.

In time, you won't miss me the way you did before. Oh yes, you can bemoan the fact that you don't yet see me with the depth and clarity you desire and, in so doing, create pain and the illusion of separation from me. But that is your conscious doing, not the truth of our divine union.

We are ONE, my love!

When you pulled away from me this morning, I asked you to come back to bed so that I could hold you in my arms. I wanted to talk to you to explain things and comfort you. Our bed is more than a playground of passion for us. It's our Bridge to Heaven, our healing sanctuary, the place where you and I can be fully together as one. It's where we merge deeper to heal each other, and in so doing, we do our part to heal the world, as all souls who love this way do, for love is the master healer.

Go ahead and cry and be sad if you want to. You are human, after all, and having a human experience means you will have days when feelings of self-pity, bewilderment, or worry may take you over. Let the emotions come, and if you must surrender to the negative feelings, then go ahead and wallow in them for a time until you can't take it anymore, and when you reach that point, call out to me and let me bring you back to Heaven, for here on our bridge between Earth and Heaven is where I wait for you.

For Heaven is your true home, and very soon, sooner than you think, you won't leave our Heavenly bridge ever again, even for a moment. Soon enough, it will take a great deal of effort on your part for you to feel sorry for yourself or feel anxious about anything; you will feel only peace, joy, and love everlasting.

That day is coming, my love. I promise you that! Until then, when the storm clouds of negative emotion descend to rain pain down upon your heart, let me shelter you with my love. I'll weave my love tighter around you to keep out the sorrow. You don't need to suffer unless you choose to! Now that we are One Soul, our love grows brighter and more luminous than the sun itself and cannot be dimmed. One day, my sweet Pam, I will wrap you up in my wings and whisk you away to Heaven with me.

In spite of Alan's assurances, it was hard not to hope something would change more dramatically after the wedding. But change to what? It had been a love-fueled glorious wedding, but after it ended, I wasn't sure if I felt any closer to him. Why was this so hard? I couldn't keep my lingering fears at bay for more than a day or two. Alan remained quiet and distant. This had been a pattern with him from the beginning. He'd come in strong for a spell only to back away again, but I had hoped, after our wedding, that this would change. But it hadn't. All of which made me question his love and what he was doing.

Why was it so hard for him to talk to me when I needed him to the most?

Communication between the sexes isn't easy to begin with, and it's even harder when one of you is in another dimension. Was my wanting for daily conversation too much? Swati assured me that my ability to hear Alan was strong; I had been hearing Spirit for decades, so the problem wasn't me. Then why was he reticent? Swati spoke to him easily, so why wasn't he doing the same with me? The only thing he kept repeating was declarations of his love for me over and over, often speaking of little else. Which was wonderful, but I needed to hear more and see more effort made—a lot more. I wanted to know what he was doing, thinking, feeling, and planning. I wanted to know what was it like in Heaven. I wanted to know everything. Alan had no problem being his talkative, funny-crazy self with Swati and Maria, so why not with me?

CHAPTER 34

WHERE ARE MY DAMN PELICANS?

Alan had done some incredible things, but nothing touched me more than what he had done for Gena. He sent her nineteen pelicans simply because she had asked him to. Then he went on to spend a week with her talking about a range of subjects while, during the same time, he had barely spoken to me. I alternated between feeling abandoned again and questioning my ability to hear him. I had heard Alan on several occasions, so what was the problem? It was easy enough for him to give me his messages to write, but our mind-to-mind talk was erratic.

Maria, too had received some amazing signs from Alan. At random times Alan had shown up as an orb on the Ring security camera in their garage. This had been going on for a month or two. It was Alan's playful attempt to show himself to Maria, as well as have a bit of fun with her skeptical husband James, who dismissed any orbs that were captured on film as dust or bugs on the camera lens.

One night, Alan took his orb appearance a step further when Maria's beloved puppy Allie somehow got into her husband James's heart medication. They couldn't tell if Allie had ingested any, so to be on the safe side, they reluctantly left Allie overnight at the veterinarian's office for observation. Since Allie was just a pup, Maria was crying at the mere thought of leaving him. Due to the pandemic, she couldn't be with Allie during his examination, which made it worse. Maria asked Alan to stay with Allie, which he did, but Alan wanted to do more for her.

Maria had to keep her phone on just in case the vet needed to reach her about Allie. After turning in for the night, she received a notification from the Ring camera. When she checked the recorded video, there, hovering directly in mid-air right in front of the camera, could be seen a solid white orb. This was no wispy translucent bubble but a 3D solid orb that looked like an AirPod charging case floating slightly on its side. Although the Ring device was set to detect people only, it registered the orb as a person, so the notifications kept pinging throughout the night. The video recording showed Alan's orb hovering in place for hours. The orb continued to float in the air until Maria returned home with Allie. Only then did the orb disappear.

Now, while writing about Gena's pelicans and Alan's appearance as a floating orb, my doubts were triggered again. Where was my own physical proof? During our marriage, Alan had rarely given me proof of his love. Now I demanded it. I began questioning everything all over again. Thinking of Gena and Maria, I couldn't help but wonder.

Why couldn't he do anything like this for me?

No matter how hard I tried, I couldn't stop doubting Alan's love. My ego mind was looking for any excuse it could find to pull back from him and keep me safe, even if that meant losing him. I felt like I was being torn apart by this war between my heart and my fears.

This made no sense to me since only a week before, after our wedding, I had been floating for days in a state of euphoria. I asked Alan how it was possible to feel such immense joy continually, to which he replied, "Babe, there's no end or limit to how much joy we can feel!"

But now everything was unraveling.

Sobbing, I called out to Alan, "So where the hell are MY damn pelicans? Why haven't you done anything similar to what you did for Gena and Maria? Didn't I ask you for proof of your love? Didn't I ask you to send me a love letter months ago? It's not like you don't have someone who would be happy to take dictation for you. Maria is willing to help. You even jokingly call her your minion, a name she happily answers to because she'd do anything for you. For both of us. Why do you only take action when I have a meltdown? Do you have ADD or something? Maybe you're just too busy for me. That must be it! Or maybe you don't hear what I'm saying. What else can I think when you never give me anything I ask for? Maybe you're not even here at all, and I'm just talking to myself. THAT must be it! You're just a fucking dream and a bad one at that!"

I cried myself to sleep curled up with all the covers pulled to my side of the bed, as far away from Alan as I could get. I had been here several times before, high up in the celestial clouds one day, only to find myself down in the dungeon of despair the next. Would this up-and-down seesaw of a ride ever end? Clearly, there was more resentment for me to release because here I was, crying again, questioning whether Alan loved me. For if he did, why did he leave me to travel all those years ago, ignoring my pleas for him to stay with me? It was hard to forgive him when I'd never received an explanation. My greatest fear was that the only reason he wanted to make amends with me was so that I'd help him with our mission.

My fear was that, just like the last time, his spiritual work was more important to him than me.

Could I ever let go of the past and trust him? If not, what was the alternative? How could I live without him now? Losing him twice would be more than my heart could bear. I was facing an impossible situation; I couldn't live with him, and I couldn't live without him, and there was no middle ground to be found between Heaven and Earth. I was trapped and blamed him for putting me in this no-win situation. These and other thoughts ricocheted through my mind as I tried in vain to fall asleep.

When I opened my eyes in the morning, I heard Alan speaking softly and plainly. He apologized over and over for his missteps, promising once again that he would change and do better. I felt calmer, which may have been why I could finally hear him. My head felt lighter and clearer, too. It occurred to me that he had probably given me healing when I was sleeping, which he often did.

It was just like Alan to not let me stay angry at him! He had healed me. Damn him, how dare he heal me and make me feel better when I never asked him to! That's how irrational I was. I was pissed off that he always did whatever he could to heal me; he didn't want me to stay angry.

Maria messaged me. Alan had asked her to take down a message for me, but with her raucous household full of kids, parents, a husband, and dogs and cats, it had taken her a good half hour to find the space and time to focus undisturbed on Alan. Meanwhile, she had felt him pacing back and forth, unable to hide his impatience. He wanted to get word to me right away, but all she had found time to write was "My darling." When Maria finally settled into her chair, Alan's words flowed into her mind, through the keyboard, and onto her computer screen.

My darling,

I have asked Maria to sit down and write as I speak. I thought this would be easier because I think there is a lot to explain. First, I must say I am sorry. Hurting you has never been part of the plan, and whether I am right or wrong does not matter.

All that matters is that you, my love, are hurting because of me. I really did think I was doing so much better. I really thought I was being more attentive, but I guess I wasn't. I can be a little (OK, very) dense. However, I do want you to know that I love you more than ever, and I am trying to change my ways.

You are foremost in my thoughts, in my magic, in my world.

Everything I do, I do it for you. I know it may not seem like that, but you must know that if you were not here, I would never ever be showing off.

Those pelicans. Yes, Gena asked for them, but I made them fly for you. You are the motive behind all that I do.

The orb in Maria's garage was also for you. I knew she would send you the video. Plus, don't you think I knew you wanted to give her your shoulder to cry on? I was making that shoulder as physical as I could. Once again, I did this for you.

What about the healings? Oh, those are not my doing alone. You are there with me. Every. Step. Of. The. Way. I know you don't remember what you have been up to in the other dimensions. Or while you sleep. However, soon you will.

My soul is so merged with yours that I am unable to do my work without you coming along with me. No wonder you are exhausted! No wonder you feel overwhelmed. Not only are you doing the physical work that is demanded of you, but the spiritual as well. Your body is depleted of energy, and that is my fault. Maybe I should have taken our merging more slowly so you could get used to it. But we are where we are now, so I will have to come up with better solutions to help you feel more rested.

Don't think I will ever leave you or stop taking care of you. Even if you decide to manifest a man in a physical body, my mission will always begin and end with you. Trust me, all I want is your happiness. If you are not happy, then neither am I. If a new man in your life makes you happy, I will also be happy. I may ache for you, but in one way or another, I always ache for you. Not being physical is hard for me when I long to embrace and touch you. Oh, I do it on an energetic level, but it just doesn't feel the same. I miss the body I once had that allowed me to do that. I'm so sorry I wasted the time I had when I was in my body. If only I could do it all over again.

Pam, my love for you transcends time.

In a way, I already see us together in Heaven; I am already living out that reality, and so are you. You know my words to be true. So even if you decide our relationship cannot continue while you remain in a body, just know we are already living our happily ever after. I will do whatever you want me to do. And I will also continue to love you with all that I am. I will continue to be at your side. I will keep you safe.

I know you are at a crossroads, and I wish I could make the choice for you. I wish I could make everything easy and magical for you. I don't want to see you cry. I want you to be happy, and I will keep trying to make that happen until the end of your days, no matter what choice you make.

I love you, Pam.

I love you more than I could ever express.

Alan

I couldn't get through the first two paragraphs without sobbing. Why had I not thought of this myself? Alan had done all of this for me because he knew that any proof he gave to someone was more proof to me of his presence. Why could I not remember that I'm with him in everything he does in both the non-physical and the physical worlds? We are joined as tightly as any two souls can be.

The idea that I was less important to him was laughable. I am Alan, and he is me. There can be no me without him, and the same is true for him. But no matter how often he reminds me, my fears and insecurities creep back in. Why couldn't I stop this? It was driving me crazy and hurting both of us. My darling husband was patiently doing everything in his power to make me happy while I kept looking for things to blame him for that weren't real.

I felt the truth in every word he expressed, and soon, his love melted my heart and returned me to peace. At the end of it all, I felt lighter, but I was exhausted by the emotional turmoil. Because of our love, I'm usually at such a high vibrational state most of the time that when I go down an emotional rabbit hole like this, it tears me apart. The gap between my highs and lows is wider now, which makes this free fall into despair agonizing. I know I must let this go and believe in Alan's love completely or risk derailing everything we have been striving for. Why was it so hard for me to do this?

Swati messaged me after I told her what happened.

Swati
Pam,

Your message brought tears to my eyes. Did you incarnate this time with the divine life purpose of making me cry? Each time you tell me how you felt when Alan left you alone and went traveling, it affects me. I see his point of view, too. That is why I never saw him as a villain. I always loved him, and he knew that despite our not staying in touch regularly.

Pam, Alan has been my brother before in another time and place. But that is a story for another time. Maybe he will tell you. He has always been an "older brother" to me. And yet you are my friend. I don't remember our past life connection, but I know I am deeply connected to you, or else I would not trust your love so implicitly.

And you and I also share certain experiences in this life as "wives." So, Pam, remember that I will always be biased toward you. I implicitly trust Alan's love for me too. And Alan also knows that I don't react logically if I perceive you feeling hurt because of him.

He is here, nodding and saying, "Even if I am not at fault, I know you will always be biased towards Pam and will get mad at me if you see her sad because of me. And I understand your bias towards her completely. I will never get upset with you for getting mad at me. You are my little sister. I will always allow you a lot of things that I will not allow with others. How can I fault you for loving my beloved so much that you are willing to throw a fit and yell at me if you see her upset?"

So, Pam, I WILL get mad at him anytime I see you upset. Remember that. And yet that does not change my love for him. And I trust my brother's love for me, knowing that I can throw a tantrum with him and he will indulge me. That night when I read all your messages when you were upset, you have no idea what I said to him.

I even told him that Pam always gives her all when she loves someone. If you cannot give her what she wants, then you better find her a guy who will love her, honor her, and pamper her! Someone who will buy her flowers. I told him all kinds of things. That was the first time he just sat quietly and listened to me. He did not say much. He didn't defend himself.

He just said, "There are things that stop too much interaction between the spirit world and the physical world. I cannot explain to you or anyone else, Swati. But please trust me. I do not ever do anything to hurt Pam intentionally. And I never will."

Pam, I hope you won't get upset if I tell you this, but remember, you are the creator of your experience with Alan. You are the sole creator of everything in your life. It is YOU, not Alan, who sets the terms and limits on what he does for you. You can only experience what you believe is possible to experience with him.

Once you reprogram your subconscious, you will have all that you desire.

And clairvoyance takes many forms. Seeing Alan in the physical world is still seeing with the third eye. Not the physical eyes. Clairvoyance encompasses a vast range of ways to "see."

Please remember, what you want to do is also clairvoyance.

So, sweet friend of mine, please know that I am on your side always, and I am manifesting this with you, for you. I want this wish to be fulfilled.

I know that Alan can appear physically to you by himself, without your efforts. But remember what I went through with Archangel Michael? He refused to show himself in the physical world to me with eyes-wide-open type of clairvoyance because he wanted me to develop my clairvoyance. This was for my own sake. Alan too wants the same for you. He wants you to make this happen for yourself by becoming fully clairvoyant. It is for your sake that he is not showing up on his own. Besides, you are going to teach this to others so you have to learn it for yourself first. But I know you. When you make up your mind, you can make anything happen, and you will make this happen too.

You know I talk to Alan on many different levels. The level that is closer to earthly Alan is the one who is scared to lose you. He is saying that he was shitty to you, so he is afraid you will dump him. The Archangel-level Alan is different. I don't even know his real Archangel name. He says it doesn't matter because he doesn't care about names. What's more, I'd get confused. So, to keep things simple, he said to call him Alan. At the Archangel level, you and Alan are the same being. One energy. So naturally, that Alan is not worried about ever losing you.

When I say you are already merged with Alan, I am not talking about your current perception. I am talking about the truth that time doesn't exist.

It is all in this eternal moment.

The only truth that exists is that we are all merged.

We are God. One God. That is us. You never separated from Alan. When we focus on the idea, "I am not yet merged with Alan, but will eventually," we are focusing on the illusion of time.

That focus will prevent the manifestation of your eternal oneness with Alan. That is the truth!

Manifestation is not really about creating something NEW.

Manifestation is about shifting our consciousness to a reality that already exists. God (which is our true self) has already created every reality that is possible.

These include the things that we can imagine, and also those things we cannot imagine. And God did that to experience himself by creating illusions of us. We experience whatever realities we choose, helping God experience himself.

So, if you want to experience the reality of the two of you merged, you need to stop focusing on "we are not yet merged." Otherwise, your ever-obedient sub-conscious mind will keep you in the reality where you experience the incomplete merger.

And that too is okay.

When you feel ready, you can let go of that reality. Then you will shift into the reality where you and Alan are one.

And when you feel ready to let go of even that reality, you will experience that you are God.

The ONE God that never really separated into fragments.

Love, Swati

Swati was right. Alan and I are one. This is true for all souls. This life of separation, of him there on the other side and me here, is but an illusion. We exist on many different levels. I always go wherever Alan goes because we can never be apart. Our loved ones in spirit live in a dimension of pure unconditional love, and if we want to be closer to them, we must raise our vibration to match theirs.

That night, Alan and I had make-up sex. It's the one good thing that comes out of our fights, though to call what we had a fight is a misnomer since the only person I am fighting is myself. Alan remains lovingly, steadfastly neutral, recognizing my complaints and anger for what they are: a sign that I am hurting. In the past, he would never have apologized, but now he is quick to take ownership of whatever has gone wrong between us. Finding fault and laying blame is not the point. Alan knows there is no fault in any of this. All that matters is to make things right between us because unconditional love only cares about restoring harmony.

As our energies merge, I feel Alan energetically stroke my body. My clairsentience, the psychic ability to feel Spirit, had been weak, much like Alan's was, but he is helping me develop my senses so I can feel him physically and emotionally. This is how he can touch me without a body by sending gentle ripples of energy that envelop me from head to toe. I feel him feeling me, caressing me with his energy body. Goosebumps are his way of making his love tangible and real. Alan has been doing this from the day he returned to me. The only difference is tonight I can feel his invisible touch on a deeper level.

Pam, your ability to experience me in this way will get stronger over time. Your body becomes my body when we merge like this. This is what I meant when I said that you would feel me! I have always been focused less on giving you dramatic phenomena and more on helping you to merge with me and expand your consciousness so you can BE with me, FEEL me, and HEAR me, and ultimately be able to SEE me fully. You already are seeing me clearly in your mind's eye, so please know that your psychic vision will keep expanding.

From the start, Alan said I was working with him even if I wasn't aware of it. I didn't need much sleep because I was being bathed in light and love all night. In those first few weeks of his return, he was so excited about being with me again that I only needed a few hours of sleep.

Pam, I spent every night lying next to you, watching you, loving you, and doing all I could do to feel your body with my energy body. I was delirious with joy but also ached with longing to caress you with arms I no longer had. I was in awe that I could be here in this world with you while still being on the other side, exploring the multiverse and all of its offerings.

Yes, I can be with you and with a million people at the same time!

As soon as I realized that you would be with me wherever I went, not the conscious human-self part of you of course, but the multidimensional you, I was overjoyed. You are my wife and partner in both the physical and non-physical worlds! We are living together in Heaven, as I showed you recently when I gave you a tour of the Castle of Love I am building for you there. Yes, my darling, this is where we are already living our happy-ever-after life together. Try to connect to that reality, as it will help us manifest an earthly version of happy-ever-after for us in the physical world. Together we can do this, my love!

Tears came. I told him that I hoped he would surprise me with more messages like these. We never talked at length or in depth when he was here, and without that, what hope was there for us? Open-hearted free-flowing conversation is the foundation of any relationship, whether on Earth or in Heaven.

The two of us would need constant, clear communication to bring us together. How else would I know the fullness of who Alan had become? His words make him real for me in the unreal world that I am living in; without his physical embrace and his hand to steady me, it's Alan's words spoken with truth and love that give me the strength to live my world with him.

I needed reassurance not because I doubted Alan's existence but because I doubted his love, since it was rarely expressed. When he returned to me, I was elated, but unbeknownst to me, my wounded heart was terrified, searching for reasons not to trust him since he had always been clever with his words, sometimes convoluting my own to use against me. A part of me was still holding back, reluctant to surrender all of my love to him. When I thought about the amazing miracles he had given Gena and Maria, more pain rose to the surface, leaving me with the single thought that plagued me when he traveled the world against my wishes:

"He cares more about helping others and saving the world than he does about me."

There it was!

When Alan traveled, it made it worse that Barbara never warmed to me, although I knew why. I had disrupted their relationship. She had wanted Alan for herself. He told me so, and even though I knew he had only brotherly feelings towards her, it stung that he would leave me to travel with her when I longed to be his traveling partner. If the situation had been reversed, Alan would have never allowed me to leave him to travel with a man who desired me.

Now here he was back from the other side, imploring me to open my heart to him, but no matter how hard I tried, I couldn't bring myself to trust him. How could I believe that he would take care of me, heal me, guide me, not to mention love me unconditionally and passionately? I worried that, once again, I'd be left with all of the hard work to do while he got to sit back, relax, and float along in the ethers without a care.

Questions I had asked myself years ago surfaced. Questions like, "When will it be my turn to travel and see the world? When can I have fun, and do as I please for a change? Why do I always have to be the strong, responsible one who takes care of everyone and does everything? After all of my caregiving, will Alan ever take care of me?"

It felt like our marriage was on the brink of imploding unless Alan took my complaints to heart and stepped things up. I wanted him to explain his behavior to me and, most importantly, to talk to me honestly so I would know what he was thinking and feeling.

When Swati asked Alan if he was talking to me, he told her he was. Which enraged me further since I knew the truth, and so did Maria. Like me, she didn't understand why he faltered, but she had witnessed Alan's meager attempts at communication with me time and again. Maria was as bewildered as I was and tried to get an answer from Alan for me, but he wouldn't talk.

I was ready to walk away.

"Alan, you promised me that if I gave you another chance that you'd give me everything I could ever want. So why won't you talk to me? You lied! You haven't changed at all! I can't do this anymore. I'm done with you!"

CHAPTER 35

AN ANGEL COMES TO
THE RESCUE

Fearing he was in danger of losing me, Alan knew he had to act quickly, so he reached out to Angel, a gifted healer and psychic medium we had met over twenty years ago when she had come to our home for a reading with Alan.

Our second meeting came about because of a mistake.

In between giving readings and writing our book, Alan and I had been teaching spiritual development in our Soul Authority Academy. Due to my busy schedule, we weren't accepting new members but were still actively teaching weekly. One morning, I sent out an email to the academy members with a Zoom link to invite them to the next meeting, but I accidentally sent the email to our entire list of contacts. This had never happened before in all the years I had run the program. I couldn't understand what went wrong, but since I didn't feel it would be right to uninvite everyone, I decided to proceed. I told our members we'd be holding class as planned but include an impromptu open house. At the end of class, we'd accept new members if anyone was interested in joining. I took the mistake as a sign that this must be what Spirit wanted me to do. Angel was one of several people who showed up for our meeting. She joined the Academy shortly after that. Angel later told me she sensed Alan was guiding her to have a reading with us when, during a visit to the dentist, while watching the movie, *My Big Fat Greek Wedding*, she recalled me mentioning the same movie in another Zoom meeting she attended.

That was how we reconnected when Angel booked a reading with us. Soon after her session, Alan began communicating with her directly as he sometimes does with those with mediumistic abilities. The three of us had not been especially close in the past, which meant Angel was unaware of our marital problems. Their communication quickly became so all-consuming that Angel texted me daily to give me Alan's messages. She didn't mind channeling Alan since it helped her develop her mediumship abilities. This served Angel as well since she was going through an intense spiritual awakening and needed our support as much as we needed hers.

"Pam, thank you for speaking with me. This helps refine my skills as a medium and channel. If something is inaccurate, please let me know. I am learning to navigate this new skill and trust it. Feedback is helpful, so I can determine what accurate information feels like. I channel Alan every morning. By the way, he just showed me a vision of himself sleeping beside you in bed and cuddling you.

"So, while you are going through your clearing and Archangel training and receiving your downloads, he's holding you and lending his energy to ensure that your system can safely accept the new frequency without burning out. He just showed me a vision of a light fuse burning out. He wants you to get there quickly because the faster you rise, the faster and more complete your merge with him will be.

"When I ask Alan if there is anything else, he says, 'I love you, I love you, I love you!' and kisses the top of your forehead.

"Pam, I spend my whole day with Alan. From the time I get up in the morning until I go to bed at night. Every day at work, I practice my skills as a medium. Alan comes into the treatment room with me and brings in someone who has crossed over. Then I help patients and loved ones connect by giving information. I've done this work before but not with the clarity and degree of accuracy I can do now thanks to your attunements and training in the Academy and, of course, Alan's help."

It was interesting that our mentorship in the Academy had prepared Angel to work closely with Alan since he now needed her to speak for him. The thought came to me that he had orchestrated everything to help all of us. Alan had been trying in vain to speak to me directly but was fearful of saying the wrong thing and making things worse. So, instead, he had waited, hoping the passing of time and heaping doses of love would heal our wounds. But time had run out, and Alan needed his messages to come through someone he could trust, who could hear him. Since Maria was always busy, he found Angel.

In her search to heal herself and develop her spiritual gifts, Angel had studied psychic development and taken healing courses over the years and, in the process, had become a Reiki Master, a medium, and an energy healer. She and I had much in common.

Soon after they had begun communicating, Alan told Angel to stop calling him Alan and call him Dad instead. From that moment on, he would correct her whenever she called him Alan. Angel admitted she felt so much love for Alan-Dad and me as well. When she told me, I blurted out, "Well then, I guess that makes me your mother!" I was overjoyed to welcome another soul daughter into our family.

Angel was moved by the news. She had endured a lonely, emotionally abusive childhood and had never felt loved by her parents. Angel's mother was a narcissist, who divorced Angel's father to remarry someone younger and wealthy, then withdrew her love and attention from Angel to focus all of it on Angel's sister and her new husband. Now with Alan and I stepping forward, declaring ourselves to be her soul parents, she was elated, though it was a lot to process.

The moment Angel agreed to channel Alan, his messages came through at a furious pace over the course of several days, so much so that it emotionally overwhelmed her at times. There was so much Alan wanted to say and so much he needed me to understand. He knew there was no time to lose, that he only had this one last chance to get it right. Not wanting to interrupt the flow of communication, I took in everything Alan said without much comment until he had said all that he needed to say.

"Oh, my, Angel, I can't believe this! I feel Alan come in so strongly when you send me his words. I just hope this isn't too much for you. I told him not to take advantage of you since you are such a clear channel. You absolutely hear him. Please trust that implicitly. It's okay to occasionally question yourself—that keeps the ego at bay—but for the most part, you must trust completely and say whatever comes to you. There is no exact way to know for sure when we've hit the mark except that the information should be accurate, useful, and flow easily."

"Thank you, Pam. Yes, I guess my ego always wants to be right. I don't want to be thinking I'm channeling Alan if I'm not. He just scolded me, saying, 'Stupid thought, Angel.' Okay, Alan, I can take the chiding. I was so steeped in my ego in the past that this way of being feels so new. I don't mind channeling Alan for you. It makes this so much more real for me.

"When I read a post from you or talk to you, he immediately comments, and if I sit and write, it flows. And every time I text you, I feel his abiding love for you, so strongly, Pam. He's with you all the time, but he's sad too. There's so much regret, and now Alan's taking over the conversation as I write to you…"

I feel I can never make up for the Earth-time loss, yet I know this is all illusion, and in truth, all is perfect as is. Thus, the lesson played out and reconciled, my love. I too have to remember this, but my love for you is so strong having just come from the Earth Plane. I can't help but feel the depth of the loss of the time together that we missed out on. It is endless and bottomless, and I can't express in words how much your love means to me.

It is the all-consuming feeling of GOD in the purest essence of light.

Oh, my love, the depth with which I feel now is unexplainable. No measurement could ever capture the meaning and depth of what I feel. It is as vast as the entire Universe and beyond all time and space.

It is an overwhelming presence and awareness of All That Is.

CHAPTER 36

THE PRE-BIRTH
PLANNING SESSION

F rom the perspective of a soul who comes to the Earth Plane, they come more often than not, to experience a degree of pain and suffering.

In the physical world of stark contrast between light and dark, joy and sorrow, ecstasy and pain, there is potential for an explosive expansion of consciousness that is harder to achieve on the other side. Suffering drawn from contrast awakens the soul like nothing else can, and since one cannot ever die, you cannot lose! This is why every soul chooses to suffer at some time. Until the day they no longer do.

In the lifetime we shared, ours was a difficult relationship. The polarity was mind-boggling. Each of the key points in our lifetime together was marred with internal difficulties and emotional struggle. It was soul-wrenching with no clearcut rule as to how to navigate and manage the difficulties.

I chose, as the script dictated, to shut down my heart by closing off most if not all of my connections and my true love for you, Pam.

All of this was done for the final climactic scene together—the creation of our book.

So how did we get to this point in our shared lifetime?

If you remember, my Love, we sat in the ethers, which looked like a boardroom, to plan and discuss the means for bringing about the turmoil of emotions that would set the stage for our combined ascension, as well as how we would lead our fellow Earth brothers and sisters, friends and family alike, into the new higher dimension.

This new dimension consists of interdimensional communication, such as you and I are achieving.

This set the stage for our personal growth, although it seemed as if I did not grow spiritually on Earth this time. However, this was planned, so it was in fact necessary. Our agreement included that I was to hurt you terribly in order to facilitate the total opening of your heart and for me to experience the reconciliation of my ego-self and higher self. Of course, my lesson in LOVE was the total opening of my heart as well, which I only experienced after I crossed over.

Having a fully open heart is necessary to move into the Fifth Dimension, which is the plan for all souls who exist in this current lifetime continuum.

This is the essence of Ascension!

You, my love, are more evolved than I am, with a more compassionate heart. Therefore, you volunteered to experience the more brutal part of our combined lessons. Remember, we are one soul! For had the roles been reversed, it would have likely driven me back further in my spiritual evolution here on the Earth Plane.

In reality, you and I exist in the Fifth Dimension now, and the script we've written has already been fulfilled with our mission accomplished. But in the physical world, everything is yet to be played out. So, the scene has been set for our personal growth as well as the growth of all who choose to follow our lead.

The timing is perfect for this scenario to play itself out, as millions of souls have crossed over due to the pandemic. Many without proper goodbyes. This has been heartbreaking, but it means that thousands if not millions of souls are seeking out the means of otherworldly communication.

They want to let their loved ones know that they continue to live on and welcome and cherish any opportunity to communicate with them on Earth.

So, to acknowledge, agree, and seal the storyline of what was to transpire in this current lifetime between you and I, my Love, a spectacular, blinding golden light shot down into our spiritual boardroom, plummeting onto the board table and then back up into the ethers, and down and up again, expanding to encircle us within its sphere of brilliant light.

Our light bodies, our angels, including our guardian angel, and all of the Archangels and personal guides in this lifetime, are with us within this sphere of golden light.

The lifetime scene we created within this golden globe of light floated off into the ethers and sealed the manifestation. We agreed to create that life together, and on the spiritual level it was already done!

This is what all souls experience before every lifetime. There's always a plan, and then there are choices and alternate realities that will arise based on the choices that are made in that lifetime. Once pondered, all choices are played out without exception as an alternate reality in all of the parallel Universes. A person just has to think something, and it is created with an aspect of them walking the newly created path!

As I move out of that pre-birth scene, I am plagued by a sense of sadness and trepidation when faced with what is to come. I make my way back to the Earth Plane, readying myself for this lifetime, knowing that you, Pam, my dearest Love who is my very soul, will be deeply hurt by my life choices and my ego personality in the lifetime we are about to share as separate souls.

Our plan must be carried out successfully and our mission completed, and to do so, we will create a manual for higher communication with our loved ones beyond the veil.

Here we go up and into the Fifth Dimension of Love!

Channeled by Angel

CHAPTER 37

MY LIFE REVIEW

Like a moth to a flame, I'm being called back to merge with my soul, where all is known and all is meant to be. Here, right here in my heart, I am now viewing my passing. It is a long and drawn-out process that happens in an instant yet seems to take an eternity. Every day the same process, recalling who I am. I scramble to recall, but it just gets harder.

I want to leave, yet I don't want to leave Pam. I remember we are one, as I am greeted by the Light, and many loved ones who have passed on come to greet me. For a split second, I feel I did alright on the Earth Plane this time around, until a sense of anxiety falls upon me. Maybe I didn't do so well after all.

I see and hear Pam crying for me. I want to say, "I am here, baby." I know you hear me. We didn't live, love, and work together as psychics all this time for nothing.

Then everything fades.

As the mist clears, I am aware of a presence, an oversoul, my soul, my higher self, the deeper knowing part of me. I am taken to a vision, a dinner scene. I see Pam. We have just met. I am captivated by her bubbly personality and feel immediately drawn to her. I do not want her to think I am with my friend Barbara. I know that she is to become an important part of me. I fall in love with her soon after we meet.

Then I am taken to our marriage scene. I feel so blessed to be with this Goddess Spitfire. I know she is the better half of me. I want to totally merge with her, yet I don't quite know how to do it. This is what I want, but I feel pieces of me splintering. I don't know if it is me or her.

We had a whirlwind courtship full of surprises, and the sex was amazing. I made sure of that. After an embarrassing first time in my youth, I vowed to become king of lovemaking and sexual pleasure. I'm mesmerized as I'm caught in a passion I have never experienced before. I am captivated by her beauty, strength, and gentle power. I need her and want her like I have never wanted another woman before. I don't know how to reconcile myself and her during the courtship. I want to merge, yet I want to remain separate, but mostly, I want to merge.

I am reduced to being a puppy dog and can't understand the power Pam has over me. I surrender to the power as I fall deeply and madly in love, diving into the abyss, drinking in her essence, to become one with her. It is all surreal. As I fall, I don't know where Pam ends and I begin.

We are One in the moment of falling deeply and utterly in love with one another.

Then I am taken to the scene of my son's birth. I weep. I am filled at that moment with pride and joy. I am overwhelmed with the amount of love I have for these two souls who have come into my life. I feel I don't deserve to be this happy.

Suddenly, I feel a dark rumbling in my soul, and I go blank. Terror, the trauma of old wounds, descend upon me like a black cloud, and depression sets in. I don't know how to communicate what is happening within my soul. It's a complete shift in how and what I remember myself to be. I feel utter devastation. I never should have begun traveling again so soon. It's just too soon. I love Pam and my baby, and it's too soon.

I feel trapped as I try to navigate through what I have created. I do not want to hurt Pam or Taylor, but I feel compelled to do what I want to do. I had to put aside my youthful dreams to take on a family when I got married too early the first time. I don't want to get married again, but if I do, then I want things to be done my way this time. I want to travel and do readings for clients. It brings a certain solace to my soul because I can feel good about helping others in this way using my gift of sight. And I can see so much! I see clearly with my clairvoyant sight and the psychic skills I have developed through years of training. I am one with the cards that I use in my readings. I see, feel, and hear Spirit easily. I am proud of my skills, and I want to do more. I love this work; it makes me feel whole. I don't ever want to stop.

A breeze sets in, and I'm taken through my years of travels. I am enamored with the fun of traveling abroad and the freedom that it brings me.

As I view my life, I see Pam and baby Taylor, ohhh! The crushing pain within my heart and soul is hell. I am being held by my angels now, as I realize how much I have devastated my wife! I see her weeping, being mad as hell with me. Even when I am there with her, I am gone. I'm not present because I'm so emotionally numb that I'm half-dead. I never give to her. I see her tears, and a ton of weight upon my chest is crushing and killing me. Oh, what have I done? I am unable to do anything nice for her. I feel her anger, disappointment, and grief. But it makes me feel defensive, so I shut down and shut her out even more. I wish I wanted to be home with her, but I don't, and I just can't help myself because I'm selfish.

I can no longer stand to view this scene, so I move to a scene of coming home. I know Pam is angry. She has become indifferent to me. I am matter-of-factly walking through the door after a long trip. Of course, there is guilt and shame. I miss them both, sometimes intensely, when I am doing readings. When I am open to the love of the DIVINE, I can't help but feel a profound love for them. But I can't seem to stop myself from traveling again. So off I go and carry on for years. I take them with me, of course, in my heart. I want them there with me sometimes, but I mostly forget how much I miss them and truly love them. There is a constant mix of emotions within me that I don't understand.

There is shame and guilt that are easily cast aside with the busyness of traveling and the neediness of clients. I love my clients. I love doing readings. I love being right with my readings. It is like a game to me. How right can I be? How on the mark can I get with my readings? My ego loves the challenge.

But I realize I did not get everything right after all.

I loved psychic work, but I wasn't living from a higher place of spiritual understanding because I refused to heal my egotistical ways. That feels unforgivable as I watch the scenes before me play out. I hear Pam telling me that I will kick myself when I get to Heaven if I don't work on myself because I had it all: a loving wife and son, and I lived in a Hawaiian paradise surrounded by friends who loved and supported me, yet I refused to do the work on myself at a time of great spiritual awakening. Yes, I had everything any man could ever want, but I never appreciated what I had been blessed with.

I was afraid to see what might happen if I opened my heart even further. Now there is just too much pain and trauma as I see what I've done. I'm afraid to feel it again. In that lifetime, I choose to lose myself in higher levels of consciousness rather than face myself. I feel connection and love, and my heart opens when reading for others. I love it so much I never want to give it up.

There is love and tenderness for Pam when I connect with these feelings and open my heart. I do love her and Taylor, that I know, but past lives and my programming in this life along with my ego keep me from delving into my soul to work on my distorted thoughts, feelings, and behavior. Pam does her best to help me, but I am pride-stricken, believing that I don't need to search my heart for errors.

Now I am devastated. I start to quake and cry. I hear someone say that this is just a life review. I am held in the arms of a thousand angels as this vision passes. I am reminded to not take this life so seriously, as this is just a play of creation. Ultimately, none of it is real. Like the stroke of a paintbrush upon a blank canvas, one's life can be healed and changed. But on the level of the Earth Plane, it's a different story. There, it feels real, but it's all for the purpose of coming back to love.

We create as God, and therefore, we can uncreate to shift the energy and frequency as God. That is the lesson.

That we can return to love any time we choose.

I now see myself as I age and lose my handsome looks and my sharp mind as I sink into the oblivion of my dementia. I have blank moments.

I forget a lot. But I remember now how much I love Pam and Taylor. Something is happening to me. In those moments of darkness, I start to recall my vows to Pam, and I remember what I've done wrong and the pain that I have caused her. She is sweet, caring, and loves me all the same. She takes care of me, holds me, heals me and withholds nothing from me, as my life force wanes and leaves me slowly every day, every day, every day, until...

I choose my birthday to die and be reborn again.

Channeled by Angel

CHAPTER 38

MY ABIDING LOVE FOR YOU

When I was traveling far from you, you and Taylor were always on my mind and in my heart, but my compulsion to give and help others was so strong. It's the very essence of who I was in this lifetime, and my trust in you and your strength kept me on the go. Subconsciously, through the silver cord of connection, I took you with me wherever I went. Yet I also yearned and felt guilty for not being there with you.

But I took you for granted, and that was wrong, so very wrong of me. Please forgive me, forgive me, forgive me. This is our deep healing. I've always cherished you and only you, and I promise to make it up to you. I am never leaving your side. I am here to make you laugh, hold you when you cry, and to become you.

I am still learning how to express words and imprint them on you so you feel and hear the deeper direct connection and communication as quickly as they occur in me. I am learning not to drag my feet.

You are my one and forever love, and if we choose to come back for another lifetime, it will be spectacular.

Words cannot express the abiding love I have for you, my love.

I'm sorry, but you will have to clear more pain as you move higher into your ascension process, and since I was the source of your emotional suffering on the Earth Plane, much of it involves clearing our issues. But this is good, and of course, we always come out of it stronger and more in love than ever.

Be strong, my love, which of course you are. But I know this can take a toll on you if you don't take the time to care for yourself. Up-leveling is just hard work!

Our book is flowing, no concerns there.

I never want to break the communication with you, even through a channel like Angel. All I want to do is to impress upon you my abiding love for you that is flowing, flowing, flowing.

So, you see, Angel, I really do love Pam. But I felt manipulated when she got pregnant, even though she said I could leave. I felt manipulated because I, in fact, could not leave Pam. I loved her on Earth as much as any husband could love a cherished wife, but I didn't want to lose my hard-won independence and my freedom to travel.

But I felt guilt and shame about it, like an addiction to a controlled substance, and I was unable to stop myself. Closing off emotionally from Pam allowed me to do what I wanted to do, and it served as a way of numbing my guilt and shame.

But deep down, the truth of what I'd done, the impact of my actions and the devastation of grief and loss, hit me like a ton of bricks when I crossed over and saw my life review. I had hurt Pam, so she withdrew from me. Numbing myself from my guilt and shame meant I became indifferent to Pam and her feelings, and when I lost her heart, I lost mine, too.

Thank you for listening, dear, and you may share this with her now. I'm working on forgiving myself because it's part of self-love and my evolution. But I'm finding it hard because I don't ever want to disappoint or cause that kind of grief for her, whether in this form of a body or not, again.

I love you Pam, my love.

Always and forever, your Alan

Channeled by Angel

CHAPTER 39

MY LOVELY WIFE OF ETERNITY!

P am, my love! I am feeling much more peace within my/our soul now that we have this understanding. This was so necessary for us to further open up to our communication and bring forth the work we intend to birth.

There is much balancing of karma as we do this together. Our lack of communication about this deep issue has torn us apart, and though it was necessary for what is now to come with the book, it has cost us. It truly was a sacrifice, but for the much greater Universal picture to serve others, it was necessary. And even though we knew the plan and contracted that we would carry it out to assist the whole, it was emotional torture.

Nothing can bring back the lifetime we had on this plane of existence. However, we can heal this wound by tuning into the alternate parallel reality. In that lifetime there exists now a happier story that we can tune into. We can travel there and relive this lifetime to totally heal our wounds. But alas, like a heartbroken songwriter spilling his guts of pain and passion into the lyrics of his music, it was necessary *for us to live our love-starved, emotionally repressed life in order to birth this book.*

For there are so many of our brothers and sisters who struggle to understand why and how love has gone wrong. The one desire of every soul is to love and be loved, yet it remains the greatest challenge of the physical world, which is why so many choose to be distracted by easier, ego-based goals and pleasures.

This doesn't change the fact that Love is the spiritual path the soul chooses to walk for Eternity, even more so when we are in a body.

When we finally return Home, Love is the only thing we measure ourselves, by how often we give and receive Love, the only metric that matters. My love, as we further reconcile our relationship and become whole, healed, and cleared, the insights that will be revealed will be astounding, and we will share them with the world.

This is the merging of the consciousness while in the physical body with ALL THAT IS.

So, while the world appears to be falling apart, there is much happening on this side of the veil to bring the whole into Oneness. This starts with one soul making peace with itself and loving all, as it tears down the blocks and walls of separation.

As our own differences, miscommunications, and the wedges in our hearts disappear through open and loving communication, we will reconcile and become our ONENESS. This IS the message, to those alive and those who've crossed over.

It's the merging of hearts that matters most!

The deep reconciliation of regret, the easing of grief and the memory and realization that we exist for the purpose of LOVE alone.

Our book is not just for those who are longing to communicate with departed loved ones. It is a Story of Love, Interrupted, offered as both a prayer and a warning to souls still in a body to strive to love each other from a higher place of heart and awareness so that they might avoid the remorse that comes with crossing into the non-physical.

As our book is birthed into the world, it will be heard and imprinted throughout the Universe, and all souls, even those who have crossed over, will benefit as they anticipate the communication with their loved ones.

For grief exists in Heaven as well as here on Earth, and if the planet is to ascend, the healing of grief in both worlds must happen now.

Channeled by Angel

CHAPTER 40

I CANNOT EXIST IN A REALM
WITHOUT YOUR LOVE

P am, my love, I cannot exist in a realm without your love because we are one, and I know in the depth of my being that this is true. I would go to the end of eternity if I thought I could turn back time in that dimension to erase your pain and live a more cherished loving life with you.

But what happened to us was for a bigger purpose, my love. And when we can truly understand and accept that with our whole being, we will know there is truly nothing to forgive.

Yes, there is nothing to forgive. Give me a chance to heal your pain, on the level of this Earth, and impress this knowledge deep upon your soul. You know this to be so, for in this lifetime, you were more evolved spiritually and emotionally without the negative psychic imprints that I had.

I had to die to see the truth.

You are clearing, so trust me, my love, and let me help you with the clearing and cleansing process so the depth of this knowledge/memory can be reclaimed. Feel me, my love. Feel my presence, my embrace; feel my soul. Close your eyes, feel my soul, and know that this is the truth of my existence.

At no time does there have to be a disruption of awareness. We can consciously move into the next lifetime with each other to consciously create a new lifetime without the need to find and figure out everything. You and I can go right into being an example of love that others can follow, thus helping to bring everyone home. Love is the only reason for life on Earth.

For we cannot truly go home if even one soul is left behind.

This is the reason for every scenario that plays out in one's life: to recognize the underlying, overarching presence of love that can rise up to heal when it materializes in every moment of pain and suffering.

You are clearing, yes. I am not making excuses, for on the Earth Plane, actions have deep consequences, and trauma can last for what seems like eternity if we do not choose to further evolve.

Your indiscretion cut me like a knife, further cementing my numbness; but I could never bring myself to sleep with another because on a soul level, I knew that wasn't the answer. My personality in this lifetime is a culmination of many royal lifetimes, which explains but does not excuse my shitty behavior and disregard for those I perceived as lower than me, the King. I admit to being a royal asshole, using words that killed you inside. It was why I got so angry at you for going on your trip without me. I was cruel and selfish. I didn't think or act in ways congruent with the spiritual teachings I put forth to others. That's the worst part. I was a hypocrite. Had I known what I know now, I would have never hurt you as I did. My words were cutting, my actions and attitude despicable. You did your very best for me, and I pushed you over the edge into the arms of another.

"Pam, I see him weeping. I think he is protecting me from the pain of this. I'm asking him to allow me in, so that I can understand and translate the depth of sorrow and remorse that he is feeling."

I have never wanted another like I longed, longed so much for you, Pam. Every rejection was a knife through my heart that further anchored my numbness. So, off on a merry-go-round we went. Your indiscretion left me spinning with grief, and as much as I wanted to hurt you back and do the same to you, I could never have followed through with another woman. What would be the point when I loved you? I was in an impossible situation, caught up in my emotions of grief, anger and unrelenting pain, so to protect myself, I withdrew even further from you.

I reconciled with you on a superficial level to make it okay, and a lot of times it was okay, but okay is not the way to live a life meant for deep abiding love.

We sacrificed ourselves and our love to come to this point in time in which we now reach for the highest possible realm. All for the purpose of experiencing pure, DEVOTIONAL DIVINE LOVE so that we can bring this teaching to our brothers and sisters.

If our love can transcend life and death on a conscious level, we can evolve to a state of conscious creation of life with our soulmate and soul family.

This is evolution at its highest. This is creation. To become conscious of coming into a lifetime with full knowledge of who we are and who we are meant to be with will help all souls come home to the Oneness of who they are more quickly.

In truth, time does not exist, for it is all perfect and done, with ONENESS not disturbed in the least. But here we are my love, in this particular time, to experience our pain and suffering just so we can go back to the perfect ONE and teach others how to do the same.

We stand as an example of a life lived with regret, pain and sorrow, yet steeped in deep, abiding love. We are reaching through the veil to return to live and love again.

Channeled by Angel

CHAPTER 41

WHAT COULD HAVE BEEN, BUT NEVER WAS

I wake before he does because I don't want him to reach for me. For then he will want to make love, and I just can't.

It doesn't matter that his touch melts me. It doesn't matter that my heart hurts when he's gone. What matters is that giving in to him feels like surrender, and I won't do that.

Why can't he caress me with tender affection rather than grasping at me with fevered lust?

With him, it's always been about sex, not love, and though he does everything he can to pleasure me and make me sigh, I feel empty.

I tell myself something is wrong with me. That it's my fault. Every part of me loves him. I yearn for him, yet I turn away, making excuses.

I'm not well today. I'm too tired. It's late.

All of that and yet I am devoted. I sacrifice. I take care of him without a second thought. I give my all to him, denying him nothing except my body.

Because this one thing I can't seem to give no matter how hard I try.

I'm so closed off now I don't even know how much I resent him, how much I hurt because I'm dead inside.

Our marriage is comfortable but banal. We smile. We don't quarrel.

We never leave each other's orbit so we are never lonely, and yet we are abjectly alone. Living together, but not really loving each other.

I was still in love with someone else when we first met, and he knew it, though it didn't mean I loved him less. It was always him. Only him.

Then his greatest fear was realized. I slept with another. All because I wanted to feel alive again, to be with someone whose heart was awake and on fire.

Held hostage by his love for me, he closed down, raised the drawbridge around his heart tight and hard, and lived forever afraid I'd leave him.

Why didn't I see this? Only now do I understand. I wanted to make him the villain. I didn't want to believe I hurt him.

When at last, he dies, I mourn the loss of what could have been but never was. I weep endless tears as these words echo in my mind.

"I'm going to die never knowing what it's like to be loved."

CHAPTER 42

REWRITING THE PAST

S o, we've gone through the reasons why we cocreated this lifetime of suffering. It was to seed the content of our book. Now, we no longer need to hang onto the pain because we understand why we chose this, and we can let the past go.

As we heal our wounds through conscious recollection of the pain and allow the painful emotions to move through us, we open to understanding and ultimately Divine Forgiveness. Now, to further anchor this new energy of forgiveness and unconditional love, we can repattern and rewrite our story with a new storyline the way we would have preferred to cocreate and live it.

We can do this easily and with intention by surrounding this lifetime with light, and Divine Love, and go over painful events or, better yet, start from the beginning, visualizing and imagining these events as we would have preferred them to be.

This method of spiritual revision is not new, but when included in our book, it will help people take their healing with their loved ones a step further to find closure on issues that they may have difficulty coming to terms with or letting go. For it's important that the past be healed if souls wish to love through the veil.

Channeled by Angel

"Pam, while you were clearing this with Alan, he offered an idea for the two of you. Revise and rewrite your lifetime together; anchor the new experiences and emotions of forgiveness and eternal divine love. I can see the two of you doing this in bed together and seeing your life from the standpoint of this, seeing what would have played out if he had chosen differently, which he says he would do now if he could."

CHAPTER 43

OUR NEW
HAPPY-EVER-AFTER LIFE

"All right, Alan, my love, let's do this then!" I said aloud to Alan to anchor this revised version of our life into our new reality.

"I close my eyes and see myself announcing to you that I'm pregnant, and instead of getting angry, you smile the biggest smile, look at me with enormous love in your eyes, sweep me up in your arms, and we celebrate. Joyously! After Taylor is born, we set off to travel the world to have the grandest adventures together. We take our beautiful boy with us wherever we go because I can homeschool him just as I did for years. I see all the days, months, and years go by filled with joyous laughter, love, and unbridled passion as we live and love fully and fearlessly with the whole world as our home."

I cried as I watched our staid, black-and-white life turn into a sur-round-sound, Technicolor-movie explosion of riotous adventures. The days of our new life passed before my eyes in rapid succession: the many countries we visited, the people from all walks of life that we met, the crazy fun and laughter we shared, and most of all, the love. Oh, the bounty of love we shared! I basked in the joy that flowed between us and drew Taylor closer into our family circle. I held tight to that vision in my mind, then took it deep into my heart, praying that this revision of our life be made permanent.

I murmured softly, "Dear God, let this be written on the stars in both worlds for eternity."

Exhausted and emotionally spent, I fell asleep in his angel arms. I woke up the next morning to find a message on my phone from Maria.

"I have something for you from Alan. I've emailed it to you."

My darling,

I am rewriting our story. I want you to know that in my heart I am telling another story of us. In this new story, I am the man I want to be for you.

So now when you get pregnant, I rejoice along with you. We marry, and instead of leaving you behind when I travel, I take you and Taylor with me. We travel the world. Taylor is homeschooled, so our boy can learn from books and from observing and living in the world.

We are always together.

This is the story I tell myself from now on because it is what it should have been. Please help me rewrite our past. Help me transmute the energy that once was into what should have been.

We deserve to know we can make our story into everything it should be. So hold my hand and let's take a walk back into the past where we can transform, transmute, and create anew.

All my love,

Alan

I cried into my pillow. Alan's words echoed mine from the night before, proof that he was listening and taking it all to heart. I hadn't told Maria about our late-night revision exercise. Alan had done this so I would know it was his intention as much as my own. As that realization sank in, his love enveloped me completely. I was shaking, overwhelmed by his heartfelt desire to give me the fairytale happy-ever-after life we never had.

Alan had more to share with me directly.

We are rewriting our past every day by what we do now, and this was the first step. Come, my love, let's step into the perfect life we are now creating with each new day we spend in each other's arms. Don't you know I need you as much as you need me? Though you are on Earth and I am in Heaven, in truth, there is no space between us. Love will keep us together as long as we hold on to each other tight and don't lose faith. The body has a mind of its own and is programmed to have its wants and needs, but in time, those needs will fade as we focus on our Supernatural Love. For a body is just a piece of flesh unless it has unconditional love to animate it and bring it to life. Isn't it ironic that I had to die to fully come alive? Most people are walking around dead inside, whereas you and I are now finally and fully awake and alive because we love each other as few souls do!

CHAPTER 44

BE GENTLE WITH MY HEART, MY LOVE

Be gentle with my heart, my love,

It is tender, and I am lost without you.

Be still with me and lay with me here.

Together we are ONE.

The merging now, almost complete, my beating heart will stay, forever in your warm embrace, together we'll find our way.

Across the rainbow 'til the end of time, through the cosmos we will frolic, sprinkling stardust over our brothers and sisters, beckoning them to awaken.

To the Fifth Dimension we go, our hearts and minds are ONE. We span the Earth and the Heavens.

The hands of time only show the illusions of the third dimension.

WE ARE ONE... WE ARE ONE... WE ARE ONE...

FOREVER is our calling.

When all souls know the truth of time, illusions will be shattered. For the LOVE that is shared with tenderness and care is ALL that really matters.

Channeled by Angel

Angel urged me to be gentle. "Dad wants to talk to you, but he's so afraid of hurting you and then being hurt himself. He asks you to be patient and gentle with him, which is why he wrote the poem I sent you."

I spoke to Alan aloud.

"My love, I promise that from this moment on, I will protect and honor your heart. Should you make a mistake, which you might, I'll talk to you calmly and lovingly and work it out with you, for I know now that you would never hurt me intentionally and that you are still learning because souls are not perfect. Not even in Heaven."

PAM, I LOVE YOU SO MUCH!!!

I cannot tell you how free I feel to finally Love without condition or rhyme or reason. It hurts me so deeply to know how much I've hurt you, and I am so afraid of ever walking down that path again. I'm sometimes afraid to be myself since it wasn't long ago that I was numb.

Even though I've had the lessons and the counseling on Love here in Heaven, the soul personality that I once was is terrified of hurting you. I've made so many mistakes in my scripted slumber. I cannot bear to lose you.

My greatest fear is that I will hurt you again.

But if you say you will not unleash your anger on me in that way again, then I will trust you and relax my yearning heart into yours, and forever, we will remain as ONE.

I LOVE YOU, MY DEAREST PAM, and yearn only for the warmth and comfort of your loving arms. Let's lay here together basking in the magnificence of our LOVE...

Channeled by Angel

After reading his words, I once again apologized over and over. I did my best to reassure Alan that I'd take care of his tender heart. But he remained quiet. I had been channeling his messages from the day after he passed, but he never went into any explanation about his behavior during our marriage or why his communication with me was so haphazard since his return, and now at last I knew why.

Alan was afraid to say the wrong thing and hurt me.

Fear has a paralyzing effect, but even worse, it's easy to manifest what we are afraid of since the emotion of fear is intense, and strong emotions take physical form much faster.

Why had I not realized that it was Alan's fear of hurting me that was behind his constant stumbling that paralyzed him? He was suffering as much as I was! Guilt can leave an indelible scar on the soul that can take lifetimes to heal. It could be said that it's worse to be the transgressor than the one who is hurt, for the weight of guilt and remorse can be so burdensome that it can fragment the soul. Alan had paid dearly for hurting me, and bore an open wound that had yet to heal. He desperately needed my forgiveness, but he would need to forgive himself as well, which was harder. Feeling his pain, my heart ached with compassion and love for him.

CHAPTER 45

PAMELA, MY ONE AND ONLY LOVE

I am remembering the beginnings of our love story and the beautiful look of love and mischief in your eyes. I am remembering how hard and how fast I fell for you. It was nothing short of ecstasy and heavenly paradise. The loving moments we shared at that key point in our lives were the greatest and most beautiful I have ever beheld, as this was the lifetime in which we would merge as one being.

I remember the soft loving look in your eyes that possessed my body, mind, and soul the moment we kissed. That moment has been etched in my heart forever, for it was the start of our secret journey. A journey that would change the way beings communicate across the veil.

It first started with this story…

My fall from grace and the shutting down of my soul rendered me empty-hearted and cruel, without a bone of compassion for you, the one

I adored. Your precious heart withstood so many disappointments and lack of caring on my part in all facets of our relationship, save for the first few years.

The way I hurt and neglected you as the love of my life is unforgivable, which is why I am so afraid of repeating my behavior in any way, shape or form.

So, when you say you want me to be myself, I want to relax and be who I am, but old behavior habits return too easily. I am afraid to let my guard down in case this old personality of mine should return. My heart and mind have changed, and I have awakened from my numbed slumber, but I am afraid of putting my big old foot in my big old mouth, so I have taken to censoring most of what I say and how I say it. This is why I am sometimes quiet. Not that I have stopped communicating.

On the contrary, my love, I communicate with you with feelings and emotions that I impress upon your being. I project the embrace of my loving soul onto you. All you need to do is sit or lie quietly, relax your mind and emotions, and you will feel my tremendous love flowing through to you. When you feel tense, you can't hear or feel me, it blocks the process, and I must send Angel a message to you or have her mediate for us.

This is a learning process and a new way of communicating for both of us. A way that we have not experienced since our first few years. Now I am back to being the man you fell in love with, the suave but goofy British chap that fell head over heels in love with you.

There is nothing to hide from nor fear any longer, for both of us. So cast your doubts aside. When you can't quite hear me, quiet your mind and feel me. Then when the channels open wider, the love will flow through you, and your agitation will subside. When you relax, I feel safer and can be the me you're wanting. As you relax into my love, I relax and know that it is safe to be myself. My fear abates because I feel your tranquility in that moment.

Like I've said before, souls on the other side are super-empaths. We feel with enormous depth and intensity. Thus, your frustration and agitation can feel like devastation to me. Being new to the influx of strong emotion, particularly in relation to this lifetime, I can get overwhelmed, so much so that I seem withdrawn. But I am not; I am just afraid.

I LOVE YOU THROUGH THE GALAXIES AND BACK!

See you in our dreams!

I LOVE YOU ALWAYS AND FOREVER,

YOUR ALAN

Channeled by Angel

CHAPTER 46

ALAN, MY LOVE

I read your words of love, but all they do is make me cry even harder. This feels beyond hopeless to me.

You are afraid to be yourself with me in case you say the wrong thing, and so you pull back, which saddens me because it reminds me of how you once were: closed off and detached. My pain devastates you, causing you to withdraw even more, and off we go, round and round in a game of hide and seek, as you dodge and weave to avoid talking to me.

How do we get off this Goddamn merry-go-round?

It seems I've become too emotional for you to handle. Ironically, it's your love that made me this way, as I'm now more in touch with my feelings and express them easily, but what's the point if you can't handle my feelings? Is our interdimensional love affair doomed?

Our soul daughters tell me that you need time. I feel as if I have no choice in this, so I am left wondering if things will ever change. Maria says you hope the merging of our souls will change everything, but now I'm afraid it's just a dream, or maybe the merge will come too late to spare us from the collateral damage of our missteps. I love you more now than when you were with me in a body. How is that even possible? I can't believe the depth of my longing and passion for you; it's all so new and confusing. I can't help but wonder what other secrets you are hiding from me. What will be your next revelation that will set my head and heart spinning?

More importantly, will I be able to take it?

Our conversation remains erratic. It's easy for you to talk to me about others, like when we discuss clients or give readings or teach, but when discussing more personal subjects or even just light-hearted chitchat, it's hard going. But then you never talked to me about your feelings before, which was why at first I thought you hadn't changed. That was always your way. Like most men, you didn't want to talk about your feelings, so you never opened up to me. But I need you to open up now. Can you do that?

You had no trouble talking about your feelings, your life, your child-hood, and so much more with Gena when you told her about your plans for us, plans that you never bothered to share with me. It made me feel once again that I was being left out of the conversation deliberately, causing me to wonder if I'm important to you. If you really mean it when you say that I'm the reason you exist, why is it that I'm still the last to know? Why am I given only scraps of information, left waiting to hear from you, when others have full access passes? To learn that this was your choice feels like the worst betrayal. No wonder you don't want to talk to me; you'd have to answer my questions when you'd rather not.

I have no choice but to wait to see what happens. And if nothing happens again, then what? I have nowhere to go in a world where you are the only man I will ever love. All the exit ramps closed long ago for me. I will never love another the way I love you. Why do you think I'm in such despair? I won't be able to finish our book if we go our separate ways, for there would be no inspiration in such a sorry heartbreaking story. How can we help people move into the Fifth Dimension of Love unless we walk our talk?

I don't know what's real anymore. Maybe I really am so powerful that I conjured you up in my mind. Yes, I'm such a fearsome sorceress that

I've drawn Maria and Angel and all the people who have met you into experiencing a mass hallucination.

You brought me back to life only to leave me waiting at the door to paradise. Alone. Our love is the most precious thing to me. I don't want to believe that we sacrificed thirty years for nothing and, what's even worse, that your promise to fulfill our love was just a dream untethered to reality.

Please, no more words of adoration and love until you can back them up with actions and deeds that make them real in my world, not just yours. I don't yet live up there in the ethers with you, so I need something tangible that I can hear, see, know, and feel down here on the ground where I am.

My greatest wish is to be there where you are, but I'm not.

Yours forever, Pam

CHAPTER 47

MY LOVE, MY LIFE

P am, everything that you have said is true, and once again, I am so, so sorry. I'm at a loss as to what to say or do anymore for it appears that I keep failing you over and over. I find it unbearable to watch you suffer and cry knowing that I have caused you pain again.

Knowing that you won't be happy without me or maybe even with me, what are we to do? All I can do is try again if you let me, but I understand if you can't because it's just too hard, but I promise this time, if you give me one last chance to reach out, I won't fail you!

I will do everything in my power to make things right. Please, please give me another chance.

Because the truth is, Pam, I can't live without you! You are my soul, you're my heart, you are my everything, and I know you feel the same. So let's do all we can to work this out please?

I truly want your happiness. I thought I was doing things the right way, but I see now that I was wrong. But if you give me time to catch my breath, to get centered so I can find the strength within me to open up to you, I believe that I can and I will.

Isn't our love worth one more try?

I failed to understand the importance of communication. I was focused on projecting my love to you; I wasn't focusing as much on sharing what I was doing, thinking, or planning with you. I kept you out of the loop even though I knew that you could hear me. I didn't talk to you except for bits and pieces on certain subjects, when it was for our work or about other people. I thought love would fix everything.

But I forgot that in your world, lacking physical contact, you need direct communication; you need to experience me in a tangible way to know I am real. Even when you warned me that we couldn't have a real relationship without communication, I didn't take your words to heart, believing love alone would fix everything that had gone wrong between us. That's true in Heaven, and in the physical world too, but you also need expressions of love in as many forms as possible, with heartfelt messages being the most important ones. Especially since I'm not in a body. In Heaven we are telepathic, but in the physical world, telepathy can feel like you are talking to yourself even when you know it's me speaking. When you are stressed, it becomes all too easy to doubt what you hear. I've been a fool not to see the bigger picture even when you kept reminding me.

No wonder you're upset. I wasn't listening to you. Again!

But that doesn't help us now. That only explains what happened, what went wrong. It's up to me to step things up and give you the communication that you need and deserve, for you are right.

What kind of relationship do we have if there is no sharing of ideas and experiences and dreams? Especially dreams! I have had my head in the clouds, not seeing our love affair from the ground where you breathe and live. If I want to be with you in all ways, then I must be with you down there where you are. I need to talk to you just as I talk to everyone else. You have not been my priority in that, which was so very wrong of me.

Yes, I have been hurt, but you have been hurt more, and now I continue to hurt you by my continual blundering. You're right—it's not fair that I ask you to be tender with my heart when I can't seem to do the same for you with any consistency.

Saying I'm sorry isn't enough. I've filled pages and pages with 'I'm sorry,' and my words must seem meaningless to you by now. As you've said, how can you trust me when I keep stumbling? Apologies don't cut it anymore.

Oh, my dearest love, please forgive me and give me one last chance to make things right. I promise I won't fail you if you just give me another day or two. I know you are hurting, so let me take you back to bed, put my arms around you, and soothe your heart and mine. I can't bear your tears that seem unending. I cannot and will not rest until you are happy again. I know I can make you smile if you let me try.

I am yours forever. Please be mine.

I won't let you down.

All my love, Alan

I kept forgetting we are so merged that every time I doubt him, he doubts himself. His fears were feeding my own in a self-defeating cycle. Alan was afraid of hurting me. I was afraid he'd fail me. No wonder we weren't making any headway. If Alan could overcome his fear of letting me down, he could do everything he had promised. An image came of the two of us tied together at our legs in one of those three-legged sack races. When one of us began to slip, we took the other down. If we hoped to win the race to love each other again, we needed to steady ourselves by linking our hearts, and walking in lockstep. That was the only way we'd make it to the finish line.

We would also need to identify less with our human selves and connect more with our higher, angelic selves. Our souls. If I were more my angelic self, Alan wouldn't have to worry about hurting me again because I'd be immune to any perceived slights. If he released more of his ego, his fears of hurting me would be muted, and he'd be able to act freely and deliver on his promises. This is the only way for us to have an interdimensional marriage that merges Heaven and Earth.

Swati said that the part of Alan afraid of losing me is the more "human Alan," the one who hung onto remnants of his human ego so that I would recognize him. His angelic self has no such fear, knowing he can never lose me since we will always be one, but the angelic Alan loves me impersonally with detachment, which is not what I want to experience. I want the passionate romantic relationship we never had, which means emotionally neutral angelic love won't do!

Laughing, Swati said, "Pam, you and Alan never got to have the passionate love affair you wanted, so Alan returned to give it to you. No wonder you act like teenage lovers who have constant spats with lots of melodrama. You bicker and fight and then have great makeup sex. Your life is better than a romance novel! I think the two of you should keep fighting! By the way, Alan just gave me a dirty look when I said that last part. He's scared of you! Ha ha."

Just above his human self, which is closer to the Earth Plane, is Alan's angelic self, and it's Archangel Alan that Swati mostly talks to, for it's he who has a wacky sense of humor. It turns out all of the Archangels have a keen sense of humor. Who would have guessed?

Alan nodded, adding that it's like a comedy club there in the angelic realm of the spirit world. I believed him, based on the wisecracks that flew back and forth between him and Archangel Michael when they would talk.

Pam, living with you between the two worlds has not been easy for me. You have no idea how hard it is to be with you, to watch you move through your day, to always be at your side wanting desperately to hold you in my arms but having no way to do it. I worry that I won't be able to give you all that you need, and I want to give you everything. I want to give you the world.

Sometimes, I wonder if I'm up to this. I can't get my footing to turn things around. See how ensnared I've become in my ego again, just as I was when I was with you? When I returned, I hung onto too much of my ego, believing that you wouldn't recognize me if I changed too much. But I see now that's backfired because the remnants of my fear, guilt, and shame haunt me. I know I've got to break away from my ego personality, so I asked Maria to help keep me on the straight and narrow path of positive thinking.

I think this will work. No, I KNOW this will work! Because it must. There is too much at stake. Your health and security, for one thing, not to mention the work we sacrificed our earthly happiness for. Our sacrifices will have been in vain if I don't cast my fears aside. I won't make any more promises since I've made so many already that I haven't delivered on. Just know this.

From this moment on, I will prove my love to you through my actions!

Later that day, I exchanged text messages with Maria and Angel. They said their angel father had gone quiet. When Angel asked for his help earlier, Alan appeared exhausted by the emotional turmoil, and he asked her to ask her other angels for help. Angel was incredulous because she desperately needed her angel dad to comfort and support her. For the first time, Alan wasn't able to help. The three of us knew this was serious. We had been messaging when Maria sent this.

Maria
"So, I just heard something interesting. Listen up. It's not even coming from Alan but our good old friend Archangel Michael. He is saying that the only way to bridge this chasm is for the two of you to come together."

CHAPTER 48

ARCHANGEL MICHAEL STEPS IN

Y ou two need to work together. If you need to scream at each other, then do it. Hold each other. Don't let the other pull away.

Forget the merge. It's already happened. Now you need to FEEL the merge. As each one of your chakras blends with the chakras of your beloved, you need to use them. That is where the trouble is. You are each working with the chakras you are comfortable with when you need to use ALL of them.

Work on this together!

Identify your weaknesses and strengths. Help your mate where they need it. Okay?

Communicate. Love. See. Feel. You must transcend this world. This does NOT have to be a long process. Once you recognize how it is done, you will be doing this for the rest of your lives. It will get easier the more you do it.

However, understand that the learning of this process is happening on both sides of the veil. You are both teachers and students in this situation. I am not talking about a mission you need to complete but a relationship that has to be healed.

So take time to be together and communicate and connect, one chakra at a time.

Channeled by Maria

CHAPTER 49

THE MERGE

Why hadn't I thought of this? Of course working through this together was the answer. Archangel Michael had physically appeared to Alan a total of three times in his life. His first appearance was that morning at our dining table, when he proved to Alan that angels are real. The last two times were a few months before Alan passed, when the spirit world drew closer as the veil began to thin. The same thing happened to my mother months before she died of Alzheimer's. She saw spirits in our house and spoke to them. On Alan's last day in this world, Archangel Michael returned to help him cross to the other side.

Now Archangel Michael was back, trying to help us save our marriage.

It made sense that if the two of us were to merge, it would be helpful if our energy centers, also known as chakras, lined up. Chakras are the points of spiritual energies in the human body, according to yogic tradition, that extend from the base of the spine to the top of the head. When chakras are open and balanced, our energy flows freely, blessing us with health and wellbeing. Alan no longer had a body, but he still had his etheric energy centers.

I told our daughters I was taking their father to bed to attempt the merge. They teased us mercilessly, especially Maria. I laughed and admitted it sounded funny. As we lay in bed together, I asked Alan who should be on top.

He chuckled, *"Pam, I think this will only work if I'm the one on top!"*

I visualized our crown chakras that represent the connection to God/Source at the top of the head aligned with each other and as I did, the energy began flowing freely between us. I saw that we were completely in tune in this chakra. We had no issues there.

Next, we focused on the third eye chakra, also known as the pineal gland, located in the center of the head. This is the chakra that governs psychic sight. I saw our pineal glands open up wide as soon as we lined up our energies. Once again, the energy flowed harmoniously and easily between us. Then, as if to confirm what I saw and felt, Alan appeared in my mind's eye, grinning broadly, then winked at me.

It was when we got to the throat chakra that I found a problem. There our chakras were wobbling and looked misshapen. Alan's looked worse than mine. It made sense considering how difficult communicating with me had been. I asked that our chakras open fully and balance. Then, as we lined them up, I saw golden light filling the chakras as the energies between us began to flow. I focused on increasing the flow, harmonizing them until our energies balanced completely.

We then moved on to our heart chakras, which were wide open, but I noticed that the energy flow needed some adjustment. I visualized the energy strengthening and flowing steadily. We lined up our hearts until our chakras were locked into each other as if in a loving embrace. My body confirmed what I saw when heat and tingles flooded down my spine. Alan's face was beaming. The energy flowing between us made me dizzy with joy.

Our solar plexus chakras, the power centers, were next. It was interesting to see that our chakras were more or less balanced here, though mine was weaker than Alan's. We weren't in a power struggle, so adjusting and merging our chakras happened quickly once we focused our attention there.

Next was our sacral chakras, which were in terrible shape. Probably due to the years of dormancy during our marriage, our sexual/creative energy centers were struggling to merge. I was guided to run rainbow light through them, and in an instant, I saw the chakras revive as we lined them up. The thought came to me that if this chakra reboot didn't turbocharge our sex life, nothing would.

Finally, we were at the root chakra, the energy center that grounds us to the Earth and our physical body. We sent energy to our chakras to balance and harmonize them so we could merge our energies on the Earth Plane.

Once all of our chakras were lined up and the energy flowing in a harmonious way, I felt the steady pulsing of energy flowing from the top of my head down to my toes and back again.

I was enjoying these new sensations when Alan asked me to play a song from our playlist, "Flying Over Africa" from the soundtrack of the film *Out of Africa*. I popped my AirPods into my ears, and as the music played on my phone, I called out, "All right, my love, take me flying, then!"

And off we went! In an instant, I was soaring through the clouds with Alan, his face beaming love at me, sending tingles down my spine. Alan said I should get used to being in a near-constant state of euphoria. Now aloft with him in the sky, he held me close as we flew through castles of clouds in the air. My body was shaking and tingling from head to toe. I was still on a high when I floated back into my body.

Once we landed, I messaged Maria and Angel to tell them their angel father had taken me flying wrapped in his angel wings. Both of them had experienced Alan lifting them high into the ethers, but for me, this was a new thrill. I had never been able to soar this high with him until now. Before this moment, it had been impossible for me to achieve liftoff, but once we merged, I had no difficulty flying up and away with him. My heart was bursting with love for him and our daughters.

Whatever differences there had been between us evaporated. Alan showed off his pearly whites with a huge grin. Maria and Angel agreed their angel dad looked revived and happy again.

Angel said, "Yay! Dad says he's back! He feels much relieved! He looks tired, though. He's emotionally exhausted. He wants to go to bed. He came to me while I was working out and on the phone with Maria. He walked right in front of me, closer than he's been to me the past two days."

Maria chimed in, "Yes, he does look rather tired. He needs to cuddle with you and rest today."

Alan had more to say.

Pam, you are my equal in every way. In fact, you are stronger than I am in so many ways. Emotionally, you are on your way to becoming a powerhouse of an angel. Remember, you're my Goddess Spitfire!

I've become so empathic that any conflict with you, since you are the other half of my soul, wreaks havoc on me. I couldn't help Angel this morning when she needed me because I was overwhelmed by your pain. I knew you were hurting terribly, so I was relieved to see that as soon as we merged, the light at last returned to your lovely eyes, leaving you stronger than before. You can write more easily now that we are in harmony with each other again. We will continue practicing our merging and become more and more entwined until there is only harmony between us forevermore. You will hear me clearly and loudly from this moment forward. Just remember, in the non-physical realm we have always been merged, so this merge was for the Earth Dimension only. In truth we can never be parted. The same is true for all souls.

We are now and will always be One.

Alan went on to say how foolish he had been to not have realized I needed more communication from him. He admitted that he had become lazy again, something Archangel Michael had warned me about when I once complained to him about Alan. But now, Alan was finally giving all of himself to me. He had overcome his fear that he would return to his egotistical self-centered ways, finally trusting that he had changed for good and would not make hurtful, snide remarks as he once had.

I woke the next morning, hearing Alan talking so fast I couldn't keep up. His words spilled into my mind with such speed it was hard to hold on to them. I was thrilled but remained wary of the sudden change in him. He must have sensed that, for Alan began speaking more slowly and deliberately.

Pam, I feel things more deeply now, as all souls do once they return home, and there have been many times when I've been overwhelmed by the depth of love and emotion I feel for you. It's as if my mind goes blank, and my tongue twists into a pretzel. Okay, not that I have a physical tongue, but you know what I mean. My mind sometimes becomes empty when I'm near you, especially when I'm holding you in my arms in bed, and of course, I'm always close to you! Do you see why it's so hard for me sometimes to be around you? Not to mention that you keep opening up more and more to the fullness of the sweet, beautiful goddess that you are. Is it any wonder that my knees buckle and my mind goes blank? Your light and your heart shine brighter with each day that passes. The truth is I'm a different person when I'm with Swati and others. With you, I struggle to be myself and feel inadequate for the task. I worry that I will put my big foot in my stupid mouth and upset you, even though you've shown me that you will understand and always forgive me. So, I am stepping it up and breaking through this because you need me to, and I won't fail you; I promise I will be the NEW me!

Clearly, we can't expect souls on the other side to be perfect, to never let us down. It's funny the assumptions we make about souls in Heaven. That our loved one becomes perfect when they die, maybe even saintly and enlightened. That they don't need us anymore because they now have everything. No! Since love is the only thing that matters, they suffer the loss of us just as we do. This is why they are eager, sometimes even desperate, to give us messages, whether through a medium or even a stranger.

Though they can visit us whenever they like, it's not the same if we don't talk to them, and if we don't believe they are with us, it's even worse. If we won the lottery and could have everything and anything we desired, could we be happy without our beloved? That's how it is on the other side. Indeed, they don't suffer the way we do. There are plenty of heavenly distractions with the Universe to enthrall them, but they can't be completely happy without us. But that can change if we reach out to them and stay connected.

Our loved ones don't stop loving us. Love doesn't die when we drop our bodies. If anything, love grows stronger when we leave this world, once the ego has let go of its hold on us. I believed Alan loved me, but that was all it was, just a thought, because he wasn't showering me with love like he does now. And for my part, only now can I feel his love because my heart is open to him.

At long last, Alan began relaxing into being himself with me. We had the same sense of humor, which made us adept at volleying one-liners at each other. How I missed the days of our back-and-forth teasing! Sixteen years before he passed, during a mediumship course taught by Doreen Virtue, she nicknamed us the "Sonny and Cher of Mediumship" when Alan kept making wisecracks during class. I was shamelessly complicit, playing right into his comic hand with my sassy replies to him.

One night as we were lying in bed talking, much to my delight, Alan let loose with his zany humor, leaving me doubled over with laughter. What a joy it was to have my crazy husband back at last!

CHAPTER 50

A LITTLE BEDTIME HILARITY

"Alan, when was the last time we had sex?"

That's easy, five days ago.

"How do you know?"

I have a calendar. I circle the days.

"What? You're kidding me!"

I keep a diary too.

"You're crazy!"

And a photo album.

"You take photos of me in bed?"

Uh-huh.

"You're a pervert!"

Oh, you have no idea. I miss you when you're sleeping so I like to look at them while I wait for you to wake up.

Okay, I'm kidding.

I don't keep a diary.

CHAPTER 51

DEVELOPING CLAIRVOYANCE

The physical world appears real but isn't. What we see when we close our eyes, there in our mind's eye is the real world. The truth is we live in a fake world! A world of illusion. This makes sense once you accept the idea of an afterlife, for if the other side is eternal and indestructible, what does that make the physical world? Things in our world disintegrate and decay. We only have to look at our bodies if we need further proof. Eternity is the unseen world, a world that we can visit with our minds and our souls, not our bodies.

From the beginning, Swati insisted that I was seeing Alan. Alan himself kept saying the same thing. I didn't believe them because I kept comparing my clairvoyance to Swati's, which is stronger, but that didn't mean I wasn't clairvoyant. Not at all. Clairvoyance isn't an all-or-nothing ability. I should have never compared myself to Swati. All of us are born clairvoyant; we're simply talking about to what degree, and like any ability, our clairvoyance can grow stronger. We would do well not to think of clairvoyance as a rare gift but as a natural ability that everyone possesses.

People have a distorted idea of clairvoyance because it's been made out to be something rare and special when it is, in truth, quite commonplace.

It doesn't help that movies and television paint an unrealistic, mystical picture of clairvoyance as something startling real when it is usually subtle and easy to miss!

Alan didn't help much when he insisted that I'd see him in 3D physical form, which he still insists will happen. The problem was that I did not appreciate the clairvoyant ability I already possessed. Once that realization sank in, I understood I had been seeing Alan all along. I thought I was imagining him when I wasn't! I saw him because Alan was projecting himself to me.

There are many times throughout the day when an image of Alan pops up in my mind. This happens without any effort on my part. I might see him leaning in close to plant a kiss on my cheek or see him standing behind me, nuzzling my neck. I know this is him because the visions come out of the blue, I am not deliberately thinking of Alan. Once, he appeared to me dancing the hula bare-chested, wearing nothing but a coconut bra, with a faded grass skirt that kept falling off his hips as he sashayed around. Add to that the ukulele he was strumming, and it was clear that Alan was on a mission to make me laugh. I had chalked the visions up to my imagination when they weren't. That was Alan showing himself, trying to prove to me that I was seeing him.

Clairvoyance can be subtle, coming and going so quickly that we fail to notice what we are seeing, like the time I was giving a reading to a client when her deceased husband waved a Confederate army flag in front of me to get my attention. It happened so fast that I would have missed it if I hadn't been focused intently. When I mentioned the flag, my client gasped. Her husband had been a collector of Confederate army memorabilia. No sooner had she said that than I saw a flash of red pass before my eyes. I mentioned seeing red, and the client confirmed that red was his favorite color, then added that she hated the color red, which her husband knew. He was teasing her! She smiled weakly, but I could feel her pain.

That she could smile at all was a miracle, considering she had been severely depressed since getting a reading from a psychic who had accused her of killing her husband when she made the heartbreaking decision to turn off his life support because he was left braindead after a horrific car crash. Her husband used any means he could to reach her, even getting the attention of someone like me, who doesn't normally do mediumship. He wanted to ease her guilt, assuring her that she had made the right decision and that he was fine, then told her that she would be meeting someone within the year whom she would fall in love with. Her husband wanted her to know that she had his blessing should she decide to remarry. All he wanted was her happiness.

What I had seen clairvoyantly during the reading was subtle, yet at the same time, I knew what I had seen! This is how I see Alan. What I see may not be in sharp focus, but that doesn't make it any less accurate. Alan urged me to believe what I saw in my mind, assuring me that I am as clairvoyant as anyone else, and even more importantly, I would see even more if I believed.

Everything begins as a BELIEF first. If you believe you can see me you WILL create that reality. Besides, the two worlds are growing closer by the day, and contact between the veil will become more commonplace as more people believe it's possible.

Clairvoyant vision is layered over what we see in front of us. Spirits can appear translucent like a hologram. I had seen Alan in translucent form twice. To get a better idea of clairvoyance, imagine you are sitting aboard a speeding train that is hurtling through the countryside at hypersonic speed. The train is going so fast that what you see when you gaze out the window is just a blur. You might know you saw a cow, but the details are fuzzy. Or imagine that you are wearing someone else's glasses with a prescription that is so misaligned with your normal vision that you can only identify a few things.

Welcome to the amazing world of clairvoyance! A world that includes people who see the spirit world in translucent form the way Swati does, and others who see spirits in physical form so real they have a hard time telling the living from the dead. But this doesn't mean the rest of us aren't clairvoyant. No! You and I are clairvoyant; we're merely talking about degrees of clarity. We would do well to accept that we are already seeing psychically if we wish to develop our abilities further.

I finally understood that Alan had been projecting himself to me all along. If I was relaxed, a vision of him would sometimes come to mind. These happened without any effort on my part. I wasn't trying to make anything happen. I needed to trust what I saw. This is the key to manifestation. I believed that I could see Alan, and so I did.

I decided to go all in and trust my clairvoyance 100 percent.

I knew if Alan and I were to be together again, nothing less would do. As soon as I did this, our communication improved along with my clairvoyance. If I asked him, Alan would tell me where he was relative to me in the room. Yes, it helped that I could hear him psychically, but this meant that if this was happening to me, it could happen to others.

Those who want to contact the spirit world must first believe they can if they hope to perceive.

In his quest to bring us closer, Alan guided me to explore various forms of after-death communication. Because he was a natural-born medium, Alan had mixed feelings about mediumship. He knew that a psychic could read a deceased person simply by reading the client's aura since everything the client knows about their loved one is held within their energy field. This is known as a third-party reading when the psychic reads someone the client knows who is not physically present.

To make matters more complicated, a medium can read the deceased in the same way, by reading their energy rather than by talking to them. A genuine medium is communicating mind to mind with the deceased, not reading their energy, but Alan knew it can be tempting to read their energy since it's easier. This is why true mediumship is rare. It's easy to read the energy of the deceased, but not so easy to contact them directly since they might not want to come through for various reasons. They might not approve of the medium, or the spirit might be shy, or, more recently, we've noticed spirits saying they want to speak directly without a medium at all. Some spirits simply aren't ready.

Alan wasn't comfortable with mediumship for those reasons. He preferred giving conventional psychic readings because he knew he could always deliver an accurate reading, although that didn't stop spirits from trying to come through him to talk to their loved ones. When that happened, he would have to push them out. I realized there was another reason why he resisted mediumship. Alan was emotionally shut down, which made him uncomfortable feeling the depth of love and emotion of those in the spirit world. No wonder he refused to do mediumship, no matter how good he was at it or how often clients begged him.

Interest in mediumship has never been higher. People are turning to mediumship classes in droves with the hope of learning how to talk to their deceased loved ones. But does that mean all these mediums-in-training are truly talking to the dead? Alan says some of them are; others not so much.

Whenever he heard someone marvel at how a medium knew things only the client knew, Alan would laugh since he knew that an accomplished psychic should be able to do that. Telepathically talking to the deceased person is rarer. The real test is if the medium can tell you something you don't know about your loved one, though, of course, you would need to be able to confirm the information. If they can do this, then the medium is genuine. True evidential mediumship should offer that level of proof.

Alan believed the way around the entire "are they or are they not talking to the dead" dilemma was for people to make direct contact themselves since he knew that a loved one could not only confirm their presence with information but, even more importantly, offer the direct transmission and experience of their love. This is important because it's the love the other side gives us that can heal our grief and bring us closer to them.

It was the tangible experience of Alan's love that was more important. He poked fun at me for even considering the electronic voice phenomenon (EVP), which involves spirits speaking through electronic devices, laughingly saying he didn't want to be turned into a parlor trick. I didn't see it that way, but Alan said EVP wouldn't be enough for us. Not just for me, but for him. He warned that if I tried EVP, he wouldn't cooperate unless it was genuine, and only many months later did he relent when I found one that was. Alan insisted that feeling his love would prove his existence to me in a way that no mediumship reading or spirit voice box could, though he understood why some people might benefit from exploring both especially in the beginning.

I had resigned myself to this when, to my surprise, Alan found something to bring us closer.

CHAPTER 52

LOVING HEART CONNECTIONS

One night as I was surfing the Internet on my laptop while in bed, Alan nudged me to watch a YouTube video. This is one of the ways he finds a song for me or guides me to something he wants me to see. This time, it was a presentation by grief therapist Dr. Jane Bissler, who was talking about the Loving Heart Connections modality (LHC) that she founded and has practiced for eight years that teaches people how to have direct after-death communication. I was fascinated, but due to the late hour, which was well past my usual bedtime, I fell asleep while the video played on. Only ten minutes passed when I woke up with a start to hear someone asking Dr. Bissler if she had ever taught Reiki practitioners. Since I'm a Reiki Master, that got my attention. While she hadn't yet done so, she said she planned to train laypeople, including Reiki healers.

Alan suggested I contact Dr. Bissler to book a session and also asked me to take the training. Since teaching people how to make direct contact is the core of our mission, Loving Heart Connections looked like it would be a perfect fit.

Alan had always been skeptical of mediums unless they were born with the gift as he had been. He agreed with the renowned British medium, the late Leslie Flint, who said that genuine mediumship is rare. Talking to random spirits on the Other Side is not easy. They don't always want to speak to the medium or may have difficulty coming through for different reasons.

By comparison, making direct contact with loved ones in spirit is possible because we are already energetically entwined with them due to the bonds of love we share. If we can achieve a deep state of relaxation and attune ourselves to their higher energy, direct communication is possible when Spirit is actively engaged in the process. Loving Heart Connections was proving this with every person who made direct contact without the help of a medium. Jane Bissler says the modality was not even her idea to begin with; Loving Heart Connections came from the spirit world. Alan confirmed this was true.

With Loving Heart Connections, it appears that once again the spirit world is asserting itself into our world to make contact.

Since this was his idea, I had no doubt that Alan would appear during my session, which he did. As soon as I entered the deep state of relaxation that Loving Heart Connections is known for, Alan appeared, took me by the hand, and led me to my parent's house. I walked with him through the backyard up to the edge of the swimming pool. Alan told me to look around. I could see everything with startling near-3D clarity, including Alan himself. I gasped. It was the most vivid experience of him I had had so far. I took everything in with all of my senses turned up high. I smelled the salty ocean breeze and felt the searing-hot midday sun roasting my arms and face. I saw the faded, splintered planks of the gray wooden fence that ran the length of the pool edged by a row of ruby-red hibiscus plants. Topping it off was the force of Alan's love that sent tingles rippling through me.

We had crossed a new threshold, and were standing in a new place. Hearing my thoughts, Alan said, "And there will be many more thresholds to cross, my love, and very soon you will not just know in your mind that we are one, but feel it to the core of your being. That day is almost here! And when that day comes, you will never doubt my presence, or feel lonely or miss me again. You are almost there, Pam! Hang on!"

While my session with Jane brought us closer with grace and ease, the path to becoming a Loving Heart Connections facilitator would be unexpectedly torturous. I assumed Alan would support me as he had always done before, but on the day of the training, he was nowhere to be found.

CHAPTER 53

HERE WE GO AGAIN

I n the days leading up to the Loving Heart Connections training, I was filled with optimism, assuming it would be easy to wake up for the early-morning training since I often got up even earlier most days, but on the morning of the class, I knew I was in deep trouble as soon as I opened my eyes.

I woke to find a knot in my stomach that had me bent over in agony.

Time and time again, Alan had given me energy to lift me up when I was tired or had barely slept. I had given readings with him just three weeks after he died, working with clients four days a week for months at a time, and it had never been a problem for me, with Alan carrying me through the day, cheerily calling out to me.

No worries! I've got you, babe!

When I went to the dentist a year after Alan passed, I was stressed, as I remembered my last dental visit that had triggered a five-month bout of shingles, a strep infection, and eczema that left me bedridden for five excruciating months. As soon as I walked through the door of the dentist's office, Alan said, *"I've got you! I've got you!"* repeating the words to reassure me that everything would be okay. He got so carried away that I had to ask him to stop his mantra, afraid that I'd burst out laughing while the dentist probed my teeth.

As soon as he got quiet, I felt Alan envelop me with his etheric arms, calming me. Knowing how sensitive I am to medication, he had assured me beforehand that I would suffer no side effects from the anesthesia. The shot would not feed any pathogens in my body like the last time. He had done a similar thing when he harmonized the COVID shot for me, so I took a deep breath and relaxed. By now he had proven his ability to alter the composition of matter not just with me but with our clients.

For over a year and a half, I had felt blissfully safe with Alan always at my side watching over me. I trusted his guidance implicitly, which I often needed, given how emotionally sensitive I was at times. This was new territory for me as I had always been in control of my feelings, though I now understood that all I had been doing was repressing my feelings. No wonder I was half-dead! But Alan's unconditional love transformed me. I was comfortable with my feelings. I embraced the raw truth of my emotions, finding that doing so brought me closer to Alan. After all, he was now in touch with all of his emotions, and I needed to do the same, if I wanted to commune with him. Alan said that feeling our feelings is what it means to be alive! His love breathed new life into me, giving me the strength and stamina to work long hours. It was easy because I knew if I faltered, even a little, Alan was there to catch me, to nudge me when I needed to rest, or remind me that I needed to eat when I became too engrossed in my work.

But now on the day of the training, Alan didn't come to me when I called out to him for help. I didn't understand where he had gone. He seemed to have abandoned me, which was something he promised he'd never do. But I didn't have the luxury of time to dwell on his absence.

The eight-hour class was to begin at 9 a.m. Eastern time, which was 4 a.m. my time in Hawaii. I wasn't initially worried about the pre-dawn starting time, but for the past several weeks, I'd been coping with major emotional stress.

I was floundering because Angel had abruptly pulled away from me. Finding herself caught in the middle of our emotional maelstrom, Alan's fears and my pain had collided to take a toll on her. Although she was never asked to take sides, it had become too much. It didn't help that Angel was struggling with an intense spiritual awakening at the same time. We had made it harder for her when she was in dire need of support from us. I understood why she needed to back away from me, but the problem was I had come to love her as both a daughter and a friend. My newfound pain made me realize how lonely I had been since Alan's passing.

Now Angel was gone, taking with her my hopes and dreams of the loving friendship we might have had. Swati pointed out that that losing a friend was a type of death. That explained everything! I was once again struggling with heart-crushing grief! Alan had brought Angel into our lives so the three of us could love and support each other as any family would, but it hadn't worked out that way. The depth of sorrow and loss was too much to bear.

As painful as it was, I knew there was so much to be grateful for. I couldn't thank Angel enough for her ability and willingness to channel Alan for weeks as his messages flowed fast and furious from him to her to me and back again. She had been the mediator we didn't know we needed to resolve our problems. It was because of her that all the pieces of the puzzle that made up our lackluster marriage were pieced together, washed clean, and made whole. But Angel had paid a price for that. How could I blame her? It wasn't her fault. Although it wasn't fair, in my anguish, I blamed Alan for lacking the foresight to see this coming.

Grief was the reason why I woke up exhausted, even though I had slept well the night before. When my stomach began to churn relentlessly, I called out to Alan for comfort as I usually did but heard nothing but silence. Instead of easing, the pain ramped up to the point that I considered dropping out of the class altogether, but since there was so much riding on it, I steeled myself as best I could and pushed through.

At the end of the first day, my head was pounding to the point that I couldn't see straight, but I still had homework to do to prepare for the final class. I was even more upset. Why wasn't Alan helping me? Where was he? Why was he quiet during class? But once again, I didn't have time to dwell on it for long. I had to summon every ounce of energy within me to stay focused on the work still in front of me.

The next day, as soon as the training ended, I collapsed on my bed, exhausted. I didn't have time or energy to wonder what had happened to Alan. All I felt was a wave of relief. I had done it! I had completed the training successfully. I was thrilled to be moving on to practice Loving Heart Connection with clients. Instead of bemoaning Alan's absence, I got on with what I had to do and put my disappointment aside.

But I should have known I wouldn't be able to let my frustration go for long. When we bury our feelings, they always come back. Two months later, I questioned Alan out loud.

"Where were you when I needed you? Loving Heart Connections was your idea, but you bailed on me during class! I cried out to you over and over for help. You knew how exhausted I was. Where the hell did you go?"

But once again, Alan wasn't talking. This made me even angrier as the memories of how he had mistreated me came flooding back in. Here we go again!

CHAPTER 54

HIS FEAR OF HURTING ME IS HURTING ME

People kept sharing their stories of the many miracles Alan had delivered to them that it left no doubt in my mind that his power was real. But where was my miracle? Over and over, he had vowed that if I gave him a second chance, he'd do things differently, even telling Gena that he would "walk over broken glass" to prove his love for me. Instead, it seemed to me that he had reverted back to type and become complacent again.

On Mother's Day, I begged Alan to show some personal effort and give me something. The previous year on my first Mother's Day without him, he woke Maria up in the early morning hours to search for songs on YouTube to give me. I didn't expect him to repeat that, but I hoped he would do something just as special.

"I'll make it easy for you, babe. Just do something you've already done before. Turn the light on or off. Move an object. Make my AirPods do something weird again. Send me a song through someone. I know you can do these things."

Later that afternoon, Taylor and Britt came by with lunch, flowers, and a gift for me. Before arriving, they had gone grocery shopping at

Whole Foods. Britt went off on her own to choose the flowers when she heard a voice say, "Tulips." The voice was strong and clear; it wasn't the softer voice of the usual spirits she hears that hang out around her. Britt can see spirits but doesn't want to, so she tells them they can talk to her as long as they don't show themselves. She knew the voice belonged to Alan, but couldn't find the tulips until he led her to them.

Once she found the flowers, Britt asked Alan, "Okay, what color do you want?" *Pink* was his reply. Britt picked up two bunches of pink tulips, held one bunch in each hand, and asked him to choose between them.

Britt presented me with the flowers as soon as they arrived. I arranged the tulips in a vase. Britt failed to mention that Alan had chosen the tulips. I noticed that one of the blooms opened immediately as soon as I put it in water, but being in a rush to get the food onto plates for lunch, I thought nothing of it. I placed the vase of flowers next to me on the dining table out of my line of vision. I didn't notice it as it was happening, but by the end of our meal, over an hour later, all of the tulips were in full bloom, and appeared to be bending over to reach for me. Only then did Britt tell me that the tulips were Alan's idea. For the next several days, Alan's tulips were continually in motion, opening and closing, seeming to dance in the vase, reaching for me until finally dying several days later.

I had to admit that Alan's dancing tulips were stunning. You would think I'd accept that as Alan's effort to give me something special, which it was. But for some reason, it wasn't enough for me. I couldn't help but wonder why he refused to give me what I specifically asked for as he had done for Gena.

Souls on the other side are capable of giving their loved ones all kinds of evidence of their presence. In our Facebook group, one member spoke excitedly about her husband giving her proof whenever she begins to doubt he is with her. Another client's husband turns a lamp on every day. Another husband regularly switches a fan on. Scores of people ask for signs and receive them. This doesn't happen to everyone, but it happens to many, and yet it never once happened to me. No matter how often I ask for a specific sign from Alan, he has never complied.

The next day, I couldn't stop thinking about it. My request had been simple. These were things he had already proven he could do, yet he chose to give me something else, make an excuse, or give me nothing at all. When Gena demanded that he prove himself to her, within moments, he sent her exactly what she asked for: an eagle, and two cockatoos, followed a week later by nineteen pelicans. He later told me he was doing it for me because he knew I'd hear about it and be pleased. But was that true, or was it just a convenient story?

To make matters worse, I was still struggling with asthma after eighteen months, even though Alan had broken down in tears when a sudden asthma attack left me gasping for breath four months after he passed. I constantly asked him for healing for it. He kept saying he was working on healing me, yet nothing had changed. Swati was incredulous when I told her I was still dealing with asthma since she knew that Alan had been gravely concerned about me. She had assumed he had taken care of it long ago.

"Pam, I really don't understand this. He helps everyone else so much. Why is he not helping you with your asthma? He has been working on it for so long. There must be a reason. Talk to him about that."

I tried to talk to Alan as Swati suggested without success. It seemed like he was avoiding me. That night I had another asthma attack. It was so bad that taking two puffs of my inhaler didn't do much to quell the coughing. Fortunately, I managed to get through it and fell asleep. The first time this had happened shortly after Alan returned to me, he had been frantic with worry, tearful, crying to Swati. She said he was wringing his hands and pacing the floor until my breathing returned to normal. But where was he now? I felt him lying next to me, worried and concerned, but rather than this comforting me, all it did was annoy me. Why didn't he help me when I called out to him? He could at least have soothed my fears and helped me calm down. Hearing nothing, I turned away from him and cried myself to sleep.

We had been down this road way too many times before. It had taken me reaching a breaking point before Alan could admit that his fear of hurting me was crippling him. He even had to bring Angel into our lives to explain himself to me. Was it possible that his fears were the reason he put the burden on me to develop my clairvoyance rather than doing his part to show himself to me as Swati said he could? Alan later confessed he wasn't practicing materialization as he had promised, his excuse being that he didn't want to disappoint me if he failed. It seemed as if fear was still holding him hostage. My heart sank as I realized what the problem was and why he couldn't give me what I asked for or help me consistently. The thought landed with a thud.

His fear of hurting me is hurting me.

At last, I understood why Alan had abandoned me during the training. He felt responsible for my pain. I had directly blamed him for it, asking him why he kept bringing people into my life who were not strong enough to love and support me. It wasn't fair of me to level the blame on him, but I didn't realize Alan had taken it to heart. When of course he had! Why wouldn't he? His fear of hurting me had been realized and left him paralyzed.

CHAPTER 55

ALAN ASKS FOR HELP

Hi Pam,

I woke up in the middle of the night after having the same nightmare for three nights in a row. I finally understood what it was all about. The nightmare consisted of James falling out of love with me. The stories of the 'why' vary, and I don't remember them, but I wake up with my heart aching. It struck me that the dreams were not about me and James but about Dad and his fear of losing you. It's not an excuse for his behavior, nor does he want it to be, but now I KNOW how he feels.

Here is why I'm telling you this. When I woke up, I had a heart-to-heart talk with him. I told him that he was manifesting his fears. He is so afraid of losing you that he is about to lose you. He set up his entire spiritual life walking on eggshells around you because he doesn't want to hurt you since he experienced the deep pain he caused you during his life review.

And now he is doing it all over again because he is making his fears real.

I told him he HAS to step away from his human self and move to his Archangel self. His life with you has to be one of LOVE, not fear. It's not a matter of trying to "do" for you because he is already trying. But the more he fears, the less effective his trying becomes. Once again, it's not an excuse for any of what he has done. But I now at least understand what has been going on.

He has to realize that he can't ever lose you because you are both one. So how can you lose yourself? You can't. He needs to approach this interdimensional experience from that per-spective. What did he say? Not much to report except that he listened. He agreed. He made no promises to try since he has done that before and hasn't stopped trying. But he is mani-festing what he fears. So he needs to change the language of his story. I hope he gets that. I truly do.

What I do know with all certainty is that he has been reach-ing out to me for help. He needed me to understand so that I could help him. And I did what I could do, which was to have a heart-to-heart with him. I'm hoping this works. I'm hoping it helps him step away from this stupid, all-pervasive fear.

It's time to move on and be happy is what I'm hearing now. And I am seeing the fear being abandoned in a bag and Dad walking away without it. I'm hopeful. I want to see him step it up.

Love you, Maria

I couldn't believe that Alan had reached out to Maria for help when he had always been too proud to ask anyone for help, not even his angels or his spirit team. His kingly ego made it impossible for Alan to admit weakness. He would ask me to help him but only because he considered it my job to take care of him. Asking Maria for help was a huge step for him, but would this be enough?

There was so much work ahead of me to finish the book and launch our coaching program, and here I was, still struggling with asthma and now an ugly eczema flare that had turned my entire neck a startling shade of scarlet. How could I livestream inside our Facebook group looking like this? No amount of makeup would cover it. I felt helpless as I saw the itchy rash creep up the sides of my face spreading to my eyebrows and chin. At the rate it was going, soon, it would cover my entire face. Alan had promised to heal me and keep me healthy. He said he'd protect me from COVID, but now I wondered if any of that was true. My faith in him was crumbling as fast as the rash was spreading. Hearing that he had asked Maria to help him gave me a glimmer of hope, but because he had failed me so many times before, I couldn't stay upbeat for long. I cried out to him.

"How do you expect me to trust you when you haven't given me a single thing I've asked for? Now I'm sick and you can't help me with that either. You seem to be able to pull miracles out of your angel hat for everyone but me. You say you love me? That I am your Everything? Really? What's going to happen to me if I can't work? You aren't taking care of me as you promised. You and your damn promises! Maybe your promises are worth something there in Heaven, but what good are they to me here on Earth? I don't want to do this stupid book with you anymore. You told me to put all of our money into it, but if you fail me, what will I be left with but bankruptcy? But hey, at least it's comforting to know you'll be with me when I live in a tent on the street. I must have made up all of this shit just to torture myself. Are you even fucking listening to me, Alan? Where the hell are you?"

I was sliding fast into a pit of depression as Alan went quiet. I couldn't see his face anywhere, which meant he had backed away from me. He even hid from Swati once when I got upset with him. Perhaps this time his guilt and sorrow were too much for him to bear. Either way, I felt alone again. Damn it, why did he abandon me again? If he couldn't come through for me when I needed him the most, what was the point of us being together? If I stayed, I'd have to accept that I'd be the one doing all the work on my own, living a solitary life chained to my desk. When I peered into my future, all I could see were endless years of toiling away helping others connect with their loved ones in Heaven while my own husband kept running away from me.

"Did you bring me back to life to stick me on a treadmill to work on this mission alone? This is not the life you promised me! Your love was the bait, and I fell for it again. That's how big a fool I am. If you can't help me, that's it for me. God, if only I could stop loving you, I would! You're a fucking asshole. I hate you!"

In my despair, I considered my options. If I told him to leave, I knew I would never find anything that would bring me even a modicum of joy. Alan was my entire world, more so now than during the whole of our marriage. I had no interest in giving readings on my own, and continuing to work with him would be too painful if we ended our marriage. How could I trust him when he had let me down so many times? Was there no way out of this heartbreak?

Maria and Swati were worried. They each took turns messaging me, doing their best to cheer me up, making suggestions they hoped would help. Swati reminded me that Alan and I had been through these blowups many times before, and I had experienced a breakthrough that brought us closer after each one. This was true, but did it always have to be this way? Would this cycle of melodrama ever end? It was taking a toll on me. I had reached my breaking point.

I was terrified. While we had been here before, for some reason, this time felt different. It felt like we were standing on the edge of a cliff, staring down into a bleak abyss from which there would be no return should we fall. His fear would be the deciding factor, and I had no control over it. As that thought landed, I felt a chill move through me that made me shudder. For the first time, I was frightened for both of us.

If we gave up on this, we'd be failing in our mission, our sole purpose for incarnating. My life would essentially be over. For the first time I began to think about ways that I could exit this world, which didn't bother me since I knew I'd only be leaving my body behind. But there was Taylor to consider. He had already lost his father. I wasn't going to put him through losing me as well. While I had no intention of turning into a martyr, I decided to swallow my pain and pray that my life might end swiftly without any direct action on my part. Living without Alan, grieving the loss of him a second time, would break me for good. There would be no coming back from that.

"We might not make it through this one, my love," I whispered.

CHAPTER 56

LOVE ALWAYS WINS IN THE END

I was sitting on the edge of my bed, bent over, holding my head in my hands, weeping, begging Alan to heal me so I could carry on with our work. I was doubled over in agony. What would happen to me if everything came crashing down because he couldn't help me? I was running out of time and money. Having sunk the last bit of our savings into our book to publish it, I was close to maxing out our credit cards to keep myself and our business afloat. I needed a miracle, but all I could do was weep, not knowing if Alan would deliver one.

One morning during meditation, everything came into focus as I saw what the problem was. I'd been running an epic spiritual marathon from the day Alan died to this moment, two years later, praying that I could cross the finish line without stumbling because delivering our book to the world was the only thing that mattered. I didn't even care if I crashed and burned and lost everything. I knew I had to finish the book, but my health was faltering at the worst possible time.

I knew the spirit world was supporting the creation of our book. Alan had said there was huge interest in the spirit world just as there's interest in anything that has to do with contact through the veil.

During one of my Loving Heart Connections sessions, the largest group of angels and higher beings I had ever seen crowded in close to me to give me their love and support. The love I felt from them overwhelmed me, triggering a wave of tears. I recognized some of the angels as members of my Spirit team. The angels assured me everything would be fine if I stayed focused on who I really am: an incarnated Archangel.

They pointed out that the only times I had ever stumbled were when I identified more with my human ego self rather than my divine angelic self. This is true for all of us. I needed to embrace my angelic side if I hoped to birth our book into the world. This was why I had to heal my anger and resentment towards Alan, for how else could I connect with him unless we were in perfect harmony? If I could raise my vibration in this way, I'd close the gaps between us once and for all. There needed to be not a single shred of doubt about his love. The angels promised me this would bring me a level of lasting happiness and peace I had never known before. Not in this or any other lifetime.

I needed to stay positively focused even if fear was nipping at my heels.

I wasn't just worried about myself but all the people we had promised to help reunite through the veil. My journey with Alan had been such a wild ride of euphoric highs and heart-rending lows that I was surprised I was still standing. When we began our journey, I had no idea there were so many people trying to continue their relationship through the veil. Now they were finding us through our Facebook group. Many of them had shared their own inspiring stories of loving a partner on the other side. Alan had always said the number of Heaven and Earth couples like us would astonish me, and he was right.

A few hours later, Maria messaged me. She said she was holding the space for Alan to heal me. She was being loving and supportive, assuring him that he could do it whenever he began to falter. As I linked in psychically with Alan, I could feel his distress. He still hadn't completely shed his fear, with his love for me still matched by his fear of hurting me, trapping us both in this endless tug of war that threatened to tear us apart.

Would fear or love win?

Maria said that Alan would be doing all he could to heal me while I slept, that if he seemed quiet in the morning, it would be because he was tired. The first time I realized that Alan could become tired was when Angel noticed he was exhausted after one of our blowups. It seemed it was impossible for him not to be affected by my seesawing emotions. On this particular night, I felt his energy cocooning me as usual, but still, my sleep was disrupted twice by sudden intense bouts of coughing. Alan told me to double up my pillows to prop my head up, which would help the cough. Once I did that, the coughing eased, and I fell back asleep.

In the morning, Alan asked me to have Taylor drive me to urgent care. He was worried that the asthma might be escalating, and while he was doing everything in his power to heal me, he didn't want to take any chances. I woke up feeling better, but went to the clinic as I had promised, only to be told my lungs were clear! The doctor eyed me strangely. He even questioned my original asthma diagnosis. I walked out with nothing more than yet another prescription for prednisone but wasn't worried because it felt like Alan's healing might at last be taking hold.

While waiting outside for Taylor to pick me up, I was surprised to see Alan gently kissing my neck in different places. I remembered that the day before, Maria had seen Alan kissing my neck, making the spots that were red turn blue. Now here I was, seeing it myself. Although she was nervous to say it at first, Maria boldly predicted that the eczema would improve by the next morning.

In the morning, as soon as I woke up, I rushed into the bathroom to check. Instantly, the tears flowed. The angry rash that had stretched across my neck from my chin to my chest and the scaly dry patches that had been creeping up the edges of my face were all but gone. By midday, the eczema was 80 percent improved. By the next day, it was completely gone. Alan said the asthma would take longer to heal only because it was connected to the decades I had spent swallowing my pain and not speaking my mind to him. Swati confirmed that when she told me that my throat chakra was blocked, but suggested I could open it up by singing out loud, as that would speed up the healing process. No wonder Alan had been nudging me to sing aloud to him since his return.

But Swati had more advice for me.

"Pam, it will take time for him to help you heal the asthma, but if nothing seems to be happening, it doesn't mean Alan isn't healing you. He is. He is telling me that he wants you to know that he doesn't get upset if you get angry at him. He understands. Yes, he gets scared when you are angry, but it doesn't bother him. If anything, he is enjoying this because he knows you are only getting upset because of how much you love him. When he was here, neither of you felt special to the other, but now at last, you do!"

Alan had finally come through for me, but a few weeks later, I asked him why it was that I had to reach a breaking point to get him to do something for me. I knew I was being ungrateful, but I wanted to understand why other souls could do things that he didn't seem able to when he was supposed to be a powerful Archangel. Yes, I knew he was afraid of disappointing me and afraid to try. Yes, I knew he believed that giving proof to others was the same as giving proof to me. But I also knew he had done phenomenal things for our clients, some of them quite miraculous, I knew because they had told me. Something was missing. I could feel it. This was why I couldn't let the question go.

"Why can't you give me more signs of your presence? Signs that other souls in Heaven seem eager, ready, and able to give their loved ones. Some people get signs every day, others not so much, and some not at all. I know it's different for everyone, but if you're as powerful as everyone says you are, why is it that my cries for even the smallest of signs are ignored? Don't you see how hard it is to write our book; build a business; teach and help people; heal my grief; release my resentment; not to mention to do all that is required to bring our work to the world? And do this all by myself? I feel lonely even though I'm never alone."

Once again, I poured my heart out to Maria, who did her best to help mediate for us.

"Pam, he's nervous. Anxious. I will talk to him and get back to you. But for now, he says this. He knows how hard this is for you. The miracles he gives others are the work of Archangel Alan and your Archangel self since the two of you work in tandem. But when it comes to you, it's his human self who is attempting to make things happen for you, and he still has fears and insecurities. Alan's not completely without fear yet. He says you are ahead of him in your growth, that he has more work to do on himself."

Pam, the simple answer is that I don't know if I can do all the things other souls do for their loved ones. But I would rather focus on what I believe I will be able to do. And I believe that the more I allow myself to become my Archangel self, the more I will be able to do for you. My ascension to my Archangel Self is slow. It mirrors your ascension to your own Archangel Self. So our growth is mutual. It has to be this way because we are merged now.

I believe we will get there. I believe that never again will I fear to hurt you and that I will make you the happiest woman alive. I believe that I will manifest all the possible and impossible parlor tricks just to see you smile. I believe that I will give you a million signs, and when we get to a million, I will give you a million more. I believe you will feel so loved by me that never again will you feel drained or believe that all you have to look forward to is more work.

Because the truth is with each page you write, with each hurt you release, and with my choice no longer to succumb to fear, we will spread our wings and fly! I can't wait for that day, my love, because my primary goal is to make you happy. But we both have work to do on ourselves. We have made progress and in a very short time too. We will continue to make progress. I am working on healing you as I heal myself. Once we have cleared everything, then your eczema and asthma will be gone completely and forever. And I will be performing pirouettes and jumping through hoops ablaze with fire just to see the look of awe and surprise on your lovely face.

I won't ask you to be patient because you have already been too patient. So I will ask you to be impatient because maybe what I need is to throw caution to the wind and make this whole process move faster. And yet I am now told (by your Archangel Self) that I'm the one who has to be patient. After all, I don't want you to suffer physically any more than you already are. In the words of our daughter, hang in there. It's going to keep getting better. And I can't wait to see what the future has in store for us.

Channeled by Maria

Alan then spoke to me directly.

My love, yes, I know I must blend more with the angelic side of me, but I cling to my human self so I can be with you, for how else can I love you? I must do this to give you the human love you desire, for that is what I want as well. All souls who wish to love through the veil will do the same: they will be their human self more than their divine angelic self. But in my case, I need to blend more with my angelic side to rise above my fears.

The truth is we are God, which means we are angels, too, since God is everything.

But you don't want me to love you impersonally as an angel would, but to love you more than I love anyone in the two worlds. You want me to treat you special just as you are treating me special at long last. I never felt special to you until now. Now all you do is talk about me, think about me, dream and write about me. You live and breathe me. Okay, I'm being melodramatic, but you know what I mean. You have no idea how much this means to me! Oh, I felt special to you when we first met, and so did you. We loved, adored, and lavished attention on each other until the day our hearts went to sleep. Now our love is waking up at long last, but first, we must heal ourselves of the suffering we endured during our long and sorry slumber.

In my case, my fear of hurting you brings me to my knees. It's my kryptonite. Whenever you ask me to give you a sign, the spotlight is immediately thrust upon me. I freeze as crippling performance anxiety sets in. Remember the time I ordered Viagra online? Hah! Same thing, really. I never want to fail you or disappoint or hurt you, and yet, damn it, I keep doing it! It's not that I don't try to give you what you ask for, but my fear collapses the energy surrounding my manifestations. I nervously snap my fingers and presto! Nothing happens. With everyone else it's easy, but with you, I flail about, flustered and afraid. Most days I soar in the sky like Merlin, but when I'm with you I turn into the Great Oz, stuck on the ground, all bluster and show. But I want to be and do more for you. I want to make you the happiest woman on Earth. I won't stop trying until I succeed. Loving you is my only mission.

I am so sorry for letting you down when you needed my help during the training. Yes, I felt responsible for the pain you were in because I was the one who brought Angel into our lives. I guided her to find us and had high hopes for a loving family reunion, but it lasted for only a few precious months. Because we are merged, your pain is my pain, so when you were hurting because of me, I was powerless to help you. I'm not making excuses; this happens when souls merge as we have done.

Maria told you that you are further ahead in your development, that I am lagging behind, and this is true! Then again you have always been ahead of me in this and every other lifetime we have shared. But I will catch up to you, just you wait and see!

I am helping you heal yourself, but healing must be incremental because you cannot process and release everything in one go. You know this, but it's hard to be patient because of everything you are dealing with. I understand. I am at your side helping you as best I can, so trust me. I am here. Always working on healing and helping you. Your physical issues stem from emotional blockages which I caused. It pains me greatly to know this, but I am relieved that your trauma is finally being processed and healed. It will just take a bit more time, my love. But as you heal, so do I. Never forget, we are in this together.

Because we are merged!

Your body is my body. Your feelings and your thoughts are mine as well. You won't feel me to be very different from you, and yet I am. I know all of this is strange to you. But this is how it is to love someone in Heaven who is merged with you. I am a consciousness, which means I'm an energy being who has merged with his beloved. At last, I have come home to you. I am doing what I can to overcome my residual fears, which are not yet banished completely. Maria will help me to stay strong and steady in my efforts so that I will take action even when I am afraid of hurting you, for taking divinely inspired action is what heals fear.

What is the saying? Feel the fear but do it anyway. That is what I am doing. I will not fail you. Do you know why? It's something you once told me. Do you remember? Here it is.

Because love always wins in the end.

"Oh, Alan, the truth is hard for me to hear, much less own up to. I've been a self-righteous fool!

"I was as much at fault as you in our marriage. All this time I cast you as the uncaring, selfish, egotistical cad when really, all you were doing was the same thing I was doing, protecting your heart, wanting to be loved, wanting to feel special. Why would you believe I loved you when I never had to sacrifice anything for you like you had for me? Having lived through the Second World War, you craved security, and yet you sacrificed the comforts and spoils of your life in England to be with me, while my only sacrifice came at the end of your life, and by then, it was too late for you to appreciate my loving efforts. You gave me as much as you were capable of giving. Like you, I was emotionally repressed. The Japanese and the English have much too much in common on that score! We both had trouble expressing our deepest feelings, but love is all about being open and vulnerable to the ones we love. There's no room for stoicism between two people who love each other.

"Saying I'm sorry isn't enough, but it's a start, so I am taking the first step. Oh, Alan, I'm truly sorry. Please forgive me, my love. I don't want to wait until I go through my own life review to make amends and beg for your forgiveness. Besides, I'm so merged with you that I feel everything you feel now. There is no room for anything but the full truth between us.

"Now at last we can love each other with the unbridled passion that we should have surrendered to from the start. Age no longer separates us. All earthly responsibilities like child-rearing have been met and are long gone. Resentments have been healed. Insecurities banished. Your fears are fading fast. The fact that you don't have a body to give me means nothing. You've already given me more love and joy than I thought possible. Oh, the heights of passion you take me to when we are alone! What we had in the past cannot compare to what we have now. All the boundaries between us have finally fallen away for good. Not even time and space can keep us apart! So it is that today I call out to you through the veil, shouting for you and all of Heaven to hear…I LOVE YOU! I LOVE YOU! I LOVE YOU!"

Pam, my love, your words make me cry tears of joy. During my life review, I saw why you acted the way you did, which is why I hold no bitterness towards you. None. My pain and sorrow are gone, leaving me only with the fear of hurting you again, a fear that is, as you say, melting away at last.

But that's not all. The time has come for me to tell you the real reason why I didn't want you to consult a medium or give you many signs or send you other forms of confirmation that people receive, not that there's anything wrong with any of these things, but I knew that they wouldn't do for us. This is why the signs I gave of my existence were to others who would tell you about them! I wasn't doing that to hurt you but to keep you focused on what mattered more: to trust your own heart and your own experience of me, to have faith in me even in the absence of proof.

To believe and trust, no matter what!

For if I gave you one sign, you'd only want another, and if a medium spoke for me, you would want to go back again and again because it's easier to listen to someone else than to work on learning to communicate with me yourself. All of this would have disempowered you, leaving you dependent upon others. It would have eased your grief only temporarily when I want more for you. For both of us! It's easier for people to believe in the messages a medium gives them than to believe the words their loved one whispers to them in their mind. But it's only direct communication that will reunite us. This is why people can consult mediums for years yet not be any further along with their connection to their loved one, let alone the healing of their grief.

None of this will do for us! Not when we know that direct communication is attainable! You and I are here to heal our issues and trauma so that our lines of communication can be fully open and teach others how to do the same. And now at last, we've made it! Now you feel me to such a depth that you trust your other senses, including what you see, because you SEE me in your mind with clarity. You also HEAR me as clearly as any medium, and more importantly, you FEEL my love and my energy, which are the very essence of me, and as a result, you experience a state of bliss when you allow yourself to relax. It's why you won't age like others do. My love has filled you completely, so how can you miss me when you feel me everywhere? Now at last there is nowhere in the multiverse that you can be without me!

I have proven my existence to you directly, which is the highest and best way because it's the only thing that leads to a truly satisfying reunion through the veil.

Now, my love, I want to tell you of what's to come.

I want to speak about all the souls in Heaven who want to connect to their loved ones because as you know, they want to connect to the physical world just as much as the souls on Earth want to reunite with them. On my side of the veil, there is enormous interest in what we are doing, for as you know, the two worlds are destined to become one. The bridging of Heaven and Earth was not possible until more souls awakened to the truth of all that they are. This is now happening at an increasing rate which is throwing open the portals to Heaven wider, and as a result, the spirit world is reaching out with great fervor and joy.

The two worlds will become one through direct contact. It cannot happen any other way!

My love, we had to suffer as we did so that we could teach what Unconditional Love is by experiencing the heartbreaking denial of it followed by the reclamation of our love, for the highest form of teaching is to teach by example, not by mere words alone.

People can feel the resonance of truth when they meet someone who speaks from their soul and has come closer to embodying it by virtue of all they have endured. So it is that we will teach others how to reclaim their love through the veil.

Do you not see that everything you have gone through in your life has led you to this moment? You studied a slew of healing modalities, attended a dizzying array of spiritual development classes that never led anywhere or held your attention for very long, and yet your soul had a plan. Through it all, you were preparing for the work now in front of you. Yes, you have been preparing for decades, and now is the time for all you have learned to come together.

Even before we met, you searched for what you were meant to do, turning to teachers who knew less than your own wise soul. Others will relate to your story, for they have done the same. This left you frustrated, doubting your worth, and wondering what was wrong with you. I couldn't help you when I was in a body because I wasn't meant to. Not then. But no more! Now, I am all that I really am! Now I can help you because now I see with perfect 20/20 clarity who I am and who you are.

I know it's not fair that you had to remain behind to anchor my energy into this world, but the only reason I can do what I do is because of you. Our love bond forged over millennia allows us to serve humanity with our hearts and minds wide open. You had to remain where you are when I moved to this side of the veil because through all of our lives together, you have always been the stronger of the two of us, and it takes a fierce and hardy soul to do the work we are about to do to tear down the veil.

You know in your heart this is true! You came into this world to be of loving service. You have always seen your sisters and brothers as your equals, never lesser than you, because you see God within every soul you meet. In this lifetime, you never sought recognition. Quite the opposite. You prefer the freedom of anonymity, but recognition will come to you because of the work that is now before you. But do not worry, for I will be at your side to help you cope with it and shield you from any negativity.

Yes, our story will inspire and help many, but it will also enrage those who aren't ready to claim the truth of who they really are: immortal beings who are the embodiment of God's eternal love. My love, I will be forever at your side through the storms that come your way, and yes, there will be a few tempests that you must endure, but I will shield you from the worst of it.

My love, this is why I had to die in order to live! For how else could I help you?

There are several things I am doing all at once, every moment of the day and night. I'm helping you heal your asthma. I'm helping you become the Archangel healer that is your soul's destiny since you are my partner and my equal. I'm deepening my connection to you in all of the ways that are possible. I'll continue to help you to see me. I'm never giving up trying to materialize to you, so be patient and believe in me, my love!

I cannot tell you when, but one day you will see me in physical form. I promise that you will feel my embrace again. We will walk hand in hand together along the beach, watching the sun rise over Maui as we once did. I will hold you in my arms and love you again. And again. And again. Others have done this, and so shall we! These are the glorious days of our life together that I spoke of all those many months ago. Our work to serve has only just begun. I can't promise that it will be easy to reach our goals because life in the physical world is not always easy, but I can promise you it will be a heart-expanding thrill-ride of an adventure like no other. And one more thing.

Your destiny is here.

I am part of it, but you have a mission of your own, my love. Do you recall what happened to you when you opened up as a channel, the day you were pulled out of your body and felt an entity rush in as you were up above looking down at yourself? You weren't afraid of the divine presence that had merged with you. What shocked you was seeing yourself touching people on their third eye as they fell backward. Do you know what you were doing? You were awakening them, Pam! That is your mission.

You are a spiritual teacher, an energy healer, and an Awakener of Souls.

Remember how I always pushed you to step out into the world to work without me? It wasn't because I didn't want to work with you or help you. It wasn't because I couldn't join you. It was because there is something you are meant to do by yourself, though I will be there supporting you. All the joking I've done since I returned to you about me wanting to become famous was nothing but a smokescreen for the real truth. Our book might seem to be all about me, but it's not the whole story.

Your life purpose is unfolding now that you and I have found harmony with each other and become one. I will always be at your side, cheering you on, helping you and urging you to climb high. Loving you. Most of all, loving you. Always. When two people love each other, that is forever. There is enormous, important work ahead of you that will be the hardest thing you've ever done. It will take every ounce of strength, faith, and courage you can muster. You will collapse in my arms at times, crying out to me that you're afraid that you'll fail, but I will steady you and lift you up again and again until you no longer need me to help you. I will pour my love over your tears until all that remains is joy. For you are meant to leave your mark on the world in service to others. All on your own, with me at your side. You are destined to help thousands of souls, and yes, Taylor is part of your mission. Our mission. Why do you think he's our son? But that is another story that is yet to be told. For the truth is this is just the beginning of our Supernatural Love story.

So, my darling, shall we begin?

GRATITUDE

S wati Nigam, our dearest friend, Alan's angel sister and his partner in crime between the two worlds. This book would not have been written if I had not had your loving hand to guide me through the early days of illness, struggle, and grief. You are a blessing to us both!

Maria Rodrigues Pereira, for always being there for us, including the days when I wanted to throw Alan and our book off a cliff. You never stopped believing we'd make it. You never stopped loving us, and for that and so much more, we thank God for you every day. Twice.

Taylor Warren Johnson, our son, our world. You have the best qualities of both of us and none of the worst. You are funnier, smarter, and more psychic than the two of us together. This book is our legacy to you.

Brittany Dupee, we love and appreciate you for your bright and fearless spirit and for loving our Taylor the way you do. Thanks for taking a chance on him. We love you!

Marci Weight Lyons, who stood by me through the two most tumultuous times of my life, my awakening and Alan's return. We could not ask for a truer friend. Mahalo Nui loa for your love.

Ken Kimura, for being there for me when I was lost and didn't know it. Your sunny, exuberant spirit never fails to lift and inspire me. Your friendship means the world.

Edie Uchida, your loving support helped us find our way home to each other's arms. It was a rough ride at times, but love got us through it! Thank you for all you have done for us. We love and appreciate you eternally.

Tracy Wright Corvo, you inspire me with your vision and radiant light. Your soulful photographs are a gift and a treasure I can never repay, though I will try my best. I am blessed to count you as a trusted friend. Thank you, thank you!

Malia and Martin Johnson, much love and gratitude for the years of friendship we've shared and for opening the Sedona store, which, if you hadn't done, we would have never met, married, or had our son Taylor. Look what you started! Thank God you did!

Melissa Ghrist Ricker and Darlene Cook, my extraordinary mentor and coach. Failure was never an option with the two of you in my corner.

To the members of our Soulmates in the Afterlife Facebook group for your love and support.

For our families in the spirit world: Michiko Higa, Warren Higa, Carlton Higa, John Johnson, Edith Johnson, and Rose Nobu Uno, thank you for your unconditional love and guidance.

Special thanks to Morgan Gist MacDonald and the team at Paper Raven Books, especially Heather Preis and Brian Dooley. I bow to your literary expertise.

PAM AND ALAN JOHNSON

Pamela Johnson is an inspirational speaker, author, channeler, and spiritual healer born and raised in Honolulu, Hawaii, where she met her husband, Alan, during his first visit to the islands in 1990. Born and raised in London, England, Alan was a natural-born medium who had contact with the spirit world from childhood until the end of his life in the summer of 2020. During their thirty years together, Pam and Alan maintained an active professional practice working as psychic channels and mediums, offering classes, healings, and readings to clients in Hawaii and around the world. Their first book, *Supernatural Love: A True Story of Life and Love After Death*, chronicles their two-year journey to heal their marriage so they could continue their relationship after Alan's passing. Their primary mission is to teach spouses and partners, how to awaken and develop their spiritual gifts so they can connect through the veil and continue their relationship through their membership programs, special events, and free classes in their Facebook group for partners, called Soulmates in the Afterlife.

Website: www.supernaturallove.com

Facebook Group: www.soulmatesintheafterlife.com

YouTube: www.youtube.com/c/PamelaJohnson

Instagram: www.instagram.com/pamalan808